Dr. Jim Gills has provided a very valuable service in writing this book. It is a welcome and vital resource for a correct Christian understanding of sickness and healing. Few people in this world have studied the physical, emotional, and spiritual aspects of healing like Dr. Gills, and this important book reveals a lifelong quest of searching, studying, and learning. He will take you on a journey where you will end up marveling at natural healing, learning how to maximize assisted healing, aligning yourself with God to achieve inner healing, struggling to understand those improbable healings, and rejoicing that the destination for all believers is ultimate healing. Dr. Gills gently points us in the direction we should all go because someday we will all face sickness and suffering. This book integrates the whole-person principle in a unique and effective way. I highly recommend it for anyone dealing with sickness. Read this book, but more importantly, use it and apply it.

—James A. Avery, M.D., FACP, FCCP
Medical Director
VNS-New York Hospice, NYC

Dr. James P. Gills, world-renown eye surgeon, has written a magnificent book on healing based on the Word of God. "My son, give attention to my words…for they are life to those who find them and *health* to all their flesh" (Prov. 4:20–22, emphasis added).

How can we search for cures? The causes and cures for disease are available to us through understanding the Creator's unique, intelligent, and irreducibly complex design of our bodies and minds. This book beautifully underlines God's prescription for our healing by discussing details of that design.

Dr. Gills recognizes that our ultimate healing of salvation is a gift of grace from God. This grace also provides our daily healing. "Call upon Me in the day of trouble; I will deliver you and you shall glorify Me" (Ps. 50:15).

From the cellular to the celestial, Dr. Gills carries our hearts through the healing process. Reading this book and the attendant Scriptures can bring healing and joy to you.

—J. James Rowsey, M.D.
Director of Corneal Services, St. Luke's Cataract and Laser Institute

This is, in my opinion, Dr. James Gills' best book to date. It is stunning. Amazing. Full of practical advice, put lovingly but firmly, this book has the potential to change one's life at nearly every level—physically, emotionally, and spiritually. It is an affirmation of biblical teaching—from Creation to redemption—and makes nonsense of Darwinism while extolling common sense to the hilt. I would literally say that every person should read this book.

—Dr. R. T. Kendall, Teacher, Author, and
Former Pastor, Westminster Chapel, London

GOD'S
PRESCRIPTION
for
HEALING

GOD'S
PRESCRIPTION
for
HEALING

JAMES P. GILLS, M.D.

SILOAM
A STRANG COMPANY

Most Strang Communications/Charisma House/Siloam products are available at special quantity discounts for bulk purchase for sales promotions, premiums, fund-raising, and educational needs. For details, write Strang Communications/Charisma House/Siloam, 600 Rinehart Road, Lake Mary, Florida 32746, or telephone (407) 333-0600.

God's Prescription for Healing by James Gills, M.D.
Published by Siloam
A Strang Company
600 Rinehart Road
Lake Mary, Florida 32746
www.siloam.com

Unless otherwise noted, all Scripture quotations are from the New King James Version of the Bible. Copyright © 1979, 1980, 1982 by Thomas Nelson, Inc., publishers. Used by permission.

Scripture quotations marked AMP are from the Amplified Bible. Old Testament copyright © 1965, 1987 by the Zondervan Corporation. The Amplified New Testament copyright © 1954, 1958, 1987 by the Lockman Foundation. Used by permission.

Scripture quotations marked KJV are from the King James Version of the Bible.

Scripture quotations marked NIV are from the Holy Bible, New International Version. Copyright © 1973, 1978, 1984, International Bible Society. Used by permission.

Scripture quotations marked THE MESSAGE are from The Message: The Bible in Contemporary English, copyright © 1993, 1994, 1995, 1996, 2000, 2001, 2002. Used by permission of NavPress Publishing Group.

Scripture quotations marked TLB are from The Living Bible. Copyright © 1971. Used by permission of Tyndale House Publishers, Inc., Wheaton, IL 60189. All rights reserved.

Cover design by Eric Powell
Interior design by Terry Clifton

This book is not intended to provide medical advice or to take the place of medical advice and treatment from your personal physician. Readers are advised to consult their own doctors or other qualified health professionals regarding the treatment of their medical problems. Neither the publisher nor the author takes any responsibility for any possible consequences from any treatment, action, or application of medicine, supplement, herb, or preparation to any person reading or following the information in this book. If readers are taking prescription medications, they should consult with their physicians and not take themselves off of medicines to start supplementation without the proper supervision of a physician.

Library of Congress Cataloging-in-Publication Data
Gills, James P., 1934-
    God's prescription for healing / James Gills.
        p.   cm.
    Includes bibliographical references.
    ISBN 0-88419-947-9 (hardback) -- ISBN 0-88419-947-9
    1. Healing--Religious aspects--Christianity. I. Title.
BT732.G54 2004
234'.131--dc22   2003027758

04 05 06 07 — 987654321
Printed in the United States of America

ACKNOWLEDGMENTS

I initially found the inspiration for this book while I watched my friend Jamie Buckingham fight cancer. In the year and a half before his death, he learned that his life was one of "just Jamie and Jesus." During that period, I observed God's five gifts of healing in Jamie's experience, which culminated in his ultimate healing when he went to be with the Lord.

This book contains a deep concept of God's provision of life and healing, which is determined by His profound DNA design contained in, and originating from, a single, microscopic cell. So, it is with wonder and appreciation that I acknowledge the Creator and His intelligence, wisdom, and grace.

I am grateful to my wife, Heather, my family, and the family of staff at St. Luke's for all their support and love. My thanks to those who assisted in the writing and research of this book, Gary Carter, Steve Johnson, and Susan McIntosh. I appreciate Carol Noe for her encouragement at the genesis of this project, as well as all the editing and publishing staff at Siloam for their work.

The Creator's plan for you, and His design that realizes that plan, asks for acknowledgment and thanksgiving in every heart. There can be no healing without them.

CONTENTS

Foreword xiii

Preface xv

Introduction. xvii

    The Design for Healing xvii
    The Need for Understanding and Appreciation xix
    Purpose xxi
    This Book xxi

PART I —**Natural Healing**

  1 An Intelligent Design—and Designer 1

  2 Disease and Healing 4

    The Basics 5

  3 Irreducible Complexity, Impeccable Design 7

    The Magnificent Cell 9
    DNA 10
    The Human Body 12
    The Awesome Eye 13

  4 Examples of Design for Balance, Repair, and Cure. 15

    Skin Healing 16
    Corneal Healing 18
    The Immune System 22
    Understanding the Immune System 24
      Innate (nonspecific) immunity 25
      Adaptive (specific) immunity 26
      Tissues and organs of immunity 28
      The main goals 29
      The double-edged sword—when things go wrong 29

  5 Designed for Health. 34

PART II — **Assisted Healing**

  6 Physician-Assisted Healing 39

    Medical Science, the Physician, and Healing 40
      The example of cataract surgery 41
    Genetic Engineering 47

The Issues of Care *and* Cure 51
Cure and Healing 53
   Understanding and respect 54
   Knowledge and competence 55
   Compassion 55
   Activity replacement 56
   Assurance 56
The Physician As Healer 56
Limitations to Assistance 59
The Meaning of Collective and
   Personal Responsibility 62

7 You Are Your Own Best Physician 65
Physical Alignment 67
Prevention of Disease 68
Health and Wholeness 68
   Proper nutrition 69
   Exercise 70
   Complementary methods 71
   Choices 72
God's Wisdom Confirmed by Science 73
Conclusion 74

PART III — **Inner Healing**

8 Mental Alignment With the Creator's Design 79
Mind and Body, Body and Mind 83
Worry, Anxiety, Fear 84
Managing the Negative Emotions 91
   Laughter—life's therapeutic medicine 92
Mental Healing 95
Personality 95
Hope As an Antidote 96

9 The Prescription for Inner Healing 101
Prayer 102
Fellowship 106
The Blessed Mind-set 109

10 Spiritual Alignment With the Creator's Design 116

    Obstacles to Alignment and God's Inner Healing 118
      Pride 118
      A critical spirit 120
      A spirit of envy 121
    The Great Physician 122
      Repentance 123
      Salvation 125
      Forgiveness first 126
      After the honeymoon 128
    Resting in the Bosom of the Trinity 129

11 Unveiling the New Heart 132

    Spiritual vs. Natural 133
    Love 134
    Loving God = Inner Healing 135
    The Purpose of Our Lives and Eternity 136
    Two Penetrating Insights 139

12 The Healing of the Word 142

Part IV — **Improbable Healing**

13 Improbable Healing in the Scriptures 149

    Improbable Healing in the Bible 151
      Healing and appreciation 151
      Forgiveness, purpose, and "direction" 151
      Cleansing and compassion 153
      Favoring the neglected 153
      Restoration and hope 154
      Improbable healing and our understanding 156

14 Modern Examples of Improbable Healing 158

    Improbable Deliverance From Addiction 165

15 How Do We Seek an Improbable Healing? 169

Part V — **Ultimate Healing**

16 Designed for Eternity 173

    Three Feasts and Three Courts 174
    Graduation Day! 176
    A Beautiful Design 177

How Will He Reward You? 178
The Facts About Rewards 179
A Date to Keep! 181

17 Eternity's Anointed Purpose for Life 182
The Temporal, the Eternal 183
Motivated by Hope or Despair? 184
Our Perspective: Living in Light of Eternity 186

18 A Walk Through Glory 188
Good-bye, Trouble and Sorrow! 189
Inconceivable Blessing 191
Can Anything Be Added to This? 192

Conclusion: Final Words 197
Hearing God Think 197
The Lord Has a Plan for Your Cut Finger,
   and for Your Life! 198
Healing and Wonder 200
Pride 201
Alignment to God 202
God's Prescription 203
S.T.O.R.G.E. 205
My Prayer for Heather 205

Notes 209
Bibliography 221

FOREWORD

As an intern at Johns Hopkins, I was deeply impressed when I would walk on the neurosurgical wards and see the CEOs and crown princes of various places with tons of money, fame, and advanced degrees, all dying of malignant brain tumors. It was at that point that I recognized that all of the wealth and fame in the world is not to be equated with good health. Any of those people would gladly have given every title and every penny for a clean bill of health, but it was too late. How often do we stop and ask ourselves about the importance of our health, and how often do we try to do anything about it?

We are complex beings, and total health for us involves not only the physical but also the mental and spiritual aspects of our lives. We have an amazing amount of control over our health through our choices. These choices include our diet, our exercise, the amount of rest we get, as well as our attitudes about a variety of things in our environment. We also have a choice about whether we will be spiritually connected to God or simply ignore our Creator. Although attention to annual physical examinations, vitamins, proper diet, and so forth is important, do we take the appropriate time to nourish our spirit? That spirit is the special thing that separates us from the rest of the animal world. The wonderful thing about this book is that it integrates our spiritual and mental well-being into our physical well-being and helps us to improve not only our health, but also that of those around us.

A truly successful life is not one characterized by wealth and fame, but rather by self-fulfillment and the elevation of others as well as an understanding of our place in God's big picture. He has provided for us the formula for health, happiness, and fulfillment. It is up to us to have the prescription filled. After reading this book, I believe the spiritual pharmacy will be your next stop.

—Benjamin S. Carson Sr., M.D.
Director of Pediatric Neurosurgery
Professor of Neurological Surgery,
Oncology, Plastic Surgery, and Pediatrics
Johns Hopkins University

PREFACE

Great is the Lord, and greatly to be praised;
And His greatness is unsearchable.

—Psalm 145:3

Have you seen mystery in a butterfly tenderly drying its wings under a ray of morning sunlight before it dances away on the breeze? Have you wondered at the language—or is it laughter—of dolphins? How often have you taken the time to enjoy, and *appreciate*, the spectacle of a full moon rising? Are any of us able to fully comprehend the ages, sizes, and distances of the galaxies of stars in an *endless* cosmos? And what can we make of the glorious chorus a songbird learns from its parents, or a pet dog's desire to please? All of created nature—the mystery of the whole universe—points to the presence of an Intelligence in its formation and function. However, nowhere is the thumbprint of a Creator more visible than upon human life—upon *your* life. This is the important point.

> **GOD'S**
>
> THE PROVISION FOR...
> **the prescription for**
> **all your healing**
> **has been preplanned**
> **and designed.**
>
> FOR HEALING
>
> **PRESCRIPTION**

The provision for...the prescription for all your healing has been preplanned and designed. It was present before you were formed. This is the great, unsearchable miracle of life: All the wisdom that the Creator needs to create and preserve all humankind is *already* within you—*by design*! This is a design so profound and beautiful that it is first contained within a single, microscopic cell and its DNA molecule. Life, meaning, and healing all begin perfectly, and beyond our full understanding, in that tiny dot.

Provision and Prescription for Healing

In this book you will discover that the beginning and end of your healing—the truth of God's prescription—lie with that cell. Within it are the seat of all *biological* knowledge and the expression of divine knowledge for the creation of and healthful nurturing of *your* life.

This cell is microscopic—many, many times tinier than a pinhead—and it has one job to accomplish. That job is to grow into, and to direct the development of, all that you have grown to be, or could be. This marvelous "crystal" of the Creator's wisdom is a fertilized egg. It is referred to scientifically as a *zygote*. It is a tiny "universe" that possesses vast amounts of information in its DNA. Through the genetic direction impressed upon that zygote by Creator God, more than two hundred different tissue types develop in your body, and such things as the shape of your ears, the tenor of your voice, and the length of your fingers are determined. You also receive a body with natural defenses, eyes to read these words, a mind with a thirst for understanding, and a soul grounded on the principle of love. And there is so much more! In the design of intricate and delicate mechanisms—from molecular interactions to the teamwork of organs—the spiritually open eye willingly sees the evidence of the Designer's plan for eternity with Him as well as life and healing now.

In this book you will discover that the beginning and end of your healing—the truth of God's prescription—lie with that cell.

The facts of our creation are unimaginably profound. There is massive scientific proof of the infinite intelligence built physically into the zygote, determining the individual we each become. How can we *not* be living in awe, wonder, appreciation—and worship? Within our molecules are the record and testimony of a Creator's *great care*. Within a single cell is where *your* healing resides.

INTRODUCTION

A theory is the more impressive the greater the simplicity of its premises is, the more different kinds of things it relates, and the more extended its area of applicability.

—ALBERT EINSTEIN[1]

Have you ever found yourself charmed by the twinkle in a friend's eye, the spontaneous gesture in her graceful wrist, a suddenly raised eyebrow, and the sounds of her laughter rising and falling? Yet there is so much more *beyond* the surface of beauty. Though we often fail to notice it, that friend has an inner source much finer and more complex than any beauty we can see on the surface. With such friend—and with *every human*—we must learn to search for the Poet in the poetry of life. The lines of that poem, as well as the evidence of that Poet, can be found in the most essential details of a human life. Mostly hidden from human view until our present technological era, the Creator and Poet of all life—and His created beauty—can be found in the secrets of each and every cell.

The indescribable complexity in everything around us indicates a marvelous, mysterious *design for life*. This complexity is found in the unbelievably immense and the unimaginably tiny. We can see it in distant star clusters, in the earth's weather patterns, in an elephant's memory, and in an ant's ability to find food. Though evidence of a Designer is visible at all levels of magnitude in nature, it is most eloquently expressed in the building blocks, the cells, of living things. In each single cell—microbial, plant, and animal—sits the miniature library of the Creator's intelligence for that creation. Within a grape cell, for example, is the design for the vine, its preferred season for growth, and for the flavor of the fruit that you recognize as different from pineapple.

The Design for Healing

We have been created as physical, mental, and spiritual beings with a marvelous design. All of life, in terms of sickness and healing, can be conceived of as a reaction to injury that is both appropriate and balanced. This is true for trauma, or disease, or a lost and confused spirit. The grandeur of the design—*your* design—is evident in every cell and its particular task. Each one of those cells developed from the zygote.

The zygote is the "computer chip" that contains all of the Creator's intelligent design stored in the "memory banks" of its DNA molecule.

The awesome programming of the computer chip determines all of your growth and functions of life—from eyelids that blink, to stomach acids that digest food, to sneezes that expel irritants. They all have purpose, and they all develop from the intricate instructions of the zygote. When we cut a finger, for example, there is an immensely complex response for repair in *each cell* in the area of the injury. Through an elaborate cascade of reactions, protein messages are sent and received. Vessels are narrowed accordingly, protective scabs are constructed, and cell duplication for the regeneration of new flesh begins. This all involves thousands and thousands of individual reactions amongst the *trillions* of atoms that make up the cells around the wound site. It is a process of unfathomable complexity, mystery, and mastery. And the same holds true for the body's reactions to tumors, herniated discs, broken bones, and cataracts. The bodies we inhabit for the duration of our brief lives obviously contain impeccable wisdom and purpose.

> **GOD'S**
>
> THE GRANDEUR OF the design—your design—is evident in every cell and its particular task.
>
> **PRESCRIPTION**

More than in any other era, the truth is made clear. Advances in biochemistry, molecular biology, and medicine have shown that the complexity of our own design is quite beyond complete comprehension and entirely beyond imitation. It is unconditionally beyond a detached process of evolution. It could only be derived from an intelligent source, from an *Intelligent Designer.* Intelligent design is revealed by science in the farthest planets as much as in intracellular detail. The observations of human science all point to the Designer, Creator, and Father, and they remind us of our need to appreciate Him. Sadly, we are almost universally unobservant and ungrateful.

The Need for Understanding and Appreciation

Many of us have a major fault within us: We take precious things for granted—the universe, species on the planet, as well as our body, our health, and well-being—until we suffer their lack or loss. However, when we *do* lose something important, we become acutely aware of what we once had. It is then that we begin to look for answers—to try to make sense of the suffering we endure because of the loss of something precious in our life. This principle emerges: *We might never be awakened to the intelligence of the Creator in His creation unless we also experience some suffering in this life.*

Brokenness, physical or otherwise, is not a simple *condition* that pills can cure—at least not often. You already know this if you are ailing. The emotions and reactions—the effects—that accompany suffering are as numerous as the possible illnesses themselves. This makes each person's experience, *your experience*, with illness unique.

Negative feelings and fear may become huge burdens that stand in the way of healing until we learn to lighten or remove them. Happily, your fears can be diminished if you understand God's plan.

We must learn to recognize the beauty of our design. We should be able to identify the intelligence in our design and be filled with wonder for our own existence. Why do we look without seeing, and accept without cherishing? Even the normal function of our bodies should fill us with a sense of awe and appreciation for the Intelligence behind it all. The intelligence in our design is apparent. As we explore the miracle of our design—and even the meaning of our suffering—we will recognize the beauty of our creation and of the Master Designer behind it all.

When you look at your nose in the mirror, what are you thinking? Do you find yourself merely wishing it were smaller or of a different shape? Or, rather, are you amazed by its ability to distinguish ten thousand different scents? Though you never see your pancreas, have you ever wondered what its assigned job is? Are you truly aware and appreciative of the task that each pancreatic cell executes in perfect concert with all the other pancreatic cells? Have you grasped the miracle of design that created you with sixty trillion cells in your human body, including pancreatic cells, brain cells, skin, kidney, bone, liver, and muscle cells?

When your body is suffering from the pain and limitation of

illness, have you turned to your Designer for solutions? Or do you seek for answers through a wide stream of competing influences and apparent answers? Maybe you turn to magazine articles or Web sites, for example. Or you lean toward the advice of friends or the attentions of doctors. Maybe you read whole texts on nutrition and exercise. Perhaps you have explored a large and growing number of available alternative—complementary—therapies and techniques for healing. Some of these alternatives are helpful, some hopeless, and some harmful. Hopefully you have turned to the Scriptures for inspiration and advice. True, divine guidance is the necessary element that allows the appropriate decisions that lead us in the direction of healing.

GOD'S PRESCRIPTION FOR HEALING

> WE MIGHT NEVER be awakened to the intelligence of the Creator in His creation unless we also experience some suffering in this life.

Our search for answers should start with the Creator's intelligence and mastery. It is there that our experiences of illness and healing become clear to us as part of a plan, a design. Close scientific examination and deep contemplation show us that the *alpha* and *omega*—the meaning, purpose, and glory of existence under the Creator's sun—all emerge from and are expressed through the single cell and its design for *abundant life*.

You have been endowed with intellectual tools: human science and reason. With them, you may dive into the depths of the mystery and acquaint yourself, to some degree, with the Creator's plan. And within it—once you accept it and receive the sovereignty of the Designer—you will find insights into humanity and God's prescription for healing. Only by recognizing that design can we understand God's gifts and grace. Only then will we find within our hearts the awe and true appreciation that are due the Creator. Our understanding of healing, as well as our effectiveness in effecting healing in ourselves and in others, demands that we step back from our circumstances and *see*. We need to be *ordinary* man appreciating our *extraordinary* God. Appreciating the unimaginably complex, single cell and its DNA code provides the way.

Purpose

All things showing a purity of function also show a *purpose* of function that is directly due to a plan that was devised *before* their existence. You don't have to be a professional scientist to marvel at the endless beauty in nature and to see evidence of the plan for your healing. You only need to be willing to humbly acknowledge the intelligence of the Creator and be grateful for it. In that way you will come to understand your meaning and purpose.

The blessing of healing in one life can have profound and far-reaching effects for many. President George W. Bush came to a point in his life when he realized that he was unable to control certain addictions and was out of control himself. In his heartfelt testimony, President Bush expresses the truth of an authentic healing, which occurred after he understood that he needed the Lord. In his own words, he "was humbled to learn that God sent His Son to die for a sinner like me." And, "through the love of Christ's life, I could understand the life-changing powers of faith."[2] Though he felt he had always been a "religious" person, these were new revelations to his heart—humility, faith, and dependence on his Creator. It is the vital difference between practicing faith and really *living* it.

With the meaning of faith clearer to him, and with more and more time spent in God's Word, George W. Bush found much needed "focus and perspective." It allowed him to accept responsibility for where he had been, to find control in a new, healthy lifestyle, and to envision great purpose in life by trying to be a facilitator to others. Inspired and moved by this purpose, which was revealed by the Lord, he became the leader of a nation, truly healed.

Looking to the Lord for His guidance and seeking to understand His purpose for you will lead you to the healing that He wants for you. Through that, many can be aided, uplifted, and healed.

This Book

There are countless ways we may be ill, out of balance, and suffering. Likewise, then, there are numberless ways we may be healed. God's wisdom and mercy are unfathomable. By examining five major areas in this book we will take a comprehensive look at God's provision of healing for the human body, mind, and soul. It all starts and ends with the intelligence, love, and wisdom articulated in the zygote.

Meant to peer more deeply at the heart of God and His care of us, this book can be faith-reinforcing for those who believe and a source of support for those who are suffering and need healing in their own life or the lives of loved ones. God has designed the body for healing, and He has provided wisdom about that body to physicians. This book may also play a positive role in the lives of believers who distrust medical science and complementary treatments while thinking that healing must necessarily involve prayer alone. Finally, the book describes the ultimate healing of eternity.

> LOOKING TO THE Lord for His guidance and seeking to understand His purpose for you will lead you to the healing that He wants for you.

I want to encourage and challenge you as we discuss the details of God's wonderful, loving plan for your healing. All of His knowledge and His provisions for your care are coded in your body. It is important that you understand that your health, healing, and, ultimately, eternity with Him have been designed, engineered, and given substance in the very structure of life itself. The Creator's plan for your healing lies in the cells of your body.

PART I

NATURAL HEALING

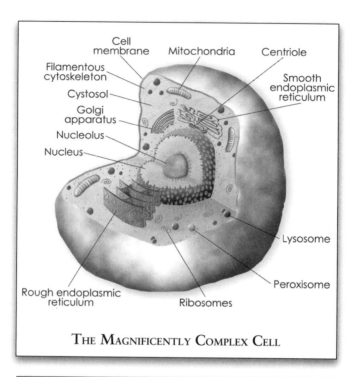

Cell membrane   Mitochondria   Centriole

Filamentous cytoskeleton

Cystosol

Smooth endoplasmic reticulum

Golgi apparatus

Nucleolus

Nucleus

Lysosome

Rough endoplasmic reticulum

Peroxisome

Ribosomes

THE MAGNIFICENTLY COMPLEX CELL

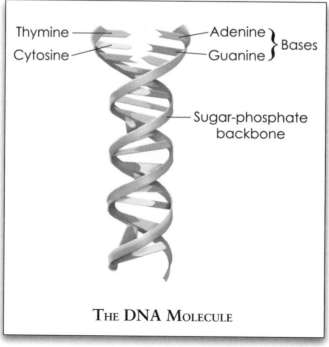

Thymine   Adenine }
Cytosine   Guanine } Bases

Sugar-phosphate backbone

THE DNA MOLECULE

Chapter 1

AN INTELLIGENT DESIGN— AND DESIGNER

Beauty is nature's brag, and must be shown in courts, at feasts, and high solemnities, where most may wonder at the workmanship.

—JOHN MILTON

The next time you turn your eyes to the sky, consider the marvel of migrating birds. Each one is a real Olympian by our standards. It is difficult to truly appreciate their tremendous annual accomplishments. Some birds fly an amazing distance. For example, the pectoral sandpiper flies 16,000 kilometers (approximately 9,940 miles) from Alaska to Tierra del Fuego in South America and back again, *every year*.[1] There is also the unexplained miracle of navigation that brings the Layson albatross home to *within thirteen inches* of the nest that it vacated prior to leaving for the winter.[2] Do you believe that? Some species of migratory birds travel two hundred to four hundred miles a day at occasional altitudes of ten thousand feet (that is almost two miles up).[3] Experiments have also shown that migratory species naturally orient themselves by the steady stars rather than the revolving moon and planets. They demonstrate this tendency even if they have been raised indoors and are seeing the night sky for the first time.[4] With additional talents for appropriate energy consumption and the advantageous use of wind directions, these birds clearly demonstrate intelligence within their construction. Our attempts to explain all of this are sadly inadequate. That is because these birds are physical evidence of the intelligence and intentions of *a divine Designer.*

There are four things which are little on the earth,
    But they are exceedingly wise:
The ants are a people not strong,
    Yet they prepare their food in the summer;

1

The rock badgers are a feeble folk,
    Yet they make their homes in the crags;
The locusts have no king,
    Yet they all advance in ranks;
The spider skillfully grasps with its hands,
    And it is in kings' palaces.

                   —PROVERBS 30:24–28

This intelligence has wholly unique expressions in every kind of creature on the planet. It is an intelligence constructed into the angles of bodies and the aptitudes of brains. It begins with a molecular intelligence that makes life as an aardvark possible for the aardvark, but also very different from the life of the accountant. This divine intelligence is ratcheted into all the individual cells that originate from a single one. It is an intelligence that oversees and conducts the most colossal, perplexing, and rousing chorus in existence. That ultimate symphony is the breathing, heaving, extravagant economy of life on this planet.

The more carefully we look, then, the more directly we are introduced to the sophistication of a design that is responsible for *all* things. The science of our present age is finally exposing this. Significant details are evident at the cellular level in dimensions of *nanometers* (billionths of a meter). Still, while mysteries of nature such as the Milky Way, whale sonar, or the improbable flight of bumblebees captivate us, we are mostly concerned with the basis of *our own* nature and *our* place in the universe. So, turning to the human body, we find the *most* astonishing proof of ingenuity, wisdom, and complexity woven into natural design. And we see that most clearly in the genetic code of the single, all-generating zygote.

For generations, prevailing scientific theories have chosen to describe the phenomenon of life as the product of frigid, physical forces and biochemical accident. Any competing concept of direction and design in nature has been ridiculed as superstition by these theories of evolution. However, a concept of design, an expression of deep wisdom, can now be understood to be a *scientific principle*. Within a single cell is the revelation of the truth that underlies all nature—including you and me. *The human body represents a scientific revelation of the presence*

GOD'S PRESCRIPTION *for* HEALING

and personality of an Intelligent Designer of great wisdom who loves and heals.

You were *designed,* and that means that you are full of meaning and purpose. Within this meaning and purpose are all the reasons to be alive and to stay alive. The Designer has a plan for you that includes awesome mechanisms for *maintenance.* The design of the human body provides countless, powerful means to respond to injury and disease. The provisions for proper, precise, and efficient operation within you, and in each individual, expose the design and the prescription for healing. *This is God's first gift of healing to us.*

Through an exploration of disease and the design for healing you can find the hand of the Designer. Through that discovery you will be able to understand the purpose and meaning of your structure and, more, your meaning and purpose in life. And so, not only is it *useful* to recognize and understand the natural design of your body to promote your health and healing—it is a *responsibility.* As each of us recognizes that responsibility, we can learn to gratefully acknowledge our health as our greatest earthly wealth; nothing could be dearer. Also there we may look for the glorious face of the Creator in full appreciation of this His gift.

Chapter 2

DISEASE AND HEALING

I will praise You, for I am fearfully and wonderfully
made;
Marvelous are Your works,
And that my soul knows very well....
Your eyes saw my substance, being yet unformed.
And in Your book they were all written,
The days fashioned for me,
When as yet there were none of them.

—Psalm 139:14, 16

If you are presently looking for healing, for freedom from pain or disability—and each of us does through the course of life—it can be difficult to understand completely what is happening to you. Common terms are sometimes confused, so it is helpful to briefly distinguish a couple now.

When you become sick, your body becomes an impediment rather than an instrument of your will. In a state of illness, your entire experience of existence thus becomes altered. Those who become ill "experience a series of intimate insults to those aspects of their existence that are most integral to being human."[1] That is, when we are ill we have lost the capacity for living in the manner to which we have grown accustomed. A disease is a physical condition characterized by diminished or inappropriate function in the body. It is an imbalance in biological systems or structures. Illness, on the other hand, is all the uncomfortable and disturbing conditions and emotions that a person struggles with when a disease is present in the body. Human illness, evidently, is illness of the whole person—body, mind, and soul.

Curing has to do with disease and eradicating it. *Healing* has to do with illness and restoring the individual.[2] We can only accomplish such restoration with mental and spiritual adjustments. *True healing requires physical cure as well as mental and spiritual wholeness.* We will refer to that as *total health.*

The Basics

The primary characteristic of both cure and healing, more than anything else, is understood to be *balance.* The human body—*your* body—was designed to maintain balance and make adjustments when natural balance is overturned. Take the relatively simple examples of heat and cold. When you become chilled, you start to shiver. By this mechanism, your body is trying to generate heat and reestablish appropriate body temperature. Likewise, when the environment is hot, it raises the body's temperature, and the response is sweating. The evaporation of sweat off the skin is intended to rebalance, to lower the temperature in the body to its preferred level.

In this section we will focus on disease and cure through the body's innate, designed abilities. What is our design for body balance maintenance? A deeper discussion of *healing* admittedly requires a fuller approach that addresses all aspects of a person. However, when we speak about innate biological mechanisms, a more scientific, empirical approach to the body as a grouping of organs and systems is most helpful.

GOD'S

A DISEASE IS A physical condition characterized by diminished or inappropriate function in the body.

FOR HEALING

PRESCRIPTION

Diseases can approach the body from the outside in the form of microorganisms, such as viruses, bacteria, and parasites. Trauma or disease may result from accidents, abuse, or exposure to chemicals and other harmful substances. Some diseases, such as cancer, originate *within* the body. In that particular case, something has tipped the balance that normally checks errant cell growth.

If we define the basis of all disease as a response to injury, then the basis of the cure of disease is the *appropriate*—in other words, *balanced*—physical response by the body's inborn mechanisms. The body has many, many such mechanisms that exist simply to respond to upset in the normal balance of function. Some of these still remain beyond our ability to explain. However, even the most *unremarkable* event of self-cure can be interpreted as a fantastic performance of coordinated and perfectly appropriate responses to injury. Each tissue in the body displays an almost inexplicable complexity in its rejuvenating and renewing capacities. And this is observed in even the most mundane—least urgent—examples of response to disease and illness. We are wholly mistaken when we take these for granted. Even the natural healing of a simple paper cut is a demonstration of our body's finely tuned sentry and repair systems. These functions derive directly from nature's fabulous design, all contained, initially, in the zygote.

Though each human body is unique, each is also the same, built upon the same model, upon a common wisdom and intelligence. When you think about the intelligence of another individual, or of yourself, you are thinking about that person's ability to problem-solve and to manipulate abstractions. Now, though, you must understand that the *whole body* exhibits an intelligence. Your immune system, for example, has a memory and "learns." You experience well-being—to the extent that you do—because your body is continually monitoring, laboring, regrowing, and fighting *intelligently.*

> ILLNESS IS ALL THE uncomfortable and disturbing conditions and emotions that a person struggles with when a disease is present in the body.

How is it all accomplished? Why is it all accomplished? Most theorists would try to have you believe that such wondrous abilities and capacities merely evolved from a great universal emptiness—from nothing. However, current cellular study provides evidence, at the molecular level, that the human body is the most lavish, intricate, and misunderstood piece of *engineering* in the universe.

Chapter 3

IRREDUCIBLE COMPLEXITY, IMPECCABLE DESIGN

To see a world in a grain of sand
And a heaven in a wild flower,
Hold infinity in the palm of your hand
And eternity in an hour.

—William Blake[1]

I was first introduced to the wonders of the body and its cells as a medical student at Duke. I became acutely aware then of the inadequacy of the presiding theories of natural selection as an explanation of the phenomenon of life. It was becoming evident to me, early on, that the great design of nature, of which the human body is the most eloquent example, would lead us to acknowledge it all as supremely intelligent handiwork. For this acknowledgment, however, it was equally clear that we would also need to be humble.

The evidence of design, evidence that forces of random chance could never match, is irrefutable. However, the popular ideas of our era still dictate to us the false "religion" of Darwinism and its materialistic assumptions. These assumptions refer to humanity's *unintended* emergence from meaningless accidents. This would infer that accountability and responsibility would be to *ourselves* alone. At every turn, however, we can now contradict Darwinism and its stubborn denial of the design that is intrinsic in the coil of nature, which includes us. I have discussed this in more detail in my recent book *Darwinism Under the Microscope*.[2]

The design that we are speaking of, the *intelligent* design, is identified primarily by its *irreducible complexity*. This is a difficult yet important term. An irreducibly complex system has been defined as one "composed of several well-matched interacting parts that contribute to basic function, wherein removal of any one of the parts causes the system to effectively cease functioning."[3] Think of it this way: If you build an automobile engine without cylinders, the carburetor is instantly useless. So why build a carburetor—or conceive of it—if it is without meaning and function? This means that both cylinders and carburetor would have to be built *together*, with the *intention* that they work together. Attributing the independent development of both parts to luck, under the condition that one part cannot function without the other, must be beyond anyone's reasonable belief. This is exactly what Darwinism asks us to believe, though.

Theories of evolution hold that a system, such as the human eye, evolved by small, progressive alterations over time. It is clear to anyone not blinded by the pride of human supremacy that the eye presents an immaculate example of irreducible complexity. The irreducible complexity of the human eye is apparent because its separate parts would be inherently non-functioning as isolated components or as integrated component parts at a lower level of complexity. In other words, according to current, popular theory, all the individual components of the eye would have had to evolve at the same time. They would also have had to evolve at the same level of complexity to be properly integrated and function as a complete eye. This could not be possible left to mere chance. Therefore, the human eye presents to us evidence of creation according to highly intelligent design, rather than alleged evolution.

> THE SINGLE CELL IS the initial point of explanation for the body's natural ability to preserve and cure itself.

Truly, such complexity of design with a purpose, the template of our physical existence, can be illustrated in the myriad details of the body. It originates in DNA and can be observed at both microscopic and macroscopic (larger) levels. In this chapter we will first look at irreducible complexity at the microscopic level by discussing the basic building block of the body. This is the single most powerful challenge to the primacy of Darwinian interpretations, and it is the initial point of explanation for the body's natural ability to preserve and cure itself. It is the single cell. If the following facts stir the grace of wonder in you, I encourage you to cultivate it by reading Richard Swenson's fine book *More Than Meets the Eye*, which helped form this discussion and provide facts.[4]

The Magnificent Cell

- Each of the 60 trillion cells of which you are made derive from the zygote alone.
- Each cell—any cell, kidney, heart, or skin—consists of about 1 trillion atoms.
- Cells are the incredibly complex building blocks that form 200 different tissues such as brain, pancreatic, muscle, and heart tissues—each with its very different properties and responsibilities in the body.
- Each cell communicates with its neighbors across a cell membrane that is thinner than a spider's web.
- Each cell is filled with extremely tiny energy-burning "engines" that are 200,000 times smaller than a pinhead.
- Each cell generates an electrical field *and* possesses an intelligent, internal clock that switches off and on in cycles of 2 to 26 hours. The length of cycle depends on the cell type.
- Most wondrously of all, each cell contains the molecular code of life, the biochemical blueprint for your height, eye color, liver function, and the sound of your laughter. This is DNA.

The cell was terribly underestimated by Darwin and others of his era. A different understanding—such as the kind humanity now possesses—would have changed the entire course of the history of science and medicine. Darwin perceived the cell as a simple sac without complexity or meaning in the overall view of life. However, advances in molecular biology have, in our time, shown the cell to be a vast "galaxy." Its constellations of objects and intricate orbits are all coordinated in intense, important, and incessant activity. The complexity of a single cell cannot be overstated—it is mostly beyond our imagination. Look a little closer at a "typical" cell.

The thin cell membrane referred to above not only "holds everything in" (making the cell a structural building block), but it is each cell's mode of communication with its neighbors. This way a cell becomes the member of a community that eventually upgrades to tissue and organ levels of integration. Across this membrane we can measure an electrical potential, or difference, that is the evidence of an electrical field. This field can, at times, be larger than the electrical field emanating from man-made power lines.[5] The cell membrane is also a busy two-way border that absorbs much needed oxygen and nutrients into the interior of the cell while it simultaneously expels waste products into the fluids that surround the cell.

GOD'S

FOR HEALING

DNA IS THE initial source responsible for all your development, growth, maturation, and continuing existence from the moment of conception.

PRESCRIPTION

Inside the cell one finds tiny "factories," known as mitochondria, floating and producing energy in the form of adenosine triphosphate (ATP). Astonishingly, it is possible for an adult human to be producing ATP in quantities equivalent to his or her body weight on a daily basis.[6] This, as any observable activity in the cell, is regulated, turned on, and shut off precisely by internal clocks. *Internal clocks!* Is it possible to imagine the existence of these mechanisms without the wisdom of a specific design?

DNA

The centerpiece of each cell is its nucleus. And the primary function of the nucleus is to provide a repository for deoxyribonucleic acid (DNA)—*the stuff of life.* This is the chemical molecule that encodes all necessary instructions for the construction and replication of living things. Dalmatians, daisies, and Dalai Lamas all have their own versions of it. You have it—and have over 99 percent of it in common with all other humans. DNA is the initial source responsible for all your development, growth, maturation, and continuing existence from the moment of conception.

The DNA molecule is an exquisite filigree of the Creator's art. It has a spiral-shaped sugar-phosphate "backbone," and nitrogen bases—only four of them—are paired off along it: *adenine* always with *thymine*, and *guanine* with *cytosine*.[7] The sequence of these four bases can be altered in an *infinite* number of ways. This is what creates diversity between you and your sister, and between a rose and a rubella virus. Strings of these base combinations are called *genes*. The less than 1 percent of genes that are unique to *you* provide your own special physical attributes and probably many elements of your personality. And there is a complete copy of all that information, locked in your DNA strands, in every one of the 60 trillion cells that make up your body.

- The DNA molecule contains all its information in 3 billion molecular pair combinations. The information contained in the DNA molecule of a *single* cell would fill 200 volumes of the Manhattan phone book.
- The DNA from a single cell, stretched out, would extend over 5 feet in length.
- One strand is only 50-trillionths of an inch wide.
- Removal of DNA from all of one individual's cells and stretched out from end to end would extend in a strand from a minimum 10 billion miles to a possible maximum of 170 billion miles.
- A strand of DNA stretched from you to the sun would weigh a slight $\frac{1}{50}$ of an ounce.

Is it genuinely feasible to claim that these details are possible minus a design? Darwin refused that idea because he did not know what we know. The irreducibly complex individual cell and its functions are exactly the basis upon which we can claim the existence of not only natural mechanisms for healing, but also a design for those mechanisms—a design for healing. It is at the cellular level, and at the level of the molecules that comprise the cell, that the processes for the body's cure originate. Each cell type has a different focus—a different job, if you will—initiated by the

DNA instructions in the zygote. Each cell has an intelligence for healing, which differs from the roles of other cells. Erected on this foundation of cellular intelligence, the human body provides both microscopic and macroscopic evidence of intelligence, irreducible complexity, and design.

The Human Body

- The adult body's 60 trillion cells are absorbed and replaced at a rate of a trillion a day. This is approximately equivalent to renovating a house the size of Texas by continuously tearing down and rebuilding 1 million rooms per second! At that rate, skin is entirely replaced every 2 weeks, and you have an entirely new skeleton every 7 years.

- Lungs, with a surface area of half a tennis court, inhale 23,000 times a day (24 pounds of air), or 630 million times before your last breath.

- Each ear has a million moving parts that vibrate 20,000 times a second.

- Your heart is a fabulous, tireless organ that will squeeze life (over 60 million gallons of blood, in total) throughout and around your body an average of almost 3 billion (2,830,464,000) times in 75 years of life!

- There are 60,000 miles of blood vessels in an adult body. These make passage for red blood cells and their oxygen-binding molecule, hemoglobin, traveling over a distance equivalent to $2\frac{1}{2}$ times around the earth, at the equator, during their relatively brief 120-day life span.

- Nothing anywhere in the universe has the complexity of arrangement of matter as the human brain, with each neuron (brain cell) talking to 10,000 others. If you are using 10 percent of your brain at this moment, it is making a thousand, trillion computations a second.

Such facts are astonishing and breathtaking. They would actually be unbelievable if one remained irrationally attached to the theory that we are accidents of nature. The human body is a work of art prescribed by DNA; it is a masterpiece of conception and execution; it is the grandest scientific disclosure of a universal Designer. The body can only continue to exist, to operate, by preserving an equilibrium of function. That is the reason we can be sure that the design includes the provisions for our growth, regrowth, maintenance, and cure. We must learn to be grateful.

GOD'S

FOR HEALING

THE BODY CAN
only continue to
exist, to operate,
by preserving an
equilibrium of
function.

PRESCRIPTION

The Awesome Eye

> To suppose that the eye with all its inimitable contrivances for adjusting the focus to different distances, for admitting different amounts of light, and for the correction of spherical aberration, could have been formed by natural selection, seems, I confess, absurd in the highest degree.[8]

That was Charles Darwin's own testimony of his doubt, as far as he could allow himself, about the origins of the human eye. Yet, all the separate components of the body would now be equally surprising to him as indications of deep design and divinely inspired complexity. Darwin's theories, which were to become the great sham of modern humanity's attempts to place itself in the center of the universe and creation, are not valid. The human eye, which mystified Darwin, is so sophisticated that it still eludes full explanation by modern science.

- The eye makes 100,000 separate motions a day, and the eyelids will blink over 400 million times in an average lifetime.
- The cornea is the initial light-focusing structure of the eye. The balance of corneal clarity—and,

therefore, sight—is highly dependent upon the ability of each highly specialized corneal cell to control its own absorption of water, nutrients, and oxygen.

- The iris contracts and dilates to control passage of light to the back of the eye. It is the most data-rich structure in the body. An iris possesses 266 identifiable characteristics, compared to the rather scant 35 displayed by the hand's fingerprint, which is currently used for identification.

- After the focusing accomplished by the lens, light and images strike the retina, which blankets the back of the eye. The cells of the retina—rods for dim and peripheral vision, and cones for color and fine detail perception—translate light photons into electrical impulses for the brain. The retina's continuous "exposure" and "development" of its pictures would take a Cray supercomputer 100 years to simulate what is occurring in the eye every second.

Briefly consider the complexity of the eye, the cornea specifically, in terms of healing. The cornea consists of five layers. Within one layer, the endothelial cells are able to recognize disease and trauma at relative distances that would be equivalent to a mother in New York City responding to her child crying in San Diego. These forewarned cells then begin producing a new protective barrier—the Descemet's membrane—on the back surface of the cornea as a preemptive repair mechanism that prevents perforation. With such a system in place, the cornea, the whole eye, and sight may be saved. How magnificent and mysterious! What do this example and our science—our instruments, experiments, and insights into nature—really tell us?

Chapter 4

EXAMPLES OF DESIGN FOR BALANCE, REPAIR, AND CURE

O LORD, how manifold are Your works!
In wisdom You have made them all.
The earth is full of Your possessions.

—PSALM 104:24

Such facts of the human body as a whole, as well as its various parts, show it to be not only the most magnificent operating system in existence, but also the greatest self-building, self-regulating, and self-repairing mechanism in the universe. The immense weight of scientific proof indicates that the astounding observed capacity of the human body to naturally heal itself is *directed by its design*. And it does so in the event of an almost limitless variety of possible wounds, biological sieges, and breakdowns. It is in the natural processes and systems of healing that irreducible complexity and intelligent design are demonstrated definitively.

Pathology, pathogens, and trauma can bend and break us, but the stunning design of the biological mechanism we each inhabit—our body—affords us beautiful, mysterious, complex, and intricate systems for repair, regeneration, and self-cure. This is a design beyond the unrealities of evolution; this is an intelligent design of irreducible complexity.

GOD'S

THE ASTOUNDING observed capacity of the human body to naturally heal itself is directed by its design.

FOR HEALING

PRESCRIPTION

The easiest way to comprehend this is to look at some particular systems of repair within the body. Just as there are an almost infinite number of attacks, injuries, and dissolutions that we may possibly experience, likewise the body is equipped with many and varied protective mechanisms. Discussion of a few of those mechanisms is sufficient illustration of the immense power that the body has to deal with the world.

Skin Healing

Skin is the largest organ of the body. It is a fabulous material that is soft enough to allow movement, yet strong and resilient enough to resist ripping. It comes not only in a wonderful variety of shades between individuals, but it also varies in texture and thickness from one part of the body to the next. Skin is our shield from, and one important method of sensing, the external world. In contact with the external world, skin is inevitably prone to suffer lacerations, abrasions, burns, punctures, and exposure to irritants. You may be suffering from one of these at this moment. If you are, you will be pleased to hear that scabs, blisters, rashes, and inflammation, familiar to all of us, are the painful testaments of skin's tireless self-curing processes at work. They are not the *injury*—rather they are evidence of the body *healing* itself.

Our blanket of skin is organized into two layers: the *epidermis* and the *dermis*. The *epidermis* is comprised of several sheets of cells at the surface, in contact with the elements that surround us. Below those sheets lies the *dermis*, made of elastin (elastic fibers) for suppleness and collagen (protein fibers) for strength. Nerves, blood vessels, hair follicles, and glands are found in this important layer. Meanwhile, the epidermis is continually being renewed: old cells are sloughed off and replaced from below. The skin's responses to injury and insult are an enhancement of this continuous, silent process.

On occasion of an injury to your skin—such as a cut—a highly complex series of reactions is *immediately* initiated. This series requires involvement by many kinds of specialized cells. It also requires the production of, and appropriate use of, specialized proteins for rebuilding as well as communication and coordination through signaling pathways. No link in the chain will engage in the absence of other links. The entire process is specific and interconnected to an unbelievable degree.

Though healing begins at the edge of a wound, new tissue must form at the site of loss rather than in surrounding undamaged tissue. This is remarkable in itself, and it offers a formidable challenge to any system of reconstruction. The immediate healing response in the skin is a nervous constriction (narrowing) of the blood vessels. Then, within the first five minutes after trauma, *vasodilation* (opening the vessels) allows a flood of platelets borne by blood plasma into the area from the capillaries. *Fibrinogen* is a protein synthesized by the liver, which is broken into fibrin strands at the wound site in the skin. These strands are then woven together to form substantial portions of the blood clot, which will stanch the blood flow. Can you sense the intricacy of the systems integration this requires?

Within 1 to 6 hours after injury, polymorphonuclear leukocytes (white blood cells) are mobilized and attracted to the site by chemicals in the blood plasma. Their purpose is to fight bacteria and remove debris such as dead cells. *Macrophages* (Greek for "big eaters"), cells of the third tissue response, present themselves within 24 to 48 hours to remove clotted blood and damaged tissue.

Granulation tissue is highly *vascularized* (populated with blood vessels) tissue that eventually replaces that initial fibrin clot. Specialized cells within the granulation tissue, called fibroblasts, manufacture collagen for the production of an extracellular matrix (like scaffolding). That stage invites the next phase of reconstruction with the introduction of the vascular endothelial cells upon which falls the burden of angiogenesis, which is the formation of new blood vessels. These new vessels have the task of delivering nutrients to, and removing waste from, the new tissue. At this point, the scar at the wound site appears red due to this increased vascularization. As the level of vascularization slowly diminishes and the collagen matrix matures, the redness fades.

Other cells in the wound area, *myofibroblasts*, are now responsible for the process of wound contraction by which the edges of the wound migrate toward the center. At that point, the body stimulates *mitosis* (the division of cells into daughter cells) and the migration of epithelial cells over the basal (deeper) layers. Basal cells continue to divide beneath the familiar scab until the epithelium is properly layered. The scab is eventually sloughed off, and the epidermis begins to keratinize, or firm up, with the production of the protein keratin. This is the same protein that makes your nails strong.

The body, skin, and cells also know when their job is complete and wound-healing processes can cease! Researchers have found that *integrins* (proteins that help cells stick to surfaces) tell cells when their wound-healing activities should stop. The first integrin (alpha3beta1) helps cells respond to the chemical signals produced by a wound and move into the wound area. The second integrin (alpha6beta4) turns off the instructions issued by the first integrin. In this manner, cells move under direction of the first integrin, then are slowed and eventually anchored by the second integrin. *Never are the instructions in conflict.*

Trauma can present a powerful test to the skin's healing processes. A scar is rarely as strong as the tissue it replaces, and more severe wounds may result in the permanent loss of structures such as sweat glands or nerve endings. Additionally, advanced age, poor immune system health, dietary deficiencies, surrounding environmental extremes, and preexisting medical conditions can all hobble the speed and efficacy of the healing mechanisms. However, overall, the skin repair process works while demonstrating a high level of specificity and interconnectedness much more elaborate than the inner workings of a Swiss clock. Do you believe that a beautiful, precise clock can suddenly appear in a woodpile or a meadow without a designer and hands to put the pieces together? There is no explanation for the incredibly complex and ordered process of skin healing outside of the existence of a *design for healing* created by a caring Designer. The healing in a "simple" cut finger is a remarkably potent manifestation of irreducible complexity and a Creator's intelligent design for your healing. It originates in the zygote, and it asks for nothing less than our deep gratitude for its Creator.

GOD'S

FOR HEALING

THE HEALING IN A "simple" cut finger is a remarkably potent manifestation of irreducible complexity and a Creator's intelligent design for your healing.

PRESCRIPTION

Corneal Healing

Events in the eye's cornea provide an exciting example of the body's natural ability to repair itself as well. We have already touched upon them, but my friend and colleague Dr. James Rowsey gives a deeper description of the process. He refers to it as *molecular direction by the Creator.*

Whether the surgeon's incision is made to transplant a cornea, which is Dr. Rowsey's area of expertise, or to remove a cataract, which is my specialty, the responses at the cellular level remain true to the same valued end of healing the cornea.

Dr. Rowsey explains:

> During surgery, the wound healing response in the cornea *immediately* follows the incision. How fine and remarkable that is! Each part of the cornea undergoes a different healing response while communicating information of the overall healing response to adjacent cells. This alone is astounding: each cell type has a different focus, a slightly different intelligence for healing. Even more, varying responses *within* a certain cell type are demonstrated throughout a single healing event. Take, for example, the various responses found in the corneal epithelium, which has the responsibility of covering the surface of the cornea to protect the eye from infectious agents in the air.
>
> The epithelium is unavoidably "injured" by the surgeon's incision, and *cells at the incision line* recognize this by the sudden disappearance of adjacent cells and their contact inhibition. You may picture this effect as similar to the experience of 50 people standing upright, squeezed into a bus. After 48 people get off the bus, the remaining 2 recognize the new conditions when they find a lot more room to move around and are no longer bumping shoulders with others.
>
> The underlying nerves are immediately irritated by the reflex release of *inflammatory mediators* (chemicals of communication). This reaction causes immediate pain, the same as if a foreign body had suddenly entered the eye. In fact, the same wound healing response occurs when a speck of dust finds its way into your eye. The nerves transmit information to the brain, and the brain then dispatches *neuropeptides* (molecules behaving as

transmitters), specifically substance P, back down the nerve from the central nervous system toward the eye and its incision site. The brain and nervous system are part of corneal healing! Substance P causes tears to flow in an attempt to wash out the "foreign body" and initiates the migration of corneal cells into the void of the incision line. This migration is a thing of wonder.

First, the area of incision is flooded by fibronectin from adjacent cells. Fibronectin is a protein that acts like a "biological glue" to facilitate cell migration. The corneal cells nearest the incision have their internal machinery activated by substance P and, recognizing the fibronectin outside the cell's plasma membrane, mobilize filaments—fibrils—*inside* the cell in the direction of the incision. Fibrils *inside* the cell are temporarily anchored to the *external* fibronectin *through* the plasma membrane. The cell then "crawls" over the fibronectin.

The second element of the migration requires that the trailing edge of the cell continually release its anchor while the leading edge continues to recognize new fibronectin and orient the cell forward toward it. That is an amazing feat. All of the cells are "holding hands" with the attachments of their adjacent membranes. If they cannot release that handholding endeavor they cannot actually slide to fill the space made by the scalpel.

Once cells cover the incision they are attached permanently with new anchoring fibrils (type 4 collagen, tenascin, integrin, and type 7 collagen), which prevents any cell displacement caused by instinctive blinking. The new cellular attachment to the basement membrane makes the surface of the incision watertight and resistant to the invasion of microorganisms such as bacteria.

There is yet another level to this marvel. Created nature is parsimonious. That is, it is conservative in its use of resources, and it rarely uses two or more types of molecule when one will suffice. Remember the

GOD'S PRESCRIPTION *for* HEALING

incredibly complex genetic library of DNA? It performs its astounding job utilizing combinations of a mere four bases. So, the healing cell movement we observe in the cornea—that which follows a map of fibronectin—is the same process observed in growth, in the development of a fetus, and in birth.

Meanwhile, as epithelial cells migrate, the cells farthest from the incision, along the line of the incision, begin to divide to replace the cells that have moved. The cells at the bottom of the epithelial defect contract their plasma membranes to avoid being hit by any injurious agent. This is similar to the startle response we experience when we hear a loud noise. Such a sudden sound causes us to reflexively shrink our shoulders and pull our head down, to avoid being hit.

Impressively, the fluid from the tear film enters the area of incision and, swelling the body of the cornea, allows nutrients, inflammatory mediators, and white blood cells to enter the area of the defect more readily by passing through the cornea. If the patient does not have adequate tears, the cells continue to be irritated and dry out. The corneal surface with inadequate moisture is interpreted by the cell as a danger signal, and the cells begin to increase the production of prekeratin fibrils. Keratinization, the same process that occurs in skin repair occurs at this point. Balance is the key in the process.[1]

Microscopic events in the cornea such as these could not be known at the time when Darwin wrote his theories. He was already bemused by the eye's abilities observed at a macroscopic level, and he doubted the accuracy of his own ideas when he pondered the human eye. Darwin's doubt would, of necessity, have been magnified a thousandfold if he had had access to the same biochemical data introduced in this section. Corneal healing exhibits incredible interrelatedness and profound complexity. More, however, there is an observed directedness to all the processes in the eye that develop from the information stored in the zygote. This is inexplicable without appeal to the concept of a purposeful design for healing.

The Immune System

You are familiar with the coughing, sniffling, aches, and fever of a cold. If you were led to a quiet moment of reflection on your bed, a box of tissues in one hand and a remote control in the other, you would wonder what could cause you so much misery for a week and then disappear. Many might be inclined to explain absences to teachers or bosses as the effort of "fighting a bug." These simple, common words demonstrate a fundamental understanding of the actual natural processes at work.

However, how many of us would connect the throes of flu with an infected finger, an acne pimple, or cancer? We are depending upon our immune system moment by moment, day by day, from beginning to end. We depend on the intelligence, vigilance, and vigor of the system to prevent and to cure illness even when we least expect it and are least aware. For example, brushing one's teeth is an undeniably healthy act. Yet, each time you do it, you release a small surge of bacteria into your bloodstream known as *bacteremia*. The only reason this never endangers you is exactly due to the protection of your wonderful immune system. However, the threat posed by such an invasion is significant enough that those with heart valve problems must take antibiotics before and after visits to the dentist to assist in a fight of which most of us are never normally aware.

The immune system carries out its many roles as advance warning system, guard and barrier, and a war machine with more precision than an atomic clock. You may in fact be aware of this through your reading. However, it is difficult for anyone to fully fathom the complexity, harmony, intricacy, and integration on multiple levels demonstrated in even the "simplest" feat of your body's triumph over infection and disease. The tools of advanced science have not been able to fully discover the logic of the design of the human body's immune system. One thing that *is* clear is the absolute necessity for such a system in the environment of this world in which we live; *it is the definition of survival.*

"From the time of conception, the human organism faces attack from a wide variety of infectious agents. We must have ways to identify them and defend ourselves against their invasion, colonization, and toxic effects."[2] From first instructions in the zygote's DNA, the fully developed immune system mounts a defense that includes structures at macroscopic and microscopic levels. This means the participation of master glands, tissues, vessels, and areas where special cells are harbored as well as the functions of structures such as select soldier cells, chemical factory cells, and cells that clean up. Subcellular components, measured in mere nanometers, include proteins that complement the action of the cells, and chemical messengers. The interactions within and between all levels are hugely complex.

The infectious agents that concern us, and can kill us, are nearly innumerable. They are microbes—biological entities—that act as tiny invaders breaching the individual's external limits "through the gastrointestinal, respiratory, and urogenital tracts and through breaks in the skin."[3] Since there are microbes that enter the body but do not cause disease, microbes that invade and cause disease are referred to as *pathogens*. The individual body that the pathogens invade is called a *host*. That is, when you have caught a cold, you have become a host for a pathogen.

The pathogens that infect humans fall into four categories: *Bacteria* possess no cell nucleus, but with their double-stranded DNA, bacteria can double in population within twenty minutes under optimal conditions. Diseases caused by bacteria include pneumonia, tuberculosis, and strep infections. *Fungi* are found primarily as single-celled yeasts or multicelled molds. Diseases caused by fungi include athlete's foot. *Parasites* are invertebrate animals, often with organ systems, that require a host for at least a portion of their life cycle. Malaria is a well-known disease of this type, and one in which the parasite demonstrates the use of two separate hosts (human and mosquito) for separate phases in its life cycle. *Viruses* are quite unique in the world

GOD'S PRESCRIPTION FOR HEALING

THE IMMUNE SYSTEM carries out its many roles as advance warning system, guard and barrier, and a war machine with more precision than an atomic clock.

of living things. Science is not even sure that viruses can be considered *alive* though they are obviously organic. Viruses cannot reproduce outside of a host cell; they consist of a short strand of genetic material in a protein coat.[4] Prominent examples of viral diseases are common colds, smallpox, and AIDS.

Protecting the body from pathogens or harmful foreign substances is a complicated war for life and health. It means constant battling in a search-and-destroy mode. The immune system's twin goals are to clearly identify its enemy and then to destroy it without harming the body. How is this achieved?

Understanding the Immune System

The field of immunology—our understanding of the immune system—was born with a discovery made in 1890 at a laboratory in Berlin. Researchers there at that time injected a rabbit with a dose of tetanus that was small enough for the rabbit to survive it. They prepared a serum from the blood of that rabbit. It was then observed that this serum was capable of neutralizing powerful samples of the tetanus toxin in other individuals.[5] This was the beginning of a revolution in medicine and ushered in the era of vaccinations. Discoveries continued to be made into the twentieth century, and still we are learning about this wonderful system today.

> GOD'S
>
> THE IMMUNE SYSTEM'S twin goals are to clearly identify its enemy and then to destroy it without harming the body.
>
> PRESCRIPTION

Immunity as defense is, to varying degrees, universal in nature. Many animals and many plants, as well, display it. However, it is the human system that represents the apotheosis—the highest degree of sophistication. This sophistication is expressed by the two levels of the body's protective immunity: *innate* immunity and *adaptive* immunity. It is important to realize at the outset that the innate and adaptive immune systems do not act in isolation of one another, or of many organs in the body and the nervous system, including the brain. "In any immune response, the components function in concert, in tandem, or in conflict."[6] This is a colossal project of the finest engineering and irreducible complexity. Integration, communication, intelligence, and balance are the hallmarks of our wonderful immune system. There is no way to look at it and not glimpse the Creator's wisdom within.

Innate (nonspecific) immunity

Innate resistance is present from birth in all normal individuals. It is distinguished by several components, or levels, that function without prior exposure to a specific pathogen. It operates the same way each time the individual is exposed, and it responds to each individual invader with exactly the same speed and intensity. Reexposure to a previously encountered pathogen does not change its response. That is, the innate immune system has no memory.[7]

The first level of protection by innate immunity is the presence of *physical barriers* to invasion. These include skin, externally, and mucous membranes of gastrointestinal tract and epithelium of the lungs, internally. Then, there are *secreted products*, such as acid in the stomach or lysozyme in tears, which are toxic to invaders. A *cellular* level consists of white blood cells and natural killer cells. The white cells—phagocytes—are attracted to sites of infection by products of the infecting organism where they proceed to ingest and digest the invader.[8] The natural killer cells release toxins on contact with an offending cell, including tumor cells. Neither of these cell types develops a memory from its battles. The *soluble molecular* component of the innate system includes *cytokines* (polypeptides), which destroy target cells but also recruit the body's cells into the fray. These chemicals, like the cells of the innate system, are nonspecific in that they distinguish neither pathogens from one another nor formerly encountered organisms from those entering the body for the first time. *Adjustments* in pH and temperature (fever) are also reactions that seek to protect the body by killing its attackers.

The innate immune system is mustered and engaged as soon as an organism has breached one of the body's mechanical barriers; therefore, it is the first defense. However, invading organisms immediately find a fertile field within the human body and can reproduce rapidly, so the body needs a more precise, *specific*, and destructive system to help wage war. It has this system in adaptive immunity.

Adaptive (specific) immunity

The adaptive, or specific, immune defense system can become active only after the individual human has been exposed to part of, or a product of, an infectious biological agent. That which stimulates an immune response is referred to as an *antigen*. This system then learns the "face" of a specific antigen as separate from other antigens. However, just as importantly, the system distinguishes foreign antigens from self—the tissues of the host body—by-products distributed on the surface of every nucleated (possessing a nucleus) cell in the body. This ability to recognize and discern, say, a herpes virus and to treat it as foreign is *forever* retained by the body after initial exposure. This memory allows the adaptive system to increase its intensity and lower its response time upon reexposure to a "familiar" antigen.[9]

The adaptive immune system consists of two arms: First, *humoral* immunity is mediated by soluble protein molecules known as *antibodies*. The primary function of an antibody is to bind the antigen and mount a direct neutralizing effect. It frequently requires interaction with *secondary effector mechanisms* such as a complement system of serum proteins, which control enzyme cascades.[10]

Second, *cellular* immunity is mediated by a variety of specifically sensitized white blood cells, lymphocytes, which attack the contagion in "hand-to-hand" combat.[11] These cells also depend upon identification of enemies through cell-surface receptors. They can recombine their information and are, therefore, specially made for specific antigens.

Humoral immunity—Introduction of a new antigen into the body encourages the body's production of the powerful antibody molecules. Antibodies are produced by special white blood cells referred to as B lymphocytes—B cells. Stimuli from other cells—helper T cells—inspire the B cells to begin production of specific antibodies. An antibody will appear in the bloodstream carried by the B cells about three days after exposure to an antigen. An antigen is the lock that distinguishes a particular pathogen from all others. Antibodies are the body's keys to those locks, and they fit perfectly. Each particular antibody is produced, and its formula retained in the immune system's memory forever, with the introduction of *every single* antigen.[12]

GOD'S PRESCRIPTION *for* HEALING

Other life forms mutate faster than your body can keep up. The number of potential antigens is potentially limitless. However, our immune system can produce "more than a hundred million—different types of antibody."[13] How can the body mount a specific defense against an almost unlimited variety of antigens when the number of genes in our DNA is limited? The answer is almost beyond our comprehension. Proteins are made from stretches of DNA—genes. Genes for the production of antibodies are assembled from scattered or distant (along the DNA molecule) bits and pieces by a maturing B cell. The B cell selects, rearranges, shuffles, and splices DNA from any location in its library. A similar process exists in T cells for the construction of unique surface receptors.

Cellular immunity—This refers to the T cells mentioned above. They were not discovered until the 1960s, and a few sub groups have been distinguished. One important T cell is the helper T cell. Helper T cells are the conductors of immunity. They release chemical messages called *lymphokines*, which are required by B cells and other T cells to mature (to identify specific invaders) with their special abilities. The helper T cells are the target of the AIDS virus, and that is why that disease is so devastating: It attacks both antibody and killer T-cell branches of the immune response.[14]

> GOD'S
>
> OUR IMMUNE SYSTEM can produce "more than a hundred million— different types of antibody."
>
> FOR HEALING
>
> PRESCRIPTION

The killer T cell is a very advanced hunter. It seeks out its quarry, whose particular identifying markers it has learned, and it destroys the pathogen hiding in cells by destroying the cells that have been invaded. This includes the body's own cancer cells. T cells kill on contact by injecting toxins. However, unlike the method of natural killer cells, these T cells initiate a self-destruct code already programmed into every cell. In other words, the killer T helps a cell commit suicide once it has been altered and poses a danger to the body as a whole. In this way, pathogens are not given the opportunity to adapt a defense to a killer cell's weapon.

Finally, there are suppressor T cells. They have a capability to destroy virus-infected cells, but, more importantly, their special role is one of maintaining the balance of immune responses. They suppress or dampen the actions of other immune cells. Otherwise immunity could easily lead to problems such as allergies or autoimmune reactions, which we will soon look at briefly.

After the various T cells have waged their immunological war on a particular invader, more macrophages are called in to clean up the "debris." This is a helper-killer-macrophage teamwork, which is a key immune defense mechanism called *inflammation*. The inflammatory response in tissues eventually results in the healing, sometimes through scarring. Inflammation is part of the process of healing.

Tissues and organs of immunity

Above the cellular level are structures and organs that are vital to our immunity. The *lymphatic system* is one of these important structures.[15] The lymphatic system collects fluids throughout the body that have seeped out of the bloodstream and cannot reenter due to the hydrostatic pressure created by the pumping of the heart. One thing this accomplishes is to make the circulation of blood a completely closed system. However, this lymph system has been co-opted for the purposes of immunity. Because the lymph system drains the body tissues, it makes an excellent way to detect foreign invaders. Lymph nodes throughout the body act as filters and inspection stations. The three main types of white blood cells in the immune system—the macrophages, T cells, and B cells—are in the blood stream, but they are also in the lymph system and the *spleen* to accommodate such inspection and appropriate responses.

Bone marrow is one of the master organs of the system. In it reside undifferentiated *stem cells*.[16] You have probably read about these cells in the newspaper—their medical potential is enormous. These are yet undifferentiated cells that will eventually choose a vocation when called upon. In the immune system they will grow into all of the important, specialized red and white blood cells.

The *thymus* is one more master organ. It provides the location and environment for the maturation of the all-important T cells that arrive in a pre-T state through the bloodstream.[17] In fact, the *T* in T cell stands for "thymus-influenced." During the maturation process in the thymus two very important things occur. First, the T cells decide whether to become helper T cells or killer T cells. And second, they acquire one of the most important attributes of the whole system—the ability to distinguish self from nonself.

The main goals

The human immune system exhibits unparalleled complexity and intelligence of design in several significant areas. This system displays profound *recognition* capabilities. How does the system recognize a familiar antigen to attack, or components of the host body itself to not attack? This is done at the molecular level with cells of the immune system creating a variety of molecular bonds with a small, distinctive part of the antigen. It exhibits *specificity* in its ability to discriminate between self and foreign. It kills the foreign without attacking self. It has a *memory*. When your body is first invaded, the primary immune response finds the invader and destroys it, and you get better. The secondary immune response, the memory, means that with every subsequent exposure to that particular invader for the rest of your life you have an immunity—a resistance—that prevents it from making you sick again. Finally, your wonderful immune system displays *diversity*. The number of life forms that can cause disease and death is unimaginably huge. Many of these organisms also have the ability to mutate and thereby "look" different. The SARS virus that caused so much havoc is reportedly mutating into something that may be even more dangerous.[18] In response to this sort of contingency, the body is equipped to produce more than 100 million different antigen receptors, each recognizing a different foreign antigen.[19]

In looking at the cells, structures, chemicals, integration, and communication of the immune system, it is important to realize that immune responses are very powerful, and they must be controlled very precisely. If they are not, serious damage can result. It is apparent that the primary attribute and functioning principle for the immune system is *balance*—the appropriate response to injury, which is neither too weak nor exaggerated. Unfortunately, this balance cannot always be maintained, and problems result.

The double-edged sword—when things go wrong

That which helps us can also hurt us. The ability of the immune system to respond to genuine threats in a balanced manner, with appropriate toughness, is a major factor in healing and continuing health. Yet, with a system that is so complex and requiring such complete coordination between constituent parts, there is the *possibility* of malfunction. Breakdown in the immune system can lead to disease, allergy, and even cancer. *The health and balance of the immune system itself are necessary for our health, healing, and well-being overall.*

Autoimmune disease—*Auto* is the Greek word for "self." An autoimmune disease occurs when the immune system loses its ability to recognize self, and the body begins to make antibodies and T cells that attack its own tissues. The results of this reversal can be devastating. Even if you are not suffering with one of these diseases, you will be familiar with some of the names: rheumatoid arthritis, multiple sclerosis, juvenile diabetes, and psoriasis.

Autoimmune diseases do not occur frequently, and why they would at all is still not very well understood by science. A weakness in the genetic determination of labeling one's own cells combined with a microorganism's effort to divert attention from itself may be one cause of autoimmune disease. That is, there is a growing belief that mimicry by invading organisms has a role in the autoimmune disease *in individuals who are genetically predisposed.* If molecules of a microbe resemble host molecules, the immune response reacts against the obviously foreign material but also against the host tissues that *appear* to be similar.[20]

Allergy—Here is something common—an experience that many of you understand firsthand. You may think of allergic response as the hypersensitivity of one's immune system.[21] In other words, the response to threat is overdone and unbalanced. In a susceptible individual, a *normally harmless* substance is perceived as a threat and is attacked. Once such an irritant, such as pollen, has been recognized as previously

GOD'S

FOR HEALING

THE ABILITY OF THE immune system to respond to genuine threats in a balanced manner, with appropriate toughness, is a major factor in healing and continuing health.

PRESCRIPTION

encountered, an antibody signals other cells—mast cells—to release their powerful chemicals, such as histamine. Mast cells are common in the lungs, skin, tongue, nasal passages, and intestines, and the release of their numerous chemicals leads to the sneezing, rashes, and other symptoms of allergy. More ominously, some, though rare, allergic reactions can lead to life-threatening anaphylactic shock.

Immunopathology—There are casualties and collateral damage in any war; the war within the human body is no different. Some diseases are due not to the damage caused by a microbe but by the host's own response to the infection. In the fight against infection a certain amount of damage to some normal tissues seems unavoidable. Tuberculosis and leprosy are examples of this.[22]

In its fight, the body must achieve its goals in an appropriate and measured way that minimizes dangers. The immune system is guided by the wisdom that sprang from the zygote as it aims to accomplish this very difficult task. It may not always be entirely possible. There are innumerable "enemies" to ward off. It is only through the mastery of the immune system that we can ever reach maturity and consider ourselves healthy *at all*.

Immunodeficiency—Immunodeficiency is seen in individuals who have an immune system that does not exist or cannot perform at the level necessary to protect the body.

Primary immunodeficiency is inherited or congenital. Secondary immunodeficiency is acquired through infection, disease, or drug treatment for conditions such as cancer. The deficiency may be anywhere along the line of immune system communication or specialized cell development.[23] The results may mean frequent and severe infections. They may mean a fatal disease like sickle cell anemia in predisposed individuals. Or they may mean a complete intolerance for the world at large, requiring that one live his or her life in a plastic bubble.

Cancer—Cancer presents us with a special case or, perhaps, an especially *interesting* case of disease and the immune system. It is of interest because of the wide swath of destruction this disease—group of diseases—cuts through modern societies. The very sound of the word fills most hearts with dread, and many families have been broken by it. Some of you reading this may presently be enduring the fears as well as pains and disfigurements of cancer and doctors' various therapies. Others will be concerned about avoiding the "plague" altogether. There is good news for everyone in that our bodies have been designed to act upon cancer and to fight it. The immune system *is not the whole story*, of course, but it is a significant part in natural healing and in new directions for medical science.

Programmed cell death is known as *apoptosis*.[24] It is important because normal cells are born, mature, live out their useful lives, and die in an orderly manner—just as we do. An outstanding characteristic of cancer cells is the lost capacity for apoptosis. They grow without restraint outside the body's control like a foreign invader of the body. "In their ruthless pursuit of immortality they eventually kill the host."[25]

When a cell becomes cancerous, some of the markers on its surface change, and the immune system is able to recognize it as something "foreign" This aspect of the system is called *immune surveillance*.[26] Therefore, it is expected that cancer cells can be eliminated by the immune system in the same way as a flu virus is through early detection and mobilization of immune system cells. However, the immune surveillance system can break down or become overwhelmed. Environmental and lifestyle factors can contribute to this. There is also evidence to suggest that some cancers are a late consequence of earlier infection by certain viruses.[27] Cancer cells wage their war by disguising themselves so that killer T cells cannot recognize them and engage the natural self-destruct code. Cancer cells may also encourage the development of suppressor T cells, thereby dampening immune responses to the tumor.

In a healthy body there will always be errors in cell replication, and there will be cell mutations (a biochemical change in genetic material) caused by outside influences. This means that cancer cells naturally

GOD'S

FOR HEALING

MOST RECENT research has found a definite connection between a healthy immune system and the prevention of cancer or winning the war against certain cancers once they have already bloomed.

PRESCRIPTION

GOD'S PRESCRIPTION *for* HEALING

appear fairly frequently. The reason that we are not all sick with cancer is likely due to the immune system's prowess at detecting and dispatching such cells. Most recent research has found a definite connection between a healthy immune system and the prevention of cancer or winning the war against certain cancers once they have already bloomed. This is exciting news because it means that maintaining a healthy body generally, and a healthy immune system specifically, can assist us against the ravages of cancer. It also means that research into the immune system may one day lead to effective treatments and even, perhaps, vaccines against the disease.

Chapter 5

DESIGNED FOR HEALTH

Even if there is only one possible unified theory, it is just a set of rules and equations. What is it that breathes fire into the equations and makes a universe for them to describe? The usual approach of science of constructing a mathematical model cannot answer the question of why there should be a universe for the model to describe. Why does the universe go to all the bother of existing?

—Stephen Hawking[1]

No natural system is perfect. You can and should expect that. The immune system, the cornea, and the skin all have their points of occasional weakness; however, this is not the basis from which to appreciate the Creator's handiwork. Look at what they *do* accomplish for you! The odds are stacked against us biologically in a world *so* full of danger: mutating SARS viruses in the air, salmonella in our chicken, *E. coli* in our hamburger, and West Nile virus in the mosquitoes buzzing by our ears. These are a mere handful of familiar threats. With clear eyes we must observe the massive accomplishments of the intricate, sophisticated systems that we own from the moment we develop from a miniscule zygote. In the face of an impossibly huge number of threats, we mostly continue to survive. This survival and hope for healthiness would be meaningless if it were not for the Creator's intelligence expressed throughout the entire body. There is undoubtedly an irreducible complexity built into us that is still beyond our ability to understand. It asks each one of us to acknowledge and worship its Creator, *our* Creator, in deep appreciation and in awe and *wonder* of such profound beauty.

Ravi Zacharias has recently considered the heart of wonder, and wonder in the heart, in his book *Recapture the Wonder.* You may think of wonder as "childlikeness in its sublimity."[2] It is right to think so. Wonder is the emotional experience that opens our eyes wide and causes our eyes to widen and our hearts to race with excitement. The dream of ultimate fulfillment, the conscious and unconscious pursuit of life, is in wonder—in *the balance of enchantment with reality.*

The more knowledge of stars and atoms and T cells we attain, it seems, the less wonder we allow ourselves to enjoy. *This should not, nor need not, be the case.* In fact, knowledge of our human body and its many mechanisms and systems for life and health ought to excite our curiosity and wonder to no end! Deep mysteries in nature, our nature, can only prompt awe and wonder for the Intelligence, the Creator, Father, who designed all and understands everything. It is because He understands everything that He has given us the searching minds we have. Human science provides us with a tiny taste of deep design and loving care built into the zygote's DNA and the body that it generates. That is a design so unbelievably remarkable, awe-inspiring, mysterious, and *wonder*ful that we must—really must—be grateful to God every moment that we are breathing.

Even so, the evidence exposed by modern scientific method continues to be largely interpreted by most within the terms of Darwinism and the theories of evolution. That does not add up. Interpreted honestly and humbly, details of our nature actually point to an irreducible complexity that could not be the product of mindless, directionless natural selection. What science *does* tell us, if we are not proud, is that within our organs, tissues, cells, DNA code, and subcellular molecular particles is the source for immense wonder. And it is—or should be—our main inspiration for great appreciation. In the organization of our atoms, proteins, and integrated systems is the evidence that we were *created* with a marvelous, miraculous design intended not only to *define* but also to *promote* and *prolong* our physical existence on the earth according to a divine plan.

GOD'S PRESCRIPTION FOR HEALING

WE WERE CREATED with a marvelous, miraculous design intended not only to define but also to promote and prolong our physical existence on the earth according to a divine plan.

In the present era the existence of an eternal soul and the dignity of each one of us—unique and precious in God's sight—have been denied. However, *actual scientific facts*, which all originate in a solitary, fertilized egg, give us a startling account of the beautiful mind of the Creator. In the natural defenses and responses of the human body is the clear expression of God's love and His plan for, and method of, our healing. God hands us His calling card through the scientific facts of our ability to exist, to flourish, and to heal when stricken. *This is His first gift of healing.* As the creation, why do we not see this and love the Creator for it? Why are we not filled with appreciation? We must look at the body, at the amazing zygote, and see the face of God. Looking at the marvels of creation, we may rekindle our wonder through a spirit of deep appreciation of the gift.

Absolutely, within our structure is the design for healing; however, we are a mortal creation, and the human body *is* fallible. The fact that we need healing at all means that we, our bodies, have the potential to falter and fail. In the occasional imbalances of the body, we come to see that sickness is as much a part of life as health is. Restoration is the goal we reach for, and it still may sometimes be outside the reach of natural systems alone. In such cases we must look outside of ourselves for some assistance. That is the idea, truth, and divine gift that we turn to next.

PART II

ASSISTED HEALING

Chapter 6

PHYSICIAN-ASSISTED HEALING

No, a thousand times no: there does not exist a category of science to which one can give the name applied science. There are science and the applications of science, bound together as the fruit to the tree which bears it.
—LOUIS PASTEUR (1822–1895)[1]

Try not to despair—ever. A great Intelligence has gone before you and anticipated your needs. *You have been designed for healing.* We have seen that the human body—*your* very own body—is wonderful and mysterious in the complexity of that design. It is a magnificent testimony to the Creator's design of the universe. With its ability to operate and maintain itself, the human body is the *highlight of all created nature.*

Yet, it is true, we are mortal. We must understand that, as organic beings, we are caught in continuous biological battles for strength, health, and continued existence. Deadly microorganisms, injuries, and neuromuscular diseases are a few dangerous possibilities among an almost infinite number. Under so many varied attacks we can expect the human body to lose some of those battles. However, some of the resulting breakdowns need not lead to permanent impairment, pain, or death as

GOD'S

> OFTEN, THE difference between health and illness, or life and death, lies in the skillful, informed application of knowledge of the human body.

FOR HEALING

PRESCRIPTION

we usually fear. Interruptions in proper function can be influenced and even reversed when true understanding of and appreciation for the body's systems are applied to care, cure, and prevention. Often, the difference between health and illness, or life and death, lies in the skillful, informed application of knowledge of the human body. That is knowledge that begins with the understanding of the miracle contained in the cells that originate from the zygote.

In other words, the road to well-being sometimes lies in finding *assistance* for the natural process of healing. *Our collective knowledge of the human design is provided for judicious intervention. This is the Creator's second gift of healing.*

Illness is a common human experience. Even the healthiest individuals among us cannot completely escape it. Still, it may not be easy for a person to admit to the need for assistance when his or her natural healing mechanisms have become injured, inadequate, or overtaxed. However, an authentic appreciation for the miracle of the body will raise awareness and concern for the maintenance of its balance. When you are able to view life for the gift that it is, you will become committed to taking diligent care of it, just as you would tend a garden. You will desire to do *whatever you can* to remain healthy and to flourish. Taking care of your body is an *important responsibility*. That responsibility encompasses pursuing the wisdom and methods of healing provided by the collective human knowledge of the single cell and your wonderful design.

To be healed—to fulfill the meaning of your design for healing—sometimes you will need to change the food that you eat; sometimes you will need to find a bandage; and sometimes you will need to see a doctor.

Medical Science, the Physician, and Healing

> No, a thousand times no: there does not exist a category of science to which one can give the name applied science. There are science and the applications of science, bound together as the fruit to the tree which bears it.
> —LOUIS PASTEUR (1822–1895)

The essence of medical science is the observation of, appreciation for, and careful intervention in the natural design when it is needed. In medicine, at least, our practice is bound as tightly to our scientific understanding of the manifestations of the Creator's knowledge as fruit is to the tree. In our age, knowledge of the structures and functions of a body derived from a zygote is the base of the tree that bears the fruit of the physician's methods of healing.

When you are sick or injured, you turn for healing to those men and women who must do their job within their understanding of our created design. They examine, interpret tests, administer medication, and repair or alter with surgery. You anticipate their knowledge and skill to bring you comfort and relief—and to restore you. They employ techniques and apply scientific knowledge to reestablish the integrity of a body whose natural ability to defend or develop is enfeebled, broken down, or nonexistent. They apply the techniques in line with principles of nature, of the divine design of the body.

I have had personal experience with this outside of my role as a physician. After a bicycle accident during training years ago, I suffered a severe and painful break in the femur, the large bone, of one leg. Dr. Dean Cole restored my leg with a vision of universal principles—physics, columns, loadbearing—along with an intimate understanding of human bones and their growth. He introduced an invention of his own into my broken leg, which lengthened the bone from the *inside* as it healed. Over the period of a few months, the bone grew a necessary 2.5 inches that it would not have done through traditional treatment.

Deep understanding of the mechanics of the body's design within universal laws is what God has provided humanity. Doctors must use this understanding in their efforts to heal. Therefore, accepting your responsibility for your body in illness often leads you to the doors of physicians in your hour of need. *As stewards of our bodies, which are God's temples, we must seek the knowledge and expertise of those who are familiar with the design.* Those people are our physicians, and we must be willing to accept their assistance in our healing.

GOD'S PRESCRIPTION FOR HEALING

> WHEN YOU ARE ABLE to view life for the gift that it is, you will become committed to taking diligent care of it, just as you would tend a garden.

The following examples will help to demonstrate the role of physicians and medical scientists in assisting our healing.

The example of cataract surgery

This is an area in which I am very familiar, and I understand the need for, and meaning of, medical practice in alignment with the details of the Creator's design. Our bodies are made for efficient operation. However, except for the young among us, we are aware of the slowing, shrinking, and weakening effects of time. Cataracts—clouding of the lenses in the eyes—are usually one natural result of aging. Injuries, some medications, and certain diseases may also contribute to their development.

A cataract often results in blurred, fuzzy, diminished vision, and trouble with glare. It will progressively limit one's lifestyle and ability to function. Presence of cataracts may eventually lead to blindness. A most important point to consider is that *a cataract will not resolve itself; the body has no mechanism for changing it.* Therefore, it becomes the task of the eye surgeon to intervene to rectify the vision impairment and the increased hardship caused by a cataract. Cataract surgery is an excellent example of the physician's role in assisting the body's God-given abilities to heal by entering where natural processes are limited or absent.

Each carefully considered surgical step is based on sound, scientific understanding of the eye's design. This means that the surgeon, first, has respect and regard for the particular aspects and requirements of the physical entity that is made of various tissues. It also means, then, that the doctor strives for excellence in technology and technique. And perhaps most importantly, it means that there is concern for, and loving response to, the individual patient with a problem. The patient is someone who wants to see. Cataract surgery is an excellent demonstration of the effort to cure and to *heal.*

It first requires the eye surgeon's knowledge of the tissues' fragility *and* their strengths. It requires the ability to understand the integration of the eye and its tissues in the body as a whole. Ultimately, it requires a desire—the task and privilege of the doctor—to protect those tissues with each surgical movement. Through thoroughness and conscientiousness the risk of infection and complications can be reduced while function is restored to the eye.

The ultimate goal is to send the patient back into an enhanced and enlarged experience of life. So, as I have written:

> The evolution of surgical practice has been to decrease
> the level of invasiveness to the body; that is to achieve

a highly specific, successful outcome with the least disruption to the patient's physical state. The goal is a minimal level of anesthesia, the absence of discomfort, minimal postoperative inflammation, and near-immediate visual recovery with no complications. As modern cataract surgical techniques have changed to achieve these goals, so has the composition of our pharmaceutical armamentarium.[2]

A simple description of the anatomy of a human eye begins with the clear cornea at the front, which provides most of the eye's optical power—our window on the world. A colored iris sits behind the cornea, widening and narrowing to control the level of light entering the eye. A crystalline lens—our object of attention here—lies behind the iris to focus light on images that enter the eye. Finally, a sensitive retina covering the back of the eye "captures" all those incoming images in the form of photons of light. The retina sends its information to the brain, and then we see.

Good sight depends on the natural optics of the lens to make the initial images sharp and coherent. When the lens becomes cloudy, like smoked glass, light photons are trapped or diffused, and images are no longer properly focused on the retina. Vision is painlessly and progressively impaired as the cataract progresses.

> ## GOD'S PRESCRIPTION FOR HEALING
>
> CATARACT SURGERY is an excellent example of the physician's role in assisting the body's God-given abilities to heal by entering where natural processes are limited or absent.

To reestablish sight, a surgical procedure is required. The latest innovations have made this procedure brief and gentle, requiring minimal recovery time. This is done in favor of the patient, to reduce discomfort and inconvenience. And the results translate easily: *sight*!

The first step, of course, is the ophthalmologist's thorough and sensitive physical examination of the patient's eye. Once the presence of a cataract has been established, the eye is carefully measured for its axial length (length from front to back) and the curvature of the cornea. These measurements allow the doctor to determine which I.O.L.— IntraOcular (inside the eye) Lens—to introduce into the eye once the cataract has been removed. The I.O.L. is a man-made, silicone plastic lens that replaces the cloudy, natural lens that the surgeon removes. Imagine the depth of understanding for us to get this far. The eye's natural shape and function had to be considered along with universal concepts, such as the refraction of light, to produce such a wonderful thing. After these measurements, surgery can proceed.

The lens is located behind the pupil, which is dilated or widened to its maximum extent. The eye is anesthetized to eliminate sensation temporarily. A sterile field is created by draping around the eye and bathing the *conjunctiva* (the membrane covering the eye) three times with an antiseptic. I demand a scrubbing around the lids three times with the same solution. A lid speculum is then put in place by the surgeon to hold the eye open. An initial limbic (the transition area between the cornea and white sclera) stab incision is made, and a viscoelastic substance is injected into the anterior chamber, which is the space at the front of the eye between the cornea and the iris. Then a tiny corneal incision, 2.5 millimeters long, is made at the edge of the cornea. This is a very special incision because it is so small and ultimately requires no sutures to close it. The incision must be made at an angle of 17 degrees as it enters the anterior chamber. This way the incision acts as a trap valve with the eye's own natural, internal pressure, ensuring that it remains tightly shut. This technique is intended to protect the patient's eye, specifically the cornea, from the threat of infection, as well as correcting astigmatism (deformation of the cornea) at the same time.

To access the cataract, the cloudy lens, a 5-millimeter round incision is made centrally in the front of the elastic capsule (membrane) that envelops the lens. The lens is then held in position as *hydro-dissection* forces fluid between the lens and the capsule. Next, *phacoemulsification*, or the use of ultrasonic vibrations, gently breaks the lens apart. This pulverizing of the lens is brief—it must be—to lower the time of penetration into the eye. In this way the cornea is protected. Longer time periods risk damaging the endothelial cells (the innermost layer of the cornea's five layers). Pieces of the pulverized lens are then "vacuumed" out of the capsule by fluid irrigation and suction.

Sometimes a small chunk will escape into the anterior chamber of the eye. This piece must be faithfully tracked down and removed since it can easily become a source of inflammation in the eye, as well as an obstruction to light. I also take time to polish the interior surface of the capsule with an instrument called a curette. This is delicate work: the remaining back portion of the capsule is merely the thickness of two red blood cells. The procedure removes stray cells and ensures that the path for light, from cornea to retina, is clear and unimpeded. Not every surgeon does this for fear of tearing the capsule, but it is important to do it for the sake of the patient's sight.

Previous surgical techniques removed the capsule entirely. However, this sometimes led to the vitreous (the substance that fills the main chamber of the eye) becoming dislodged and causing a retinal detachment, which is very serious. I leave as much of the capsule as intact as possible for this reason, and for secure placement of the I.O.L. It is apparent that there are many considerations in a large number of ordered surgical acts that, at the bottom, are intended to heal someone and enhance their life.

After the cataract is removed, the I.O.L. is implanted to assume the position and duties of the no longer existent natural lens. The lens enters the eye rolled up, due to the incision size. Under the surgeon's guidance, it unfurls inside the eye to take its place within the capsular bag. The anterior chamber is irrigated with a balanced salt solution and, significantly, at the corners of the corneal incision. This final injection of saline along the incision induces a natural reaction in the body: a temporary "focal wound edema"—temporary swelling caused by minor irritation. Here the surgeon is utilizing knowledge of a natural body response—and using it—for the greater end. In the case of the incision, the swelling reaction ensures a close seal for the short term, and healing without sutures in the longer term. Still, the wound is checked for leakage at this point. Finally, I inject a combination of antibiotics through the stab incision to prevent postoperative infections. Surgery is complete at this time.

Surgery is invasive, so at each step at our clinic we are dedicated to reducing the natural threat of complications such as infection while searching for the best ways to restore precious eyesight. To that end I have made innovations over the years intended to increase patient safety and end up with better results. Such innovations include use of intra-ocular antibiotics and anti-inflammatories. Nearly thirty years ago, Tom Lloyd and I developed the first empirical formula—the Gills-Lloyd measurement—for fitting each individual eye with the most appropriate I.O.L. by measuring the length of the eye and the curvature of the cornea. I also combined limbal relaxing incisions, for small and large degrees of astigmatism, with cataract surgery. This had not been done before, but it is important to do because accomplishing two procedures in one operation exposes the patient to less surgery overall.

Irradiating the operating rooms in our clinic with UV light when they are vacant, filtering all solutions used in the eye, and thorough post-operative testing all reduce the risk of endophthalmitis (a dangerous infection) and help to make surgery at our clinic twenty times safer than elsewhere—at a hospital, for example. It is all about awe, honor, and appreciation of the physical mechanisms, treating the individual with requisite respect and love, and the attention to details. Our patients' well-being is our concern, and all these measures seek to enhance it.

The implanted artificial lens is a product of human technology that has learned its lessons from the far more complex natural design. As a replacement, it performs two great tasks. First, it replaces the cloudy cataract with a clear lens. Second, it can eliminate refractive problems that the patient may have had. That is, though the natural lens has an ability to change shape and, by that, alter its focal length, it may do so imperfectly. That is why some people need to wear glasses. An implanted I.O.L., lacking the sophistication of the natural design, has only one focal length. However, it can provide better focus to an eye that lacks the ability. My goal, as an eye surgeon and healer, is to put the right I.O.L. in place to meet the individual patient's needs while seeking better eyesight for the patient.

Introducing an I.O.L. with one focal length means presenting the patient with some choices. If both eyes are being operated on and, for example, lenses are selected for distance, vision will be sharpest for activities such as driving or golf; glasses would likely be required for reading. Conversely, the selection of lenses for close range might require the use of glasses for driving.

There is a compromise available: "Blended vision," previously known as "monovision," focuses one eye for distance and one eye for close-range. Over time, the brain adapts to its new perceptions and will use the one eye suited to a particular task without strain. These decisions demonstrate the need for the doctor's wisdom and understanding in the face of patient expectations.

In my book *Cataract Surgery: The State of the Art*, I noted that:

> As our ability to provide better quality cataract surgery improves, so do the expectations of our patients....It must be determined whether the patient's impression of "good" vision means seeing clearly a distance or near. Many patients feel that clear vision means seeing detail on street signs ten blocks away, while others perceive clarity as reading a novel without glasses. If the expectations of these two types of patients are confused, the patient may perceive their outcome as a significant postoperative complication.
>
> This problem is magnified when the wrong personality type is selected for monovision. As we all know, monovision offers an excellent visual compromise for many, but can present disappointment for the very discerning or critical patient. [This] can be disastrous for both patient and surgeon if a square peg is put in a round hole.[3]

The success of cataract surgery, therefore, does not depend solely on the surgeon's knowledge and skill. The doctor must also be sensitive to the patient's overall well-being. This indicates a real necessity for surgeon-patient communication. There must be significant dialogue to evaluate accurately the needs and desires of the patient, and to educate the patient. Through that we can be confident that the recipient of the new lenses will be excited by the advantages and not bothered significantly by the disadvantages.

Genetic Engineering

Not all cures of diseases are accomplished by medical practitioners alone. Researchers have an equally vital role to play. One exciting example of the human drive toward effecting cure within the boundaries of natural design is the cutting-edge research in genetic engineering.

In Greek mythology the *Chimaera* was a monster with the head of a lion, the body of a goat, and the tail of a serpent.[4] Through genetic engineering, formally known as *recombinant DNA technology*, our modern chimaeras are organisms that contain some genetic material, DNA, of other organisms. Medical science has been working with the DNA of humans and other species to attempt to cure certain diseases.

DNA provides the instructions for the construction of the whole human body. Protein production is an extremely important aspect of those instructions. The alteration of human DNA for specified, or artificially directed, protein production began in 1972 with a collaboration by two scientists—Herbert Boyer and Stanley Cohen.[5] By pooling their resources, these two men were able to introduce specific, previously targeted DNA segments (genes) to circular molecules of bacterial DNA called plasmids.[6] The cutting of the DNA is done using enzymes that the bacteria produce themselves to attack foreign DNA. Intimate observation and understanding of natural processes were obviously necessary for that enormous scientific jump. There are a number of these enzymes, so "snipping" can be done at specifically chosen places along the DNA strand. Desired fragments are then picked out and separated.[7]

In principle, at least, the process is elegant: scientists can remove genes from one organism and combine them with genes in a second organism. This allows the second organism to produce proteins, which the first organism does naturally but it does not. The second implanted organism gains the ability—through the introduced piece of DNA—to produce the proteins that the first organism naturally produces. Certain important substances can thus be produced in higher volumes this way. How does this benefit anyone? This technology can be used to ask something as simple as a bacterium to produce a necessary human protein such as insulin. A vat of altered bacteria, then, will produce large quantities of insulin and thereby help many diabetics' lives. In addition, such bacteria could be forced to produce the proteins from infectious agents, such as the AIDS virus, for the purposes of manufacturing vaccines. Other applications now include the production of clot-dissolving agent for heart-attack victims, and growth hormone for underdeveloped children.[8]

Another aspect of recombinant DNA technology is replacing defective or missing genes with normal genes. The first trials involved children with SCID (severe combined immunodeficiency disease) caused by the lack of a single enzyme due to a single abnormal gene. "The missing gene is introduced into a harmless virus, then mixed with progenitor [those that give rise to others] cells from the patient's bone marrow. When the virus splices its genes into those of the bone marrow cells, it simultaneously inserts the gene for the missing enzyme. Injected back into the patient, the treated marrow cells produce the missing enzyme and revitalize the immune defenses."[9] Similar approaches are being investigated for hemophilia, Parkinson's disease, diabetes, AIDS, and—perhaps of interest to most—as a therapy for cancer.

> Scientists are removing the immune cell known as the tumor-infiltrating lymphocyte…or tumor cells themselves, inserting a gene that boosts the cells' ability to make quantities of a natural anticancer product…and then growing the restructured cells in quantity in the laboratory. When the altered cells are returned to the patient, they seek out the tumor and deliver large doses of the anticancer chemical. They also appear to mobilize, in some unknown way, additional antitumor defenses. In the near future are anticancer vaccines…[10]

Studies have found that there are many possible solutions to serious medical problems with the use of recombinant DNA gene therapy. Cancer is only one. Others include help for patients who have inoperable heart disease. They can benefit from the injection into the heart muscle of a genetic compound known as phVEGF165. It increases blood flow to the heart and reduces angina. Such gene therapy has the potential to "become a major advancement in the treatment of heart disease."[11]

GOD'S PRESCRIPTION FOR HEALING

STUDIES HAVE FOUND that there are many possible solutions to serious medical problems with the use of recombinant DNA gene therapy.

What is our potential for cure within this technology? To give an indication of just how far this can go, you may be astonished to learn that one research company has combined a spider with a goat! Spider silk is one of the strongest materials in the world with a tensile strength that can support weight up to 300,000 pounds per square inch. This makes it many times stronger than steel. It has been determined that spider silk would be very valuable for the construction of bulletproof vests, for one thing. The problem was how to harvest large enough quantities of silk—spiders are solitary. The solution was to clone New Zealand miniature goats that have a spider's silk-producing gene added to their own genetic makeup.

The silk gland and milk gland are almost identical, and these "new" goats produce a very special milk. From this milk, spider silk can be extracted at a rate of about 15 grams per liter. This far exceeds any possible production by individual spiders. And with the recombinant DNA as part of the goats' revised genetic makeup, the silk-producing capability is passed on from generation to generation. In terms of human medicine, possible uses being considered are the production of sutures, replacement tendons, and wiring for prosthetic devices.[12]

Most of you are likely aware that the human genome—the whole map of human genes—has been laid out in its entirety recently. As we saw, DNA is mind-boggling in its complexity, and it is still not fully understood. The human DNA base pair sequence is 100 times the number of strings of single letter characters in an 18-volume World Book Encyclopedia set. That's three billion base pair sequences. Each of us differs by about one million pairs. The recently successful genome project mapped the DNA of only one individual, however. We should never forget what it is we are trying to accomplish and our responsibility for the integrity of our created design.

We must remain in awe and deep respect for created nature and our construction. We must also be humble. We won't always be able to improve on nature. The owner of the company that crossed a goat with a spider, Jeffrey Turner, commented, "You have to have humility."[13] Humility and appreciation are the only attitudes that will allow us to continue to forge new therapies for a body that was created so magnificently.

The Issues of Care *and* Cure

The medical and surgical interventions of physicians, as well as the efforts of researchers, do not describe the full effort in physician-assisted healing. It is necessary to remember that when we are speaking of healing, we are speaking of people. The burden, and privilege, of all of us who seek to assist the healing of others is to address the human-ness of those in need. To do that requires that some important distinctions be made.

It may be human nature that we are delinquent in our recognition and appreciation of the good that we have in life, and all too aware of the bad. Questions of sickness and health are no different for us from this perspective. In fact, as unconscious to our blessings as we tend to be, we usually will recognize only "health" in the negative: as a lack or absence of pain or disability. Health is this way seen as a lack of hindrance. And typically you and I do not wake up in the morning thankful for the smooth running efficiency of our body, at least, not until we lose that efficiency by becoming injured or ill.

The famous example of a hammer illustrates this. If we are building a house with a hammer, our mind is focused on the larger task of design and construction. When suddenly the head flies off of the lowly hammer, it instantly becomes infused with great meaning. We are forced to consider it for what it is: a necessary tool that requires its own repair for the greater goal to be met.[14] In a similar way, our body is abruptly thrust into consciousness when sickness becomes an obstruction to what we take for granted when we are healthy—seemingly mundane acts such as thinking, eating, or walking.

> ## GOD'S
>
> FOR HEALING
>
> ILLNESS INVOLVES A **whole range of an individual's feelings and moods—fear, helplessness, powerlessness, dependency, and vulnerability.**
>
> ## PRESCRIPTION

The human body is not exactly like the hammer in our example, however—it is not like any other object in the universe because it is the medium by which we absorb, understand, and interact with the world, each other, and our Creator. When we become sick, the body becomes an impediment rather than an instrument of our will. In a state of illness, our entire experience of existence thus becomes altered. Those who become ill "experience a series of intimate insults to those aspects of their existence that are most integral to being human."[15] When ill, we have lost the capacity for living as we have grown to understand it. Human illness, evidently, is illness of the whole person. For healing to occur there must be change, not only physically, but also mentally and spiritually.

Our whole understanding of physician-assisted healing pivots on our understanding of the meaning of *illness* and how it is distinguished from the meaning of *disease*. Perhaps the most direct way to state this is that disease is a process that causes biological malfunction, and illness is the lived experience of this. Illness involves a whole range of an individual's feelings and moods—fear, helplessness, powerlessness, dependency, and vulnerability. Disease, rather, is a neutral, objective, and scientific description of dysfunction in the biology of the body.[16] Both words might simply seem to connote a single state defined by its not being a state of health. However, when even a minor sickness could conceivably mean a confrontation with one's mortality, illness cannot be taken as a simple lack of health or the isolated experiences of pain and limitation.

This is to say that illness relates to a very personal vision of what is normal. There is no absolute state of happiness or health. Each of us is constantly balancing abilities and limitations. How can we say, except facetiously, that "John is the happiest man in the world" or, likewise, "Jane is the healthiest person in the world"? The experience of illness will be very difficult and deep for an Olympic runner who is told that, after her injury, she will be able to walk normally but will never run competitively again. Clearly, this is one personal world instantly found upside down. For another individual to whom, say, art is the important activity and competitive running never had meaning, the same bad news is not so difficult to receive. For these people, the injury and physical pain are equivalent, to a large degree; however, the experiences of them—the illness—are so vastly different that they are incomparable. Think, also, of the person who feels something is amiss and is afraid, choked with anxiety, yet the doctor can find no cause: we may think of this as illness without disease. Likewise, disease without illness can manifest itself in an individual who has had a physical weakness identified by a doctor, yet feels good, remains irrepressibly positive, and refuses to see herself as sick.[17]

GOD'S PRESCRIPTION *for* HEALING

Cure and Healing

> Disease is a territory colonized by science, with death lurking in the background, lining the horizon. And between these experiential extremes—that of the mortal self, and that of the neutral eye of science—innumerable items of experience are dispersed.[18]

Doctors employ techniques and apply scientific knowledge to reestablish the integrity of a body. Yet, can you say that this describes all that they do or all that you might hope for as a patient? Is this the path to or meaning of healing? Your answers, and the whole meaning of the physician-patient relationship, lie in the way you understand humanity and what it means to be sick, and in your acknowledgment that the Creator remains the source of all healing—even through His instruments: your doctors' heads and hands.

GOD'S

FOR HEALING

REAL HEALING BY the healers—the doctors—is a response to the partial disintegration of the patient's being and constitutes the caring restoration of balance and wholeness to the person.

PRESCRIPTION

How is assisted healing best defined under the requirements of cure and caring, with "death lurking in the background"? Primarily, the presence of both illness and disease requires a dialogue between patient and doctor that covers a wide range of potential physical and emotional experiences. Cure can proceed in an unidimensional approach—advancing scientific techniques have allowed doctors to *cure* disease without a more intimate sense of *care*. But healing may not proceed if the removal of pain, limitation, and threat of death does not allay fear and sense of loss. The personal and subjective nature of health and illness means that the states of health and illness represent a balance in each life. When a development—a lump or pain or weakness—becomes alarming enough, the *balance* is shaken; you seek professional help. At this point you become a "patient." Real healing by the healers—the doctors—is a response to the partial disintegration of the patient's being and constitutes the caring restoration of balance and wholeness to the person. This necessarily affects the efficacy of the scientific treatment.

Under a medical gaze, cures for disease and the easing or removal of symptoms certainly have a basis in a mechanistic view of the body as a scientific object. An appropriate scientific detachment is required of the practitioners in their advancing, applied technologies. Tests, probes, and needle pricks are indispensable sources of information for the physician. However, being informed by the patient about perceptions, feelings, social environment, or cultural background also has vital impact on the success of treatment. The value of a particular therapy is intimately tied to the human relationship and the communication between physician and patient as two humans.

> It is the doctor's privilege:
> To cure seldom
> To relieve sometimes
> To comfort always.

Those words hang on a plaque on one of the walls in our clinic. They are a tiny poetic expression of the sort of healing that requires the attention and assistance of a physician. Within the four short lines we read a description of the nature of health and illness, of the blessing and responsibility that is the doctor's lot, of what expectations are reasonable from the patient's vantage, and of the nature of the relationship between doctor and patient.

Several main elements characterize physician-assisted healing and treatments that seek to care as well as cure.

Understanding and respect

The human body is a natural wonder with an almost impenetrable biological design. The cure of disease is the realm of medicine that requires a scientific approach to the atoms, enzymes, receptors, organs, and systems of the body. This informs a technologically based repair and rejuvenation of impaired function and renewal of the integrity of the biological organism. There is, or should be, an element of awe, humility, and respect in the physician for the sheer magnificence of design and function in the human body, for its tissues, and every component part down to its individual cells and molecules.

Knowledge and competence

The reason that you visit an ophthalmologist rather than a gardener when you have trouble with your eyes is to benefit from the specific knowledge and training that the eye doctor possesses to apply to your difficulty. If health of the individual is the aim of the practice of medicine, this will mean that biomedical science and technology must be brought to bear on the problem. With a view of the patient as a fellow human, as a unique and precious entity, the physician has the obligation to provide craftsmanship and fully developed skills. All procedures must be carried out with attention to detail and perfection.

Compassion

We typically, and justifiably, think of medicine as a science, but our discussion of illness indicates that the practice of medicine is a *human* science. Likely this is what people intuitively understand as the "art" of medicine. Illness and suffering cannot be treated without an understanding of persons and the commensurate empathy for them. An ill person is not merely a well person carrying sickness "in their arms, but a newly constituted entity in need."[19] The patient is experiencing life in a whole new light when he asks the physician for assistance. Perhaps you know that feeling. One physician claims that "one of the most helpful experiences that we physicians can have is to be ill ourselves."[20] All doctors naturally depend upon biomedical experience and insights, but also know too well that the same treatment can succeed in one patient and fail in another. The physician, to truly heal, must comprehend pain and suffering and recognize them in a fellow human who is "just like me." This will inevitably allow responsiveness to the unique aspects and needs of the patient.

> ## GOD'S
> ### FOR HEALING
>
> THE PHYSICIAN, TO truly heal, must comprehend pain and suffering and recognize them in a fellow human who is "just like me."
>
> ## PRESCRIPTION

Activity replacement

This is perhaps associated more with nurses—as well as family members and friends—than doctors. It entails doing for others what they cannot do for themselves. It is the provision of assistance in acts of living, such as cooking, feeding, bathing, and providing humor and emotional support.

Assurance

The physician must be aware of several things in inviting the patient to trust and to transfer responsibility and anxiety. First, for the patient, the relationship can seem unequal and insecure. The patient lacks the knowledge and means to effect his own cure and must supplicate others—usually strangers—for their help. This entails relinquishing a degree of freedom of choice and autonomy. Naturally, feelings of vulnerability and lost dignity abide in the essence of this relationship. Self-image is as much at stake as biological health. A main function of healing is to reconstitute the patient's autonomy.[21] Second, the single most important commodity for the patient is hope—and healthcare providers have the ability to nurture it or kill it.

The Physician As Healer

The Johns Hopkins Hospital and the medical school at Johns Hopkins University were established in the late 1800s. One of the four founders provides a fine example of the physician who cured disease and fulfilled the demanding role of healer as well. Dr. Howard Kelly, speaking of the years of his residency, said:

> My hospital experiences…drew me into intimate touch with the problems of suffering humanity and revealed the priceless gratitude of the poor when treated with affectionate consideration; this was the final touch necessary to convert all my interests to my profession, no longer merely a means of livelihood but a shining path of service replete with rich, spiritual rewards.[22]

A letter from his father early in his life expressed the paternal hope that the son would live a life "of great usefulness to others."[23] Dr. Kelly accomplished that. He was a specialist in gynecology. He opened his first private practice in Kensington, which is a poor neighborhood in Philadelphia. Finding rooms on the first floor of a two-story house, he slept on a sofa near a window. Outside of this window he dangled a string with one end tied around one of his big toes. He felt a great burden for the poor women of the area who might be ill, pregnant, or trying to take care of their ill infants. If any of them tugged on the loose end of the string during the night, Dr. Kelly would awaken so that he could assist them.[24]

He was also ahead of his time in precautions to avoid infection in surgery. This included his invention of a water basin in which flow was controlled by a foot pedal. Dr. Kelly continually kept the patient in mind and heart. Remarking that "a patient's belly is a battlefield where germs and solutions fight, often with dire results to the host," he began to promote asepsis (absence of infectious elements) over antisepsis (destruction of infectious elements). He had observed deaths from carbolic acid poisoning (an antiseptic of the day), and he had started to advocate simple dressings and meticulous attention to natural principles over the use of gadgets and solutions.[25]

Dr. Kelly's overriding concern was to provide care and comfort for those seeking relief of pain. To that end, 75 percent of his cases, conservatively estimated, were "honor cases" that he worked for free. For years he employed a nurse to visit and care for patients who could not actually afford such care.[26]

Dr. Kelly asserted, "A true physician's great interest in life…lies in understanding thoroughly and in relieving the sick. When he has fought the battles with disease and conquered, he feels he has a vested right to the reciprocal affections of his patients for life, and this is the chief reward of his services."[27] Howard Kelly became an innovator, inventor, and dedicated physician who earned world renown. He "rallied to the clarion call of his Christian faith to battle in the cause of public health and moral and civic betterment," and he continually sought to lighten the burdens of those in need.[28]

> But a certain Samaritan, as he journeyed, came where
> he was. And when he saw him, he had compassion. So

he went to him and bandaged his wounds, pouring on oil and wine; and he set him on his own animal, brought him to an inn, and took care of him.

—Luke 10:33–34

Physician-assisted healing must, as in Jesus' story of the charitable Samaritan, express *agape* love—the kind of love Christ displays. Physician-assisted healing must demonstrate this love for a fellow human being. A philosophical or naturalistic ethic is not sufficient. The Hippocratic Oath is a nonbinding declaration—if indeed it ever was—that is largely irrelevant in an age of unbridled technological advances. Confused ethics seek to guide us in the intractable debates surrounding, for example, cloning and abortion.

Medicine is an activity with its own logic in scientific goals, but by love and fidelity to the goal of the good and well-being of the patient, it becomes a moral obligation. It is "grounded on God's love; as we love others, we love Him—and He loves through us."[29] This, really, is the definition of a Christian doctor.

Jesus gave us the purest example of the way we should approach the sick. Healing those who were sick and suffering was a daily aspect of His life. Healing the ill was central to His mission to save. Faith, hope, integrity, and respect for the patient are elements that grow out of *agape* love. It is the compassion, inspired by the example of the Great Physician, that enables healthcare professionals to recognize that, effective as our science and technology can be, they do not remove suffering.

> GOD'S
>
> FOR HEALING
>
> PHYSICIAN-ASSISTED healing must, as in Jesus' story of the charitable Samaritan, express agape love— the kind of love Christ displays.
>
> PRESCRIPTION

The motto of our St. Luke's clinic is simply this: *Excellence with love.* Those three words express our dedication to the practice of medicine bound by the love for our fellowman as exemplified in the life and work of Christ. The motto describes an attitude, a professional bearing, and a methodology in treatment, which involve:

1. A respect for human life and all its vital pieces, such as tissues and cells, as God's gift.
2. The concept of stewardship of God's creation demands that we pursue excellence in knowledge and medical technique in the attempt to restore the integrity of each individual's body.
3. A relationship with each "neighbor" who visits us founded in compassion, which leads us to seek to meet their special needs. We seek to help them heal, rather than to help them merely "get better."

Caring individuals who listen and who will pray with those who wish it staff our clinic. Our excellent group of doctors and nurses apply the highest level of knowledge and expertise—and the latest innovations—to the scientific cure of our patients' physical ailments. Finally, with an understanding of our responsibility for and stewardship of the health and well-being of our patients, we grapple with the realities of what is being done here.

Limitations to Assistance

A man was meant to be doubtful about himself, but undoubting about the truth; this has been exactly reversed.

—G. K. Chesterton[30]

Most of the world is familiar with a wooly, white sheep by the name of Dolly. Many have some idea of the principles that underlie her fame, though no one yet seems completely clear on the implications of the cloning procedure that produced her. The adventure began February 28, 1953, when Francis Crick publicly announced that he and his partner, James Watson, had "found the secret of life." This secret? Watson and Crick had discovered the double helix structure (much like a pair of circular staircases) of the DNA molecule and how it might replicate itself. In 1962, Watson and Crick won a Nobel prize for their work. Now the "genie was out of the bottle." Since then, the "DNA revolution" has broken out from cloistered walls of academia. Applications of the "new biology" have entered the stock market, crime labs and courtrooms, hospitals, and collective consciousness.

In 1993, Michael Smith won the Nobel prize in chemistry for his research in the 1970s, which produced recombinant DNA and the genetic engineering boom of the 1980s. This was a time when scientists began to seek in earnest such lofty goals as extending the human life span; eradicating diseases such as cancer, cystic fibrosis, and Down's syndrome; tailoring drug treatments to an individual's genetic makeup; and ending global hunger with disease-resistant crops.

Nothing human is perfect, however. Ironically, on the fiftieth anniversary of the Watson-Crick discovery, medical regulators in the United States called a halt to gene therapy due to the hundreds of serious reactions, such as the development of leukemia. Transgenic crops that were engineered to grow faster with built-in resistance to pests, disease, and tolerance to herbicides promised to be successful at first. In fact, the performance of these genetically modified crops has been inferior to natural strains.[31] No one yet knows what these foods do in the human body when consumed, and still we are eagerly replacing the natural strains, which contain the genetic diversity that ensures continued adaptability.

A group of miniature New Zealand goats certainly can no longer drink their own mothers' silk milk. Are we sticking our hand into a rat's nest? Where have humanity's own egoistic inclinations, undisciplined by the Holy Spirit, taken us in the name of healing? A very short list would include stem cell research on human embryos refused the right to develop to maturity, genetic engineering and interference with the already pristine blueprint of life—DNA, human-animal hybrids, euthanasia, and anacephalic (headless) clones created as "organ factories." Early in 2003 a fifty-five-year-old woman was able to give birth to a baby that was conceived of an egg donated by the woman's own daughter. Sister becomes mother, mother becomes surrogate, father…

Why? It is the natural confusion of a human mind that lacks a compass indicating God's true north. The simple ability to achieve something scientifically or medically does not imply immediate sanction of that action. Our eyes must remain on the Lord and His counsel through His Word. Anything else derives from human pride, is oriented in the wrong direction, and is destined to cause much suffering to many in the long run. That which is intended to liberate us from disease may someday serve to enslave and diminish us. The antitotalitarian writer Max Frisch put it succinctly: "Technology is the knack of so arranging the world that we do not experience it."[32] Human pride and trust in fallible human intellect alone separate us from God and His plan for us, our bodies, and our healing. Only when we align ourselves to God and surrender ourselves to His Spirit and His redemption do our purpose and direction become clear.

At St. Luke's we seek to give sight back to our patients to reestablish their independence, livelihood, and joy of fully experiencing life. To accomplish this, we utilize the newest and best information, tools, and techniques. We work hard for others' sight, but remain humble before the vast mystery of nature, and remain cognizant of our inabilities to solve certain problems. As technologies progress, modern culture has turned to an unquestioning trust and belief in the power of science to cure and to conquer any human

> ## GOD'S PRESCRIPTION FOR HEALING
>
> THE SIMPLE ABILITY to achieve something scientifically or medically does not imply immediate sanction of that action. Our eyes must remain on the Lord and His counsel through His Word.

difficulty. However, human science has not solved every problem facing humankind. Indeed, it has intensified some problems and created some new ones. Humanity runs an increasing risk tampering in areas that are not naturally in the human domain. We run the risk of blindness to the fact that we do, in fact, have limitations to what we can accomplish together.

We will only find effective methods of healing by keeping one eye on the Creator and resisting any temptation to "play God." As in all areas, we need to preserve *balance*. We must balance our needs and necessities with the needs of our design. We must balance intellect with wisdom, science with caring, and our own desires to achieve with veneration for the Creator and His handiwork. We were created with such profound intelligence; we must remain focused on our role as facilitators rather than creators. Absence of humility and appreciation will not only doom attempts to assist healing—they may very well carry us toward disaster.

The Meaning of Collective and Personal Responsibility

As we look for and endorse new ways to assist healing, we must grapple with difficult issues mentioned and others yet unseen. Such questions ultimately deal in the meaning of "human freedom within the created order and human responsibility to God and to humanity."[33] For some healers and their patients, reference to God's laws is still accepted as the ultimate source of morality. This is important because it is a morality that is inspired above and outside the limited human intellect. Unfortunately, Voltaire's legacy, the glorification of reason, has largely influenced the ethics and morals of today and common approaches to novel scientific advances. Human intellectual energies have outstripped a moral maturity that would help counsel us.

> WE ALL SHARE THE responsibility for the directions and extents to which humanity moves for the sake of healing and living.

Human pride tells us that anything, anywhere at anytime is sufficient and good. The basic amorality of humanism, best exemplified in Darwin's theories, is built on the foundation that man's self-determination and self-actualization are primary. Self-interest is a natural extension of a philosophy that sees human reason as the universal benchmark of reality and of the right and the good.[34] It is so very important that we all remain aware, informed, vigilant, and active in promoting proper, moral means to desired ends. It is the responsibility of each of us to be courageous enough to make responses if necessary. We all share the responsibility for the directions and extents to which humanity moves for the sake of healing and living.

Meaning, and the beginning of wisdom, will be found in our recognition of our position in a vast, complex universe. This requires our humility before the wonder of it all and our surrender to the Creator of all this beauty. *Our science is really His science.* Physicians and patients alike must come to see this as a basis for methods of healing. Expectations must be realistic, and we must be grateful for that which can be accomplished. It is not our place to expect immortality, nor is it our place to strive for anything approaching that, at any cost. We must be humble enough to know our position under the Creator's sun and simply be grateful to be in its light.

Mindful of our limits and responsibilities, though, we also know that God has provided us some of His knowledge of our design that we may advance the methods of healing. This is His gift. The physician uses such knowledge for the patient in his time of need. With libraries, an array of medications, and a repertoire of techniques, physicians can assist in the healing process of the wonderful human body that God created. Frequently calling upon health professionals for help is unavoidable. Yet, there is more—much more—to the whole process of healing.

My friend Dr. Charles Lasley performs gastric bypass surgery on individuals who are morbidly obese. They suffer physically, psychologically, and socially from the burdens of fantastically overweight bodies. His surgical technique reduces a patient's stomach size to a mere "pocket" that can contain approximately one ounce—in other words, very little food. Prior to surgery, these people suffer from a wide variety of ailments including diabetes, hypertension, sleep apnea, and gallbladder disease. The success of the procedure is observed in these patients after they lose 150 to 300 pounds in the months after surgery, and the disease symptoms disappear. In reality, this surgery is lifesaving for people in this position.

Dr. Lasley performs about three hundred of these procedures each year, which represents a large number of people requiring help. The causes for the initial weight problem can be multifactorial. Often there is a genetic predisposition to obesity. Also there are social factors, such as the lack of instruction on how to care for oneself, and psychological factors such as self-destructiveness arising out of achingly low self-esteem. And yet, Dr. Lasley maintains, the surgery is still viewed as a "last resort"—personal responsibility remains paramount. As a physician concerned for the patient's overall well-being, *he would rather see the same results accomplished by the patient's own means.* This is physician-assisted healing on a number of levels.

GOD'S

TRUE AWE AND
appreciation
of God's gift of
life causes us to
recognize our own
responsibility for
our own healing.

PRESCRIPTION

For Dr. Lasley and his colleagues, the transfer of responsibility from patient to surgeon is less desirable than the patient's own agency in his/her own survival, well-being, and health—if it is possible. It may not often be possible; however, it does point to another column in the architecture of healing: the responsibility we each have for our own health and, more, the appreciative, conscientious stewardship of the body God provided each of us.

Health and healing certainly require doctors' surgical and medical expertise; however, we are finally growing to understand that we must seek their wisdom in the fields of prevention. Health and healing require us, as patients, to heed their advice. True awe and appreciation of God's gift of life causes us to recognize our own responsibility for our own healing.

Chapter 7

YOU ARE YOUR OWN BEST PHYSICIAN

Health has its science as well as disease.

—EMILY BLACKWELL

Nothing can replace the expertise of physicians in our lives, and you should not hesitate to seek their help when it is required. To do that would be to deny one of the great gifts God has provided for your continued well-being. It is true that when we feel lost and perhaps weak we want someone to take control. It makes sense. The complexity of the body, its diseases, and the gap in knowledge keep most of us at a loss. Also, we have fears. The Creator loves us, however. He has given your ophthalmologist and your general practitioner understanding. He has also given it to you. You understand pain, and sometimes you understand how to remove it. However, to understand the role of the physician in healing is not the same thing as becoming passive and disengaged. Under those conditions, a doctor can treat a disease, or at least its symptoms. But it will be harder to heal unless the patient recognizes his or her own responsibility and takes an active role in the healing process. Healing is somewhat more substantial than merely swallowing a pill. You can take substantial steps on your own toward preventing physical breakdown, and you can even significantly influence the process of healing when stricken. The awareness of this is also God's gift, but you must be willing to accept it. It is reasonable to think of your own responsibility in total health as *self-assisted healing*.

GOD'S PRESCRIPTION FOR HEALING

IT IS UP TO YOU—AND you alone—to care for your body by doing certain things, avoiding others, observing closely, and taking steps to counteract or reverse the onset of illness.

There is much that you can do for yourself—and must do. For example, if you were to buy a new $250,000 Ferrari, I believe that you would certainly take care of it. You would read the manuals about its proper operation, and you would be careful to keep the vehicle lubricated and free of dents. In the end, wouldn't you be proud to show off such a car and proud of its good state of repair? How much more should you be concerned about your own human body?

If you think about it, you live in a "mechanism" of flesh and blood, which you expect to perform. You expect it to help you achieve the things in life for which you hope. There is more, of course. Designed by the Creator for fulfillment with one another and with Him, your body is a temple, God's temple. Conscientious care, respect, admiration, and appreciation for the gift leave you with a responsibility. My earlier book titled *Temple Maintenance* was written with this thought in mind.[1] It is up to you—and you alone—to care for your body by doing certain things, avoiding others, observing closely, and taking steps to counteract or reverse the onset of illness.

The body with its sixty trillion cells and cellular memory equal to the content of two hundred New York phone books needs more committed attention than a car. What kind of attention does a body need, then? There is only one way to have an awareness of the immense responsibility of caring for your body and to accept that responsibility wholeheartedly. By appreciating the Creator's intelligent design for your body and thanking Him for life itself, you will be inspired to assist in the processes of maintaining health and assisting your own healing. With genuine gratitude and wonder for what you are and have received, you really have no choice other than doing what you are capable of doing for the preservation of the integrity of your body. Your body is not something alien—distant. It is the only one that you will have!

GOD'S

> IT IS CRUCIAL FOR YOU to recognize your responsibility to maintain physical balance in your body by promoting the good and minimizing the bad.

FOR HEALING

PRESCRIPTION

Physical Alignment

> Do not be deceived, God is not mocked; for whatever
> a man sows, that he will also reap. For he who sows to
> his flesh will of the flesh reap corruption, but he who
> sows to the Spirit will of the Spirit reap everlasting life.
> And let us not grow weary while doing good, for in due
> season we shall reap if we do not lose heart.
>
> —GALATIANS 6:7–9

You can help maintain physical balance in your body by promoting the good and minimizing the bad. Healthcare costs are rising disproportionately to other costs. The last hundred years have seen the primary causes of death shift from consequences of trauma and infection to degenerative diseases such as cancer and arteriosclerosis, diseases that are mediated by lifestyle and, therefore, preventable.[2] Obesity has now overtaken cancer as the number one preventable cause of death in our country. Attitudes are beginning to change, and healthcare practitioners are becoming more aware that "the nutritionists of today are the doctors of tomorrow."[3] The concept is profound enough to have one expert write a chapter in her book entitled, "How We Heal, Making Foods Your Medicine."[4]

Western medicine as a discipline is the practice of science. Healing, as opposed to cure, is restoring balance. Self-assisted indicates the role that patients have in their own healing. Doctors can help cure symptoms, but it will be harder to heal without the patient's recognition of his or her own responsibility and need to take an active role, including making changes.

Self-assisted implies the role that patients have in their own healing. Many patients want the doctor to take control of their destinies. The patient needs to evolve from a passive self. Likewise, doctors need to consider elements that are perhaps sometimes less empirical and a little more intuitive.

However, God's gift of knowledge and understanding of the body is not limited to healthcare professionals. Healing requires that you, as patient, heed the advice of physicians and recognize your own responsibility and the importance of your own role in your own healing. This is a magnificent revelation that can help you change your life and the lives of your loved ones.

Prevention of Disease

An ounce of prevention is worth a pound of cure.[5]

Ben Franklin's familiar maxim has always been true, but never more to the point than in our present era. It expresses the most powerful aspects of your efforts to assist your own healing: proper habits, balance, awareness, and wise choices. The greatest contribution that you can make to your own healing is to make a commitment to, and work toward, the prevention of illness.

> GOD'S GIFT OF knowledge and understanding of the body is not limited to healthcare professionals.

What does this mean? It means making healthy foods and drinks a necessity; avoiding dangerous or nutritionally empty foods and substances; making regular exercise a habit; maintaining flourishing relationships and a positive attitude. And mostly it means remaining in awe of God's wonderful creation—your body—and respecting it as His handiwork, protecting it as its steward, and remaining faithfully thankful for it.

Health and Wholeness

The study of health and healing touches more profound dimensions of life than most of us think. Although the words *health* and *healing* are familiar to everyone, most of us begin the journey to health and restoration very far from ever having known what it means to be physically, mentally, emotionally, and spiritually whole.[6] *Wholeness* cannot be defined entirely by one visit to the doctor, a fad diet, one exercise philosophy, or any single discipline—total health is multifactorial. But there is a simple answer for many if not most health problems that "burden your body and spirit": Many times you can change the state of your health by simply changing what you put into your system.[7]

Proper nutrition

> It is clear that our Western diet has some serious problems associated with it. Every year, national organizations and government agencies issue dietary guidelines that seem to grow closer and closer to the guidelines God gave Moses in the Old Testament thousands of years ago. It is no accident that God's wisdom is being "confirmed" by the latest scientific findings.[8]

Choice of diet is a vital aspect of how you protect yourself. You need to know enough, and be willing, to select those foods that promote health. And you need the self-discipline to deny yourself the foods that break health down. Why do triathletes, for example, carefully regard the food they eat? "In order to: avoid sickness, improve our complexions, get smarter, steady/alter our moods, lose/gain weight, improve our energy levels, live longer and go faster."[9]

While there are no magical formulas, and what works for some people doesn't work for others, it seems that nutritional supplements like vitamins might be necessary in addition to a healthy diet.[10] The best advice from the athletes? Be sensible. Eat good food, sensibly supplemented, and work hard.[11]

According to some leaders in the medical field, the best diet is probably a vegetarian diet. That is a diet high in complex carbohydrates and lacking, significantly, substantial amounts of animal fat.

Not only are animal fats to be avoided, but also processed foods, which are traditionally high in salt, sugar, and the empty calories of white flours. Beyond that, most of us are well aware these days that substances like drugs, cigarettes, alcohol, and caffeine must be avoided to promote health in our tissues. You should always drink plenty of water as well.

In the Bible, blood is symbolic of the salvation Jesus accomplished on the cross. Blood is also the very real issue of life in our bodies. We need to keep our blood healthy. This is accomplished through balance. Blood must be prone neither to deficiency in quantity, anemia, nor to overabundance, polycythemia. Tempting sweets must be balanced with the proper vitamins and useful nutrients. Moderation and balance are the keys.

Exercise

Start healing with exercise. We need exercise. How often have you heard this? It is now known that you can best protect your body from disease with exercise. Exercise is a neuroprotector. It protects all the important connections between systems in your body. I used to run to work, twelve miles a day. It was undoubtedly good exercise for me, but perhaps not the wisest exercise. It would have been better for me to do interval exercises, using every component of my body, as well as including days designated for rest. A balanced program that includes stretching, interval training, utilization of all muscles, and plenty of rest is the kind that provides the all-important balance.

> **THE GREATEST** contribution that you can make to your own healing is to make a commitment to, and work toward, the prevention of illness.
>
> **GOD'S**
> **FOR HEALING**
> **PRESCRIPTION**

Starting Out Triathlon by Paul Huddle and Roch Frey is a handy, concise book with tips on nutrition, regimen, stretching, example [recommended] workouts, and so forth.[12] Referring to triathlon, Bob Babbitt mentions that the toughest part is getting out the door to do the training.[13] However, he stresses that it is all worthwhile in the end because of the sense of accomplishment you will have at having successfully overcome a seemingly insurmountable challenge.[14]

Among the "Golden Rules of Triathlon" are hints to help everyone succeed in any physical endeavor.

1. Plan recovery into your training schedule.[15]
2. Consistency is the key to gains, i.e., continuing and persevering.[16]
3. Injuries DO occur—take time off when injured and consult a health professional if injury or pain persists.
4. Have a plan—but be flexible. "Nothing is etched in stone."[17]

The daily workout needs to consist of three sections: warmup, the main set, and cool down. Warmup and cool down are important though often overlooked aspects. "Probably the most important part of any workout is the warmup."[18] While most of the "work" is accomplished in the main set, the warmup and cool down help prevent injury and soreness and allow maximum performance. Strength training—with weights—is as important as any other aspect of training. In weight training, remember that full range of motion is vital, as are the order of exercises, proper technique, and breathing. Weight training is not just for bodybuilders. The rule of thumb is that "heavier weights and fewer repetitions build (muscular) power and size, while lighter weights with higher repetitions emphasize endurance with minimal gains in bulk."[19] Both strength and endurance are desirable.

Developing and maintaining flexibility are neglected but extremely important elements both in athletic performance and total health. Flexibility decreases after age fifteen, but it can be regained at any age with some effort. Improving flexibility demands focused attention, patience, and the "ability to remain quiet—both physically and mentally."[20] This is accomplished through stretching the muscles and paying attention to your breathing while doing it.

Complementary methods

These apply primarily when we have already fallen ill. The word *healing* can be found with reference to the practice of medicine and healthcare, but it is more common in what has been called "alternative medicine." In their present incarnation, that is, recognized as an adjunct to traditional, physician-based care, these methods of healing are perhaps more accurately labeled "complementary medicine." The dominant strand in complementary techniques for health and healing is a personal engagement in the enterprise.

This move from conventional medicine may indicate some disillusionment with conventional approaches, an expression of greater independence, and a growing concern for natural methods that appeal to the whole

GOD'S

FOR HEALING

THE MORE productive and reputable alternative techniques should be included as self-assisted healing.

PRESCRIPTION

organism. Reginald Cherry goes so far to say, "The fact that these kinds of enterprises are such big business and attract so many eager customers testifies to the number of unhappy, unhealthy, dissatisfied people who are searching for something."[21] Still, "complementary medicine" has recently evolved, indicative of its ability to augment rather than replace the science of modern, conventional medicine.

Some of these techniques may work or help to some degree; some are not scientifically sound; others are simply scams. Alternative methods may seem simpler to understand or at least be more accessible and comprehensible to the patients' intuitive senses—and to their commitment to some sort of action as a means to the end. The more productive and reputable alternative techniques should be included as self-assisted healing.

Choices

In his book *Maximum Energy*, Ted Broer has made the following observation about the role of choice in the healing process:

> Life consists of a series of choices. The little choices that we make on a day-to-day basis are the same factors that affect our health tomorrow, next year or in the next decade....In other words, the long-term picture of your health is created by all the things that you do and don't do and all the things that you put and don't put into your body on a day-to-day basis. This ongoing string of small choices can determine whether you are going to be healthy or sick in the days ahead. Genetic factors influence the equation in some ways, but the health and nutrition choices you make today can still help determine whether you end up battling heart disease, diabetes, or cancer tomorrow."[22]

Many studies have found that in most cases these diseases—and others—are "related either directly or indirectly to nutrition...are caused in part or in whole by our nutritional choices...[and therefore] they can be prevented in part or in whole by better choices."[23]

Whether we like it or not, we make important decisions every time we sit at a table or sit on a sofa rather than walk, run, or skate. We must ensure that we make informed choices.

We can enjoy maximum energy and optimum health throughout our lives, and the keys to this kind of life are very simple. As with most things worthwhile, the way to get maximum energy is to do it one choice at a time.[24]

God's Wisdom Confirmed by Science

We live in a culture that is buried under books, gimmicks, and gadgets aimed at diet, fitness, and well-being. However, in this chapter you have become aware that you have a personal role to play in maintaining the strength and vitality of your own body. The human body is equipped with a marvelous defense system that is able to repel or overcome almost every major disease or sickness under normal circumstances. Medical research studies are confirming in increasing numbers and frequency that a healthy diet and regular exercise play a major role in the body's long-term resistance to debilitating disease and sickness. There is more than enough information available to help you assist in your own healing process. Make the choice today to become a willing, active participant in your own healing.

GOD'S

FOR HEALING

MAKE THE CHOICE today to become a willing, active participant in your own healing.

PRESCRIPTION

What we eat and what we do with our bodies at every moment alter the body at the molecular level. Every choice you make is a block in a foundation for a good life in days, years, decades ahead. Thus, the essential attribute of self-assisted healing is personal responsibility. I am responsible for the way I find myself today; I am responsible for the choices I am making today; and, therefore, I am responsible for how I will find myself "tomorrow." Goals must be set, but reasonable, achievable ones. Understand that change can be slow; patience will stand you in a better position to adapt. Habits must be developed so that there is no personal conflict.

God's wisdom is a pathway to healing and health for you that is paved with wise choices and decisions.[25]

Conclusion

In every area of life, including food and lifestyle choices and human relationships, my first accountability is to the Word of God. Everything and everybody else need to line up behind that rock-solid source of truth.[26]

Illness is a life experience that we share between one another. Moving like ripples on the surface of a pond, the effects of sickness in one life nudge other lives all around. You may be ill yourself, or you may be watching your sister or child or friend hurting, but you and they participate in the suffering together.

The fact that you picked up this book with interest means that you are already aware that the experience of illness is not an easy one to face. You may have found it to be usually deeply troubling and disturbing. And it is painful—in many different ways and on several levels. It also has much to teach us. Although it may seem to be a reasonable or obvious point about healing, too often this one point is neglected in discussions on health and healing: The ambient human environment we are embedded in is an integral aspect of healing.

The question of healing turns on more than just the cessation of pain. Our more profound experiences of illness point us closer to the truth. It is in the most difficult episodes of your life that you will learn to see and appreciate the Creator's design, plan, and concern for your existence and prosperity. We are the beneficiaries of a gift of inestimable value. We are the recipients of a design for life, healing, and eternity bound within the fragile membranes of our cells.

Illness is, unfortunately, inevitable in the human body. At these times an enduring appreciation of God's precious gift will demand

> GOD'S
>
> WE ARE THE recipients of a design for life, healing, and eternity bound within the fragile membranes of our cells.
>
> PRESCRIPTION

that you seek help. Through genuine gratefulness of your gift from your Creator, you can have the awareness of your need and the collective knowledge you need to assist in meeting it. Doctors, nurses, researchers, as well as neighbors, family, and yourself can and must play a role in the healing of your own body and those of others. We were made for this by the Creator, and that is His second gift of healing.

PART III

INNER HEALING

Chapter 8

MENTAL ALIGNMENT WITH THE CREATOR'S DESIGN

For this reason I bow my knees to the Father of our Lord Jesus Christ, from whom the whole family in heaven and earth is named, that He would grant you, according to the riches of His glory, to be strengthened with might through His Spirit in the inner man.

—EPHESIANS 3:14–16

Together we have thought about the wisdom endowed to the body by the Creator through an intelligent design. We looked at the body's natural ability to preserve balance and to reestablish that balance on occasions when it is lost. All the appropriate reactions to injury that are required for physical healing are founded on this principle. This is the Lord's first gift of healing.

You are a recipient of that gift, and your appreciation and respect for your design and the Designer requires that you seek the path to health and wholeness by making a personal commitment to constantly take care of your body. By doing this you may prevent imbalances and illness in the first place. This also entails making significant alterations in personal behavior in the event of an upset.

In the earlier chapters we discussed the occasions when you will require the assistance of doctors. Biological life, for a human, is incredibly complex. Freedom from illness and pain cannot always be realized without some kind of intervention beyond your own natural attributes or efforts. For that reason you have learned to trust the health professionals to enter the Creator's intended process of healing by restoring equilibrium and completeness to your body. They employ methods borne of the wisdom found in the physical design. The skill and understanding endowed on our physicians, researchers, health scientists, and clinicians are God's second gift of healing to us.

For many of us, the naturally wondrous body, our attentive stewardship, and the caring assistance of experts exhaust the definition of, and possibilities for, healing. But, is all healing a physical event in these terms? Does your own wrenching experience of illness, feeling your most beautiful inner self become twisted by pain, seem satisfied by that alone? Could we ever claim that any of the above elements addressed the real issues at the bottom of, say, losing a child to leukemia? What direction can we move when we observe a best friend descending into pits of despair and decay? How do we personally approach mortality and eternity?

Humans are *so* much more than clumps of tissues and the results of their labor. We are not simply physical entities as cod fish and fir trees are. We are physical, mental, emotional, and spiritual beings. All aspects of the exceptionally designed body are integrated into a unified whole, which is greater than the sum of its parts, and completeness of the entire person also mirrors this principle. So, how do illness and healing register in your inner experience?

> ## GOD'S
>
> **UNIFICATION OF ALL human components means balance and communication between body, mind, emotions, and spirit.**
>
> ## PRESCRIPTION

FOR HEALING

Unification of all human components means balance and communication between body, mind, emotions, and spirit. Wholeness and balance at the mental and spiritual levels are proven to affect the capacity of your body to heal physically. Additionally, as a thinking, feeling creation of the Creator, you also have needs for mental and spiritual healing when balance has been overturned in those areas as well. What is required for this healing of mind and spirit? What are the ways you must seek to align yourself in order to be healed? What is God's prescription for your inner healing then?

God's Word tells us that we need to be transformed and aligned through Christ in order to be the recipient of all that He is. It takes full surrender to engage this integration of the Godhead into all that we are: body, soul, and spirit. "Not my will, but Yours, be done" (Luke 22:42). This denial of self presents you to God as a holy, pleasing, and available recipient of all He is. It is the life of continual healing—health and wholeness—spiritually as well as physically. He made us to be in harmony with Him in order to run smoothly. His main purpose was to draw us into fellowship with Him.

When we were speaking of physical health and healing, we were referring to maintaining or reacquiring balance by adhering to guidelines that the body's design dictates. Physically, you align yourself with God's purpose by accepting the stewardship of your temple in which He will dwell. When we speak of balance in hearts and minds, we may think of it as realignment. That is, to prosper you must come back into conformity, into line, with the spiritual principles and precepts by which you were created. This is the path toward healing. When that is accomplished, you may be restored to God's design and His plan.

Mentally, you must seek to have "the mind of Christ" (1 Cor. 2:16), remain positive and hopeful, and constantly rejoice with great feelings of thankfulness. Spiritually, you must have God's Holy Spirit reigning in every part of your being. And, by focusing on eternal life rather than temporal existence, you seek to align yourself with God and His purposes (2 Cor. 4:16–18). Inner healing is the healing of mind and spirit. The body is also strengthened through it. *The capacity for inner healing is also determined by our design, by the nature that we were created with, and it is the Creator's third gift of healing to us.*

Dr. Ben Carson, my colleague and friend, tells a gripping, personal story of mental alignment. Dr. Carson, a neurosurgeon at Johns Hopkins in Baltimore, is known around the world for his pioneering work, such as the successful separation of Siamese twins joined at the head in 1987. However, it would have been difficult to imagine Dr. Carson rising to such heights as he was growing up. His story as a healer of others could so easily have been very different.

Early on, living in inner-city Detroit, Ben was an underachieving student who exhibited failing grades, though his mother continually encouraged him. He overcame his hurdles to finally reach the top of his class, gain a scholarship to Yale, proceed to medical school at the University of Michigan, and become director of pediatric neurosurgery at Johns Hopkins at the age of thirty-three.

Dr. Carson's biggest problems were not lack of motivation or difficult circumstances, however. His most intense problem, and most noticeable triumph, occurred at age fourteen. In his words, at this time, he confronted the most severe personal problem of his life—one that almost ruined him forever.[1] This problem was a "pathological temper" that controlled him and made him entirely irrational.[2] At the moment of what was to be his ultimate crisis, or turning point, he was arguing with a friend. Enraged by a tiny taunt, Ben went blind with anger, as he frequently did, grabbed a pocketknife, and thrust with all his might into his friend's abdomen. Fortunately, the friend's belt buckle broke the blade and saved his life, essentially saving Dr. Carson's life at the same time. Ben realized that this behavior was far from normal and that he needed help. As he struggled in the overwhelming pain of a new awareness, Ben felt a strong feeling to pray as his mother had taught him to do.

INNER HEALING IS the healing of mind and spirit. The body is also strengthened through it.

Ben knew his bad temper was a destructive personality trait that was very difficult, if not impossible, to modify. Still, as he spoke to the Lord, he placed his faith in God, believing that He could accomplish things that psychological experts claimed could not be done. He read his Bible and was particularly impressed by Proverbs 16:32:

> He who is slow to anger is better than the mighty,
> And he who rules his spirit than he who takes a city.

In misery and anguish, Dr. Carson felt a peace enter his heart as he read, prayed, and cried out for help. He has been able to control his temper ever since. He explains the miraculous transformation in these words:

> I'm not afraid of anything as long as I think of Jesus Christ and my relationship to Him and remember that the One who created the universe can do anything. I also have evidence—my own experience—that God can do anything, because He changed me. From age 14, I began to focus on the future.[3]

Dr. Carson demonstrates the results of realignment with God, with focus on His precepts, on the future, and on a greater purpose of the Creator for the creation. And through this realignment, not only has one life—Dr. Carson's own—been altered from darkness to light, but the many lives that have been touched by his immense skill in healing have also been changed forever.

Mind and Body, Body and Mind

A merry heart does good, like medicine, but a broken spirit dries the bones.

—PROVERBS 17:22

King Solomon, without a fully developed science, knew that total health and healing require *wholeness*. Intuitively, you also are aware that you are not divided portions of brain, body, and spirit, but that each is connected, part of a singularity, and therefore each influences the others. Those influences are more profound than you may know, however. Science is just now teasing out the details of the depth of the relationships. For example, recent research indicates that emotional pain excites the same parts of the brain as physical pain does.

Some illnesses heal under the energies of the body's systems. Some require medical intervention, while the healing of others can be approached through diet, exercise, and lifestyle changes. And yet other illness can be attributed to one's mental and spiritual states. Errant emotions, fears, and anxieties can kill. Conversely, realignment of your inner self can assist in your overall well-being and in your physical health.

Numerous studies have now pointed out the weight of the mind-body connection. We are being increasingly informed about the role of depression, loneliness, unhappiness, fear, and anger in the development and prolongation of diseases such as cancer, heart disease, diabetes, and asthma.[4]

Mind refers to the complete array of mental functions "related to thinking, mood, and purposive behavior." The mind is generally seen as deriving from activities in the brain but displaying emergent properties, such as consciousness.[5]

Typically we think of the mind as centered in the brain. Scholarly research indicates that our thoughts and feelings influence the body through two primary "channels," the nervous system and the circulatory system.[6] The brain, as the center of the nervous system, sends and receives electrical impulses from every part of the body. You can move a toe under the brain's instructions, and that toe also "tells" your brain, you, when it has struck something painfully. Significantly, with nerve endings in the bone marrow (the birthplace of white cells), the brain influences the mighty immune system. In addition, your brain is a gland that secretes hormones that affect the entire endocrine system.

Just how deep the mind-body connection is remains somewhat of a mystery; however, every physician knows about the reality of the "placebo effect." A placebo is an inert, virtually useless substance (a sugar-pill, if you will) sometimes administered to a patient (normally in trials for new medications) under the pretence that it is a powerful drug that will directly improve their condition. Results from the administration of placebos have indeed demonstrated improvement or "healing" in statistically significant numbers of patients. Likewise, upon learning that their "medicine" was not what they believed it to be, some patients have experienced a reversion to their original sickness. There is no explanation for this outside of the influence of thought and feelings on the whole person. You have heard the adage "you are what you eat." I would like to tell you that "you are also what you *think*."

The implications are so marked that some refer to it as the "*biology of belief*."[7] It is in there that the body with its strengths and weaknesses; the brain/mind with its thoughts, feelings, and consciousness; and trust in love for, and communion with, the Creator God in our spirits all come together.

This has all been planned and placed within you by design. This is not merely a combination of biology and psychology, though. As Dr. Daniel Fountain says, healing is also about faith. "Obedience to the teachings of Christ and the freeing power of the Holy Spirit can and does result in healing beyond that produced by medicine, surgery, and psychology."[8]

Worry, Anxiety, Fear

Not too long ago an interesting event occurred in a supermarket in Florida. After a couple of patrons began to cough and complain of headaches and shortness of breath, and the phenomenon widened to affect many more people—twenty-five in all—the store was evacuated. However, the emergency crew could find no irritants in the air or any other reason for the "outbreak." One member of the crew pointed his finger at anxiety as a possible cause.[9] It would seem that some people had merely observed some kind of discomfort in others and found themselves experiencing similar discomfort through fear and worry.

It has been determined by some that personality is an important factor in the emergence of and healing of cancer. "Cancer-susceptible" personalities tend to suppress "toxic emotions" such as anger. They also tend to suffer their burdens in life alone rather than seek comfort from others. They are also frequently unable to cope with stress. Stress is now known to suppress the immune system, and it does this more effectively in cancer-susceptible individuals, over-whelmingly so.[10]

A broken heart, loneliness, fear, and worry—these all contribute to our illnesses and play upon the effectiveness of our healing. They need not do so, however. I recently lost my friend Larry Burkett. Prior to his going to be with the Lord, Larry had survived a cancer diagnosed in 1995. In his book *Nothing to Fear,* Larry described the mental and spiritual attributes of a cancer survivor. Faith is paramount. He

also encouraged the cancer patient to avoid doubt with a single-minded purpose and to achieve peace by releasing worries and fears.[11] This is a diminution of *stress.* Likewise, another cancer survivor, my friend Reese Patterson, indicates the importance of taking charge, expressing harmful emotions clearly in a socially acceptable manner, and learning to say *no* without guilt.[12] All these aspects of one's heart and mind work to lower stress levels and elevate helpful, healthful thoughts and emotions.

Stress induces a stress response. The stress response involves changes in the body when an individual experiences a challenge or threat. The greater the perceived threat, the more intense and comprehensive the response. An extremely important point here is that the effects of the stress response are equivalent whether the threat is real or simply imagined.[13]

Most of us worry frequently about things that really are not exactly as they first appear to be. We imagine many things, and we make "mountains out of molehills." I tell my patients that worry is worse than syphilis. You can treat most cases of syphilis, but it is much more difficult to treat most cases of worry. Most of us are responsible for the disease of worry. Worry, anxiety, and fear exaggerate our physical illnesses and impede our healing. I discuss this at greater length in my book *Rx for Worry*.[14]

God would not have commanded us not to fear if it were impossible. There is a type of fear that comes from a spiritual disorder when the believer has a basic lack of trust in Christ. Such a fear is sin. When you operate in fear, you become anxious, confused, troubled, and generally miserable. A fairly new believer recently phoned our home quite upset. When we questioned her, we discovered that she had tried to convince one of her relatives to accept the Lord, using every argument she had recently learned at her Christian college. Since her relative reacted indignantly, she pushed further and became so irritated that the gentleman wouldn't listen to her reasoning. Her testimony was then jeopardized by her bad attitude.

She realized that she overreacted because of fear that her loved one would die and go to hell if he didn't trust Christ soon. We all understand that burden. She has been praying for her whole family to come to know the Lord and temporarily forgot that the Holy Spirit does the convincing.

As we mature in our walk with the Lord, hopefully we come to understand that simple, trusting, abiding faith cannot be easily ruffled. Fear, anger, bitterness, or an underlying sense of insecurity are usually signs that somewhere along the way we have stopped relying on God and have chosen to place faith in our own abilities and independently govern ourselves.

In contrast, Oswald Chambers said, "Faith is deliberate confidence in the character of God whose ways you may not understand at the time." Where and in whom my faith is established is revealed when the condition of my soul is laid bare by the onslaught of life's issues. If my faith is anchored in Him, my soul remains anchored in Him even in the thunderclouds and storms of life. If I'm abiding in Him, the storms of life will not overwhelm me; if I am solely responsible for my own welfare, I'll be gripped with fear when something invades my life that is beyond my capacity to resolve. Faith in God's sovereignty is a great balm to the soul!

Mark Twain once said that courage isn't the absence of fear but the mastery of it. We would say it's the place where fear and faith meet. *Fear* has been described as a small trickle of doubt that flows through the mind until it wears such a great channel that all your thoughts finally drain into it. Even tiny fears that go unchecked can build up into paralyzing trauma. To begin with, fear is understood to generate from six general categories: poverty, criticism, loss of love, illness, old age, and death.

Also, fear comes from mental disorders. This kind of fear can terrorize your mind and cripple your emotions to the point that you are bound by guilt, despair, and chronic bouts of anxiety. Instead of being productive, you lose confidence in your own ability and become ill at ease. If you continue in this frame of mind you can become paranoid. Paul said, "Let this mind be in you which was also in Christ Jesus" (Phil. 2:5). A phobia is what results when fear and reason don't keep in touch.

> ## GOD'S PRESCRIPTION FOR HEALING
>
> "FAITH IS DELIBERATE confidence in the character of God whose ways you may not understand at the time."

One more source of fear, if it is possible to separate fear into types, is physical fear. Physical fear can prevent the organs in your body from functioning as God intended. It is a terrible feeling to be physically afraid. The psalmist said, "I will fear no evil," not because there was no evil, because David's life was in danger many times while he tended his father's sheep and during the years when King Saul was trying to kill him. He learned early on that God was his protector—"For Thou art with me" (Ps. 23:4, KJV). There will always be real and genuine reasons for fear, but "I will fear no evil, for Thou art with me."

This doesn't mean the Christian will never suffer physical harm of any kind. No, but there is a freedom from physical fear when your confidence is grounded in God and His Word. The apostle John said, "God is love" and "Perfect love casts out fear" (1 John 4:16, 18). A relying trust in God's wisdom and love produces an abiding trust in One who has your best interest in mind. A great saint of God who lived in the 1600s, simply called Brother Lawrence, referred to this fearless abiding as "practicing the presence of God" as a lifestyle choice.

The Abbe de Beaufort describes Brother Lawrence's epiphany as he heard it in their first conversation together:

> The first time I saw Brother Lawrence was upon the 3rd of August, 1666.
>
> He told me that GOD had done him a singular favor, in his conversion at the age of eighteen.
>
> That in the winter, seeing a tree stripped of its leaves, and considering that within a little time, the leaves would be renewed, and after that the flowers and fruit appear, he received a high view of the Providence and Power of GOD, which has never since been effaced from his soul. That this view had perfectly set him loose from the world, and kindled in him such a love for GOD, that he could not tell whether it had increased in above forty years that he had lived since.
>
> ...That we should feed and nourish our souls with high notions of GOD; which would yield us great joy in being devoted to Him.
>
> That we ought to quicken, to enliven, our faith. That it was lamentable we had so little; and that instead of taking faith for the rule of their conduct, men amused themselves with trivial devotions, which changed daily. That the way of Faith was the spirit of the Church, and that it was sufficient to bring us to a high degree of perfection.
>
> That we ought to give ourselves up to GOD, with regard both to things temporal and spiritual, and seek our satisfaction only in fulfilling His will, whether He lead us by suffering or by consolation, for all would be equal to a soul truly resigned.[15]

Sometimes we think that the Prince of Peace Himself couldn't possibly relate to the horror and dismay in our lives. However, in the Garden of Gethsemane Jesus said, "My heart is ready to break with grief." (See Matthew 26:38.) Scripture says He went and threw Himself on the ground. This is the scene of a straining, agonizing, and struggling Jesus. The Book of Hebrews depicts the scene well: "During the days of Jesus' life on earth, he offered up prayers and petitions with loud cries and tears to the one who could save him from death" (Heb. 5:7, NIV). He truly was "a Man of sorrows and acquainted with grief" (Isa. 53:3). Is it any wonder that He invites us into His presence?

> Come to Me, all you who labor and are heavy laden, and I will give you rest. Take My yoke upon you and learn from Me [the precept], for I am gentle and lowly in heart, and you will find rest for your souls [the reward].
> —Matthew 11:28–29

The One who truly understands beckons, "Fear not, for I am with you; be not dismayed…" (Isa. 41:10).

You don't need to live in fear and apprehension. Your fear level is ultimately a referendum on the closeness of your friendship with God. When God says He'll never leave us or forsake us, He means it! One of my dear elderly patients, Irene Galanos, came to my office not long ago. After I finished her treatment we shared for a few moments together about what the Lord means to us. She looked at me with a little sparkle in her eye and asked if she could give me her testimony.

She began to tell me how she and her Greek family first immigrated to the United States in May of 1947 after the war. Though they were of Greek descent, they had been living in France and had suffered much during the war years. The family settled here in Tarpon Springs, Florida, where a large Greek community lives. She was Greek but spoke only French. It was difficult to be in an English-speaking country, living among Greek-speaking distant family members. The conditions were very difficult for her family because they had to start all over again financially. She said, "Although at first we lived in someone's garage, we didn't care that we were so poor because we were finally in a land of freedom.

My sisters and I had jobs during the day, and we tried to go to language school in the evening. Times were very hard. I became sick."

All her stress affected her health. She contracted tuberculosis and was put into a sanitarium in nearby Tampa, Florida. "I was very, very lonely there. It was hard, but the Lord was very near to me. A missionary came to the sanitarium and talked about the Lord. It comforted me."

When Irene was finally released from the sanitarium, since she was the only unmarried daughter, it became her duty to take care of her dying mother. Her mother had been the family's tower of strength during the war, while they acclimated to a new country, and during Irene's long illness. "When my mother died, I cried and cried and cried. I could not stop crying. After all the family members went back to their homes, I closed the curtains in my mother's home, and I sat crying day and night. My family tried to get me to go outside, but I just sat in the dark and cried. How could I go on without my mother?"

But the Lord did not leave Irene during this dark and lonely time. She remembered the Greek Bible that had been given to her. Though she was still learning Greek, she started to read it through from cover to cover. She said, "The reading went very slow. As I struggled to read line after line and paragraph after paragraph, a Light began to help me understand what I was reading—it was the Holy Spirit. God's Word was like food to me. I would wake up in the middle of the night. I was reading, reading, reading, reading, all the time. I don't say that I understood all of it because it was Greek, and my childhood language was French. But I read and read and read. I read it all the way through. I have read my Bible through many times now. I do not always have the language to explain to others, but I love my Bible. I read it and read it and read it. After I read it through, then, one day I opened the window shades and began to let the sunshine into the house again. The heavy depression lifted off me. I loved my Bible. God has never failed me even in the other illnesses that I have

> **GOD'S**
>
> To be in the right place to receive God's gifts of healing, you must manage the destructive negative emotions that frequently populate your head.
>
> **PRESCRIPTION**

had through the years, He is always with me in my reading of His Word. He always comes to me. I live by myself now, but I am never really alone. God is always near."

God says in His Word:

> I will never leave you nor forsake you.
>
> —HEBREWS 13:5

> Be strong and of good courage, do not fear nor be afraid of them [the enemy coming against you]; for the LORD your God, He is the One who goes with you. He will not leave you nor forsake you.
>
> —DEUTERONOMY 31:6

> Wait on the LORD; be of good courage, and He shall strengthen your heart; wait, I say, on the LORD!
>
> —PSALM 27:14

> Only be strong and very courageous, that you may observe to do according to all the law which Moses My servant commanded you; do not turn from it to the right hand or to the left, that you may prosper wherever you go.
>
> —JOSHUA 1:7

His Word brings encouragement and life. Renew your thought life with His Word, and take courage.

Managing the Negative Emotions

Stress, anxiety, worry, and fear are killers. The evidence for this conclusion is large and growing. To be in the right place to receive God's gifts of healing, you must manage the destructive negative emotions that frequently populate your head. Some people seek comfort in others, and even in the companionship of pets. These elements have positive effects on health, as do the growing number of "therapies," such as art therapy (learning and practicing art), for example. Exercise may be the best way to diminish stress in your life. However, another important aspect in your life has tremendous rejuvenating—and aligning—effects, though it is too easily overlooked. You may have heard that "laughter is the best medicine," and it is very true.

Laughter—life's therapeutic medicine

A clown is like an aspirin, only he works twice as fast.[16]

God placed within us a valuable, healing emotion—laughter. In the twenty-first century, even mainstream publications have come to understand and explain the healing power of laughter; however, the idea of its therapeutic effects was first viewed, with skepticism, in the mid-1960s.[17] It all began when author/editor Norman Cousins detailed in his book *Anatomy of an Illness* his astounding rejuvenation through humor. Cousins described how he had "laughed himself back to health." Diagnosed with a degenerative disease—ankylosing spondylitis—and almost completely paralyzed, he was offered only a few months to live by the doctors. Cousins checked himself out of the hospital, checked into a hotel, consumed high doses of vitamin C, and immersed himself in humor.[18] He read funny stories; he watched old comedies by Keaton, Chaplin, and the Marx Brothers. Norman Cousins eventually recovered and lived another twenty years of healthy, productive life.[19]

I am not saying that his radical approach is typical or advisable—God has provided knowledge to physicians and medical science to assist in your healing—but it does indicate the power of our humor and laughter to assist in our healing. *That humor and your capacity for it are all included in the Creator's design of your mind. And it all derives from the DNA instructions in the zygote.*

Dr. Annette Goodheart, Ph.D., MFCC, a California-based laughter therapist, is author of *Laughter Therapy: How to Laugh About Everything in Your Life That Isn't Really Funny!*[20] She maintains that laughter isn't locked away in a folder marked "For Professional Use Only." Instead, it's always there, and it's always ready to be shared. She operates on the assumption that certain laughter rebalances the body chemicals produced by fear. A heartfelt laugh will rebalance the internal chemistry disturbed by anger. Painful emotions produce stress chemicals in our bodies. By mere design, our bodies are intended to rebalance those chemicals through cathartic processes. They are processes like

GOD'S PRESCRIPTION *for* HEALING

laughing, crying, sweating, yawning, trembling, and raging.

Prior to receiving her Ph.D. as a therapist, Dr. Goodheart was an accomplished artist. She said, "Painting is a process of confronting yourself, as is writing or any other creative effort. You must face yourself over and over again as you confront an empty canvas or a blank page. Basically, what I did when I painted was to play with my colors. I'd splat some paint on and see what it said back to me. We'd have a dialogue—basically that's what I do now in therapy. Cathartic therapy as I practice has…basic steps.…You get in touch with your feelings.…You release them through catharsis.…You rethink the situation or the experience associated with the feelings, that now has become possible because the chemical rebalancing in your body allows you to think more clearly. Then, finally you take whatever sensible action is appropriate."[21]

As a therapist dealing often with people in great pain—either mentally, physically, or emotionally—she helps her clients put a different frame around the content of their situations in order to see them from new perspectives. This is the same technique an artist uses. The therapy of laughter has radically changed the "canvas" of scores of lives as Dr. Goodheart has helped them view their situations through a different "frame of reference."

GOD'S

FOR HEALING

IF WE COULD LAUGH as frequently as a four-year-old, we would have the heart rate and blood pressure of a four-year-old.

PRESCRIPTION

Her studies substantiate that laughter begins with the dilation of the cardiovascular system, which enables us to keep our flexibility. Initially, when we laugh our heart rate and blood pressure rise, then drop below our normal levels. Those constricted blood vessels that cause high blood pressure immediately react. It seems as though four-year-olds can laugh hundreds of times a day, while the average adult laughs only fifteen times a day. If we could laugh as frequently as a four-year-old, we would have the heart rate and blood pressure of a four-year-old.

As the diaphragm convulses in laughter, our internal organs get massaged. This keeps them supple. Gulping in massive amounts of air oxygenates our blood supply. Air expelled during laughing has been clocked at seventy miles per hour, which gives our respiratory system a tremendous workout. We lose muscle control as the whole skeletal system relaxes. Goodheart says, "I believe laughter is one of the things that causes our brain to produce hormones called beta endorphins, which reduce pain, and our adrenal glands to manufacture cortisol, which is a natural anti-inflammatory that's wonderful for arthritis."[22]

The most rewarding part of her work is with those people who have serious problems—emotional or physical. Therapists are confirming that we may have relatively little control over the events in our lives, but how we respond to them makes all the difference. Patients who are diagnosed with cancer can "reframe" the situation through humor and discover that depression and fear are half the battle. The tension and fear of the illness are a big part of the symptoms. How the patient responds emotionally can suppress or enhance healing. Stress increases the severity of the problem. Humor and laughter, however, can be part of the solution.

> **GOD'S**
>
> FOR HEALING
>
> HOW THE PATIENT responds emotionally can suppress or enhance healing.
>
> PRESCRIPTION

Many case studies have shown that laughter works well even for those recovering from surgery or those battling mood swings and bouts of depression. Here again, not only does the release of endorphins cause the pain—physical or mental and emotional—to be tolerable, but also the recovery time is lessened.

Pain is a God-designed feedback sensation that tells us when we need to pay attention to something potentially destructive. It is a natural part of being human. But we have a God-given, overcoming tool placed right inside of us. Ironically, when we laugh, the one thing that will disappear from us first is the fear of our situation. There is a saying that if fear is the lock, laughter is the key. Laughter is perhaps God's tool for us to "jump-start" a body chemistry that has gotten out of balance. Healthy, nonridiculing laughter provides physiological, psychological, and spiritual tools we have all had all along but perhaps have forgotten to apply. So, learn to laugh, and live, all over again.

Mental Healing

It has been observed that hopelessness breeds recklessness—or, we might say again, "imbalance." And for mental health, we must have faith and reason. Balance derives from an understanding of and appreciation for the Creator's wisdom. Without the awareness and appreciation, some people seek escape from tribulation with damaging substances and behaviors. The retreat into self-destructive compulsions and addictions is frequently believed to offer answers and rest. That is mistaken. Rather, these behaviors only complicate things and further alienate us from ourselves, our Creator, and our purpose.

When you are faced with illness, you are presented with something that might very well be life changing in a variety of ways. But, more, through that illness you are afforded the opportunity for personal transformation and growth. How can we make sense of what is happening? How can we remain hopeful—how can we live—when we are weak and fear becomes our primary sense? How do we face death? How do we face life? Who you are and how you face trouble are so important.

Personality

In their seminal volume *Handbook of Religion and Health,* Harold Koenig and his co-writers define personality as a "stable set of tendencies and traits."[23] This includes the behavior—thoughts, feelings, and actions—that distinguishes you from others. Koenig and his colleagues accentuate the role of three traits that have particular meaning to healing: hostility, hope, and control.

Stress derives directly from a lack of control, or rather, a perception of a lack of control. Both Larry Burkett and Reese Patterson expressed the huge need for the cancer patient to be informed and to be active in the medical healing process. The beautiful thing for the believer is that with a faith in God and His hand in every event of life, the sense of control *internally*, that is within oneself, is enhanced.[24] Such a sense of control means less stress, greater peace, and therefore a better disposition toward healing.

"Hostility is a more or less enduring pattern of suspiciousness, resentment, frequent anger, and cynical mistrust of others."[25] These negative elements are proven impediments to total health and healing.

They undermine and erode the wonderful gift of hope that the Lord imbedded in every human heart. Unfounded and exaggerated fears often result in such hostility, in despondency, and in a willingness to give up. How can we be healed in such a mental and spiritual state?

Biology plays a large part in the development of your personality, as do the social environments you are exposed to from birth, but we also have choices to make. Prayer and faith in God have been demonstrated to result in lower levels of hostility and higher levels of hope. You and I are free to, and we must learn to, appreciate our design, the Designer, and by understanding the true center of control in our lives, choose hope over hostility and all negative emotions.

My friend Dr. James Avery works with hospice patients, in other words, those who are dying and will not ever get better. He believes that not only is hope a real possibility in one's last days, but it is also a necessity.[26] True, the hopes of the those facing imminent death largely differ from those of us who are healthy—hopes for a peaceful death, hopes for loved ones left, hopes for an improbable healing—but the important thing is that hope flowers in every heart.

It is vital that we comprehend the immensity of this. As Dutch Shields writes, "Hope deferred is the common cold of the soul, except that this virus can kill."[27] Our Creator endowed us with the inner capacity for hope; it is part of His design for healing; we must nurture it in ourselves and in each other. *The place for hope in the process of healing is as important as any medication, treatment, or nutrient.*

"…but God meant it for good" (Gen. 50:20). Humans cannot live without hope, without the sense that something, something good, can be attained, yet we lose it so easily. There are many ways that even illness may end up in something good, but we have a very difficult time seeing this. Your ability to hope, to search for God's plan within the hardship is a central key to healing, and it was born, with you, out of your DNA.

Hope As an Antidote

Faith gives substance to hope (Heb. 11:1). Hope is important, but hope lacks substance until it is rooted in faith—Fully Assured I Trust Him! Hope is faith talking aloud, drowning out voices of defeat. An example is found in Mark 5:25–28, where the woman with the issue of blood

 GOD'S PRESCRIPTION *for* HEALING

said, "If only I may touch His clothes, I shall be made well." Hope gave her the tenacity to press forward in faith. The Amplified Bible says, "For she kept saying, If I only touch His garments, I shall be restored to health."

Hope is birthed in an attitude of gratitude that causes you to expect joyously even if you have to wait a little for the answer. You are assured of the character of God. You can develop a habit of thankfulness toward God and others. It puts you in a frame of mind to expect to receive and enjoy in the future. Cynicism and criticism squelch hope and faith. They usually are rooted in some resentment and bitterness that haven't been dealt with yet. You can't go forward when they are barricading the way.

Words are seeds that will bring a harvest. You can energize others with words of hope and encouragement into the lives of others and into your own trying times. "Death and life are in the power of the tongue" (Prov. 18:21). Regardless of what your circumstances are, you are learning the character of God—He never fails. Such words brought a mighty harvest late in the career of George Frideric Handel, the great composer of the *Messiah* oratorio. He drew encouragement and inspiration from the timely words a friend sent to him at a low point in his composing career. History records it this way:

> GOD'S
>
> FOR HEALING
>
> HOPE IS BIRTHED in an attitude of gratitude that causes you to expect joyously even if you have to wait a little for the answer.
>
> PRESCRIPTION

He was a has-been, a fossil, a relic, an old fogy, but it hadn't always been so. As a young man, George Frideric Handel was the talk of England, the best paid composer on earth, and his fame soared around the world.

The glory passed however, audiences dwindled, and one project after another failed. Handel grew depressed. The stress brought on a case of palsy that crippled some of his fingers. "Handel's great days are over," wrote Frederick the Great, "his inspiration is exhausted." Yet his troubles also matured him, and his music became more heartfelt. One morning Handel received a collection of various Biblical texts from Charles Jennens. The opening words from Isaiah 40 moved Handel: "Comfort ye my people."

On August 22, 1741, he began composing music for the words. Twenty-three days later, the world had *Messiah*, which opened in London to enormous crowds on March 23, 1843. Handel led from his harpsichord, and King George II, who was present that night, surprised everyone by leaping to his feet during the "Hallelujah Chorus." From that day audiences everywhere have stood in reverence during the stirring words: "Hallelujah! And He shall reign forever and ever."[28]

To pass words of hope to an emotionally drowning soul is to drag them into the "life raft" by hand. You can't hold back a man or woman whose hope is in the Lord. To that person, God is always bigger than the giants of the Promised Land. The truths in God's Word bring hope. Saturating our souls in His Word enables us to rise above despair. Caleb and Joshua saw the giants in the land, but knew that with God they could overcome (Num. 13). The prophet Jeremiah looked at the smoldering ruins of Jerusalem and responded in much the same way. He had the devastating facts, yet in the midst of the lament he reminded himself of the reliability and faithfulness of the God he served:

> ## GOD'S
>
> **FOR HEALING**
>
> **HOPE BREAKS OUT of the net of reasoning and moves forward in faith and confidence in God and His Word.**
>
> ## PRESCRIPTION

This I recall to my mind,
Therefore I have hope.
Through the LORD's mercies we are not consumed,
Because His compassions fail not.

 GOD'S PRESCRIPTION *for* HEALING

They are new every morning;
Great is Your faithfulness.
"The LORD is my portion," says my soul,
"Therefore I hope in Him!"

—LAMENTATIONS 3:21–24

It isn't human nature to hope against hope. In fact, such a response seems contrary to human sanity, but an irrepressible trust in God is rewarded. (See Romans 4:13–25.) His peace passes understanding and human reasoning (Phil. 4:6–7). Joyous faith founded in hope cannot be explained, but it is steadfastly based on "the substance of things hoped for, the evidence of things not [yet] seen" (Heb. 11:1; cf. 1 Pet. 1:7–8). Hope breaks out of the net of reasoning and moves forward in faith and confidence in God and His Word. Hope renews our minds.

Hebrews 6:18–19 tells us that when disappointment and confusion come, our response should be to run to the Lord, not sink into despair. God's faithfulness in times past enables us to hope again and to pass this hope along to others. Hope is "an anchor of the soul, both sure and steadfast" (v. 19).

As we receive God's Word through faith, hope rises within us. When we live it out before others as "living epistles," those who see our witness receive His living, life-giving hope just as they receive it by reading His written epistles. Their faith in Him will be enhanced when we are anchored in Him! In the times in which we live, Christians, anchored in the Rock, Christ Jesus, will be able to extend a hand of hope to those terrorized by the current events that are sure to happen before Jesus returns.

> GOD'S PRESCRIPTION FOR HEALING
>
> HOPE IN GOD AND His Word—it will transform you into a man or woman of faith.

Why art thou cast down, O my soul? and why art thou disquieted in me? hope thou in God: for I shall yet praise him for the help of his countenance.

—PSALM 42:5, KJV

It is the powerful, living Word of God, applied by the power of the Holy Spirit in the name of Jesus to any situation that quickens the life-changing promises of God. As long as you are content with a thimbleful of God, you will only view life from the standpoint of reports of illness, bad relationship scenarios, and hopeless circumstances, and your soul will be troubled as a result. Hope in God and His Word—it will transform you into a man or woman of faith. The Word of God comes alive in you when you call upon the Holy Spirit of God to awaken your spirit and soul to who God is. Jeremiah 32:17 reminds you: "There is nothing too hard for thee" (KJV).

Chapter 9

THE PRESCRIPTION FOR INNER HEALING

I looked into the eyes of Jesus, and I felt love.
I touched the hands of Jesus, and I felt power.
I knelt at the feet of Jesus, and I felt worship.
He put His arms about me, and I felt protection.
He lifted me up, and I felt mercy.
He turned me, and I felt tenderness.
He sent me, and I felt commission.

RALPH E. MCINTOSH, © 1997

Clinical evidence and formal studies have been conducted that prove the positive influence of a religious faith on healing. This includes the positive effects of fellowship and worship attendance at church, of private religious activities such as daily devotional prayer, and of intercessory prayer (individuals praying for the healing of other persons). So positive are these effects that health practitioners are finding faith difficult to ignore.[1] These research studies have been published in a variety of medical journals.[2]

Statistics reported by WebMD give the following indications for people who do not attend church or profess a faith in God:

- Their average hospital stays are longer than the hospital stays for believers.
- They are several times more likely to die following surgery.
- They have a 40 percent higher death rate from heart disease and cancer.
- They experience twice the number of strokes.[3]

In this chapter we will take a closer look at some of these expressions of religious faith that will encourage you to seek God's blessing and healing in all you do.

101

Prayer

Is anyone among you sick? Let him call for the elders
of the church, and let them pray over him, anointing
him with oil in the name of the Lord. And the prayer of
faith will save the sick, and the Lord will raise him up.

—James 5:14–15

The most widely cited study to date on the therapeutic effects of prayer
was conducted by Dr. Randolph Byrd at the San Francisco Medical
Center in 1988. Dr. Byrd studied a coronary care unit (CCU) population to explore two questions:

1. Does intercessory prayer to the Judeo-Christian
   God have any effect on the patient?
2. How are these effects characterized, if present?[4]

In this study, 393 patients were assigned randomly to one of two
groups. Group 1 had prayers made to God on behalf of the patients
by intercessors. Group 2, the control group, received no prayers from
anyone. Intercessory prayer for each member in the first group was exer-
cised by three to seven intercessors who were provided with the patient's
name, diagnosis, and information on the patient's general condition.
Intercessors selected were born-again Christians with active Christian
lives in their churches. All 393 patients received the same high-quality
cardiac care at the hospital. The identities of the individuals in the first
group, the group being prayed for, were kept secret from the attending
doctors, nurses, and from the patients themselves.

Dr. Byrd recorded the dramatic results of his statistical study about
the efficacy of remote intercessory prayer in this way:

Analysis of events after entry into the study showed the
prayer group had less congestive heart failure, required
less diuretic and antibiotic therapy, had fewer episodes
of pneumonia, had fewer cardiac arrests, and were less
frequently intubated and ventilated.[5]

Dr. Byrd concluded that with intercessory prayer to God—from a
distance and without the beneficiary's knowledge—"there seemed to be

  GOD'S PRESCRIPTION *for* HEALING

an effect, and that effect was presumed to be beneficial."[6]

In another study of patients suffering from rheumatoid arthritis (RA), the authors reported that individuals receiving in-person intercessory prayer—prayer with direct contact between the intercessor and the patient—showed significant improvement in their one-year follow-up.[7] The researchers concede that further explorations are required with more detailed examination of possible placebo effects, as well as the "varying types and degrees of spiritual and religious beliefs and practices." However, their study already suggests "that in-person intercessory prayer may be a *useful adjunct to standard medical care* in the care of certain patients with RA."[8]

> "If the subject of [Byrd's] study had been a new medication instead of prayer, this would have been considered a medical breakthrough."

GOD'S PRESCRIPTION FOR HEALING

This conclusion is an important point. William Standish Reed, founder of the Christian Medical Foundation, surgeon, scholar, and strong believer, makes it clear:

> I believe implicitly in the Healing Ministry of the Church of Jesus Christ. However, I believe that the ministry should be used in conjunction with the best medical and surgical methods—not as a substitute for scientific methods. It is my belief that the answer to the prayer of the cancer sufferers often is the scalpel of the well-trained surgeon.[9]

Other researchers have noted statistically significant beneficial effects of immersion in a personal and private practice of Christian faith. In *Prayer and Mortality*, the authors sought to reveal an association between private religious activities (meditation, prayer, or Bible study) and longer survival in certain groups.[10] Establishing controls for demographics and health status, the researchers reported that among community-dwelling adults aged sixty-four to one hundred one, "persons with no disability and little or no private religious activity…were 63 percent more likely to die" over the six-year period of the study.

"Even after controlling for social support and health behaviors, investigators found that lack of private religious activity continued to predict a 47 percent greater risk of dying."[11]

Another hospital study of cardiac patients, this one in 1999 at St. Luke's Hospital of Kansas City, found that a group of patients that received daily prayer by Christian volunteers had "shorter recovery times with fewer complications" than the group that received no prayer. William Harris, Ph.D., who conducted the study, concluded that "prayer makes an effective adjunct to standard medical care."[12]

Dr. Larry Dossey makes the point even more stridently. He states that "if the subject of [Byrd's] study had been a new medication instead of prayer, this would have been considered a medical breakthrough. Up until then, most medical people had considered prayer a nice thing. It didn't hurt much, but they certainly didn't consider it a matter of life and death."[13]

Dossey wisely points out that "when we talk of prayer we are talking about distant manifestations of consciousness. To talk this way is to break some kind of taboo. We can accept the power of the mind in affecting bodily processes, but to talk interpersonally—that my consciousness can have an effect on other persons and events—is a major paradigm shift."[14]

Koenig notes that the work of others has indicated the possible mechanisms of religion's action or influence on health—on hypertension, in this case. The beneficial effect of religion on blood pressure is most likely a combination of factors that include:

- The promotion of healthy lifestyle practices (especially abstinence from alcohol, tobacco, and promiscuous sex)
- Coping effects of religious practice
- Social support effects of integration into a religious community
- Beneficial psychodynamics of particular belief systems and faith[15]

When you are baffled and desperate for an answer to life, the Holy Spirit can lead you to prayer that is "according to the will of God" (Rom. 8:27). Jesus Himself taught us to pray, "Thy kingdom come. Thy will be done in earth, as it is in heaven" (Matt. 6:10, KJV). When we pray in agreement with the will of God, we know that all heaven is on our side. What a comfort to know that when we ask anything according to God's will, He hears us and grants the things that we ask (1 John 5:14–15).

The apostle Paul admonished us to "pray without ceasing" (1 Thess. 5:17). How is this possible? In my book *The Prayerful Spirit,* I emphasized the importance of being in communication with God continually.[16] When you wake up at night, think of His love for you and not of the world and its anxieties. Be constantly thinking about your Redeemer and about your relationship to Him as you go through your days. Staying in close contact with God will help you when the rough spots in your life occur. He is just a call away:

> GOD'S
>
> I HAVE FOUND "breath prayers" to be a true blessing and a refreshing way to go through my busy workday at the clinic.
>
> FOR HEALING
>
> PRESCRIPTION

Call to Me, and I will answer you, and show you great and mighty things, which you do not know.
—JEREMIAH 33:3

I have found "breath prayers" to be a true blessing and a refreshing way to go through my busy workday at the clinic. These prayers are short and simple requests, spoken in one breath. They can be one phrase of praise, gratitude, or worship. Try your own breath prayers—they will help you to cope with whatever situations arise in your day. They certainly will remind you of God's continual grace in your daily life. After all, it is His very breath that you are breathing that gives and sustains your life.

Here are some of the breath prayers that I use daily:

- "Give me gentleness, Father."
- "Bring healing to this patient, Father; guide me in my part."
- "Bless my children, their spouses, and my grandchildren today, Father."
- "Help me better understand and live Your truth today."

- "May I live for the anointing, Father; it's the presence of the Holy One."

Our friend Ralph McIntosh battled an aggravating bout of symptoms, including chest pains, for a few years, which the doctors couldn't define well enough to determine the right treatment. At one point he was hospitalized and tests were run, but still there was no conclusive evidence. A resulting weakness drained his strength so much that he had trouble climbing stairs without pulling himself up one step at a time by clinging onto the handrails. He knew something was terribly wrong with him, but no test pinpointed the problem.

One day while his wife, Susan, was at work, in desperation he determined to seek the Lord's healing for himself. He pulled two chairs together in their living room and sat down to have a chat with the Lord. He spoke aloud, "Jesus, am I dying? If so, I want to know so I can get things in order for my wife and family." For some time he sat there waiting for an answer. Then he sensed that he was in the presence of the Lord Jesus, communing with Him person to person. He experienced an amazing spiritual moment with the Lord, and later Ralph penned a poem titled "The Commissioning," which is at the beginning of this chapter.

From that day forward Ralph began to get well. The weakness left, and his health returned. With the healing came a renewed purpose and call upon his life. That day he received an inner healing and a spiritual commissioning. Within a few years he gave up his contracting business, and he and his wife went into full-time Christian ministry.

Isaiah had the same reaction in Isaiah 6. Our reaction to His glorious presence is worship followed by a deeper awareness of our need of redemption and a commissioning to tell others of Him. We conclude, "Here I am! Send me" (Isa. 6:8).

Fellowship

...not forsaking the assembling of ourselves together...
—HEBREWS 10:25

John Donne believed that no man is an island. Many of us live our lives ignoring that simple, difficult truth until we become ill. It is well documented that vibrant social bonds are an integral element in health, healing, and longevity.[17] In my practice at St. Luke's I am keenly aware of the beneficial effects that accompany reaching out to the individual patient in a helpful, human, loving manner. Dr. Ben Carson describes the ability of one of his assistants to touch others, his patients, as vital to his work as a surgeon. She is a receptionist, but her real ability lies in helping people "focus on the positive side of a matter."[18]

What kind of impact do our relationships have in healing? Dr. David Spiegel, M.D., a professor of psychiatry at Stanford University says that, *"The relationship between social isolation and early death is as strong statistically as the relationship between dying and smoking or having high cholesterol."*[19]

God had good reasons for commanding us to fellowship with one another. There is something about having to "rub elbows" with other people that keeps us from isolating ourselves, especially when we are struggling with emotional issues. Even children today seem far more self-centered than they were years ago when two, three, or more siblings had to share a bedroom.

Whether it's a church family, a social club, a gym, a service club, a volunteer position at a hospital, a book club, or a twelve-step support group, whatever it is, relationships provide the exercise of staying in touch with others.

Some of the loneliest people wait for their phones or doorbells to ring and complain because no one cares. Not only is it your responsibility to reach out to others; it actually is a privilege to be involved with others' lives. Even if you aren't a group kind of person, you were created to communicate—and it keeps you healthy.

Healthy relationships are important. Loneliness kills; we should avoid it like a plague. Psychologists at McGill University took a group of heart attack survivors who were being discharged from the hospital and divided them up into two groups. Both groups received the same excellent heart care from the cardiologists and their own family physicians.

> ## GOD'S PRESCRIPTION FOR HEALING
>
> Even if you aren't a group kind of person, you were created to communicate—and it keeps you healthy.

However, one group also received a monthly phone call from some of the research team. If the researcher making the phone contact sensed any psychosocial problem, a specially trained nurse was scheduled to visit the patient in the home.

Just the little personal contact that was made resulted in a 50 percent reduction in the patients' death rate after one year in the group who were cared for by occasional phone calls and visits.

Stanford researchers randomly assigned women with metastatic breast cancer to receive usual medical care plus a weekly support group designed to help them manage the stress of their illness. The support group patients lived twice as long as those who were not in the program. At UCLA, patients with malignant melanoma who participated in only six ninety-minute sessions with a support group that also provided relationship training had a 50 percent reduction in patient death and recurrence of symptoms when compared with the usual care patients receive. Over the six years of this study, more than three times as many patients in the nonintervention group died as compared to the group that received support.[20]

> GOD'S
>
> FOR HEALING
>
> WE ARE INCOMPLETE apart from the other members of the body of Christ.
>
> PRESCRIPTION

All of us need interaction with others. It causes us to forget about ourselves when we focus on others. God made us to need one another. We need listening ears, caring hearts, and it must be a two-way street in order for a family, a community, or a church to be made up of healthy, emotionally fulfilled people.

As a Christian you are admonished to encourage others, pray for others, sing together, and testify of what God is doing in your life in order to edify—build up others in Christian love. Your life is enriched when you reach out to others and let them reach out to you. We do live in a fallen world where sin and pain abound. Many times, through no fault of our own, we are victims of woundedness. Our tendency is to pull in to ourselves and avoid close relationships. We think, *If people know this or that about me, they wouldn't like me and won't want to be my friend.* This is self-deception.

Fellowship with others is a freeing experience. God has placed distinct gifting and aspects of His divine nature within you. When you fellowship with others you can edify others with your life. The body of Christ will be complete some day when all of us are together with Him in glory. It is pride that keeps us from humbling ourselves and admitting that we need one another. God created us to need one another. We are incomplete apart from the other members of the body of Christ.

The Blessed Mind-set

Alignment—the key to inner healing—really means abandonment to God and the Holy Spirit reigning within your heart and mind. The Lord created you in a wonderful way, yet the many aspects of your consciousness must be kept in check, continually, by your proximity to God and His will. Ungodly, destructive, and negative thoughts proclaim that we are bound rather than freed by the Holy Spirit. Developing God's blessed mind-set is your first step toward true alignment with His design and desire for you. Aligning by adopting God's blessed mind-set allows us to experience the consequent inner healing that every one of us seeks—whether we are aware of the need or not.

The mental attitudes that produce mental health are those in alignment with the Creator—and these are outlined most explicitly in the beatitudes found in Matthew 5:3–11. They present what is probably the best summary of the mind-set blessed of God, which is the mind-set of inner health. That mind-set produces a life that stands in direct opposition to the life produced under a burden of sin.

The first beatitude says, "Blessed are the poor in spirit, for theirs is the kingdom of God" (v. 3). Humility is listed as the first requirement for having God's spirit within us. However, we are often preoccupied with self-centeredness and pride. We are concerned with satisfying what we feel are our needs. How am I going to be hurt? What does that person think about me? How does this make me look? What do I get out of this? The mind-set described in the beatitudes is one that is centered on God and others—not on self. It is a spirit of humility and God-wardness.

The theme of humility continues in the second beatitude, which pronounces God's blessing on the brokenhearted: "Blessed are those who mourn, for they shall be comforted" (v. 4). Matthew is describing people who know the glory of repentance and forgiveness, as David did in Psalm 51. The Savior has told us that we are blessed when we mourn because we will be comforted in the breast of the Trinity. Life is temporary and so, therefore, involves suffering, but our growing relationship with the Triune God is forever. Irrespective of the earthly circumstances we must face, God's authentic healing touch is eternal and ever present.

"Blessed are the meek, for they shall inherit the earth" (v. 5). The true meaning or significance of meekness is in learning truly to abide by the Lord's teachings. The meek are those who fall in alignment with His instructions. Unless we follow Him and abide in His teachings, we will never really have anything.

Meekness is "controlled strength." Without the revelation and obedience to what the Lord would have us accomplish we would be dangerous. My friend Jim Rowsey tells a story that clearly illustrates the need for control, discipline, and observance of God's will:

> As a youth I enjoyed the sport of boxing, and my father was a Golden Gloves champion. At age ten, upon leaving a boxing match we had attended together at Madison Square Gardens, we observed a large, drunk, and bellicose man outside. He was pushing people off the sidewalk and shouting. I thought to myself as I looked at my father: this is going to be wonderful; that obnoxious man is about to get decked. However, when the bruiser neared us, my father took me by the shoulder and led me off the sidewalk. Surprised, I asked my father why he hadn't dealt with the man with force. My father's response to me was, "*You have to know who is in control.*"[21]

Your nature will sometimes tell you to drive to success or to exact justice through your own power. Meekness, however, means living under authority—God's authority. Only there can true justice or success be found.

Pride will destroy us. In our independence of Him we cannot inherit God's portion for us in this life, or the new heavens and the new earth in eternity. But when we abide in Him, we inherit the earth.

"Blessed are those who hunger and thirst for righteousness, for they shall be filled" (v. 6). It is the individuals who reach this fourth beatitude attitude who are pronounced happy and filled! A basic human flaw affecting every person born is that we are full of and bound by desire. Desires are like thorns that choke the Word of God in our lives. The empty quest to fulfill earthly desire inevitably remains unquenched, merely increasing the earthly desire. Human desire can never be satisfied or fulfilled. It is only as we truly hunger and thirst after God's ways that we will find true satisfaction. Seek after God, and you will find God Himself in the paths of obedience that He has marked out for you in His Word.

The fifth beatitude tells us, "Blessed are the merciful, for they shall obtain mercy" (v. 7). No one is closer to the very heart of Christ Himself than a merciful, forgiving man or woman who is patient with the pains and shortcomings of others. *It becomes clear that the path to one's own inner healing is found in nurturing and assisting the healing of others.* A merciful heart lacks traces of bitterness and envy and is distinguished by an unwillingness to hold grudges or aggravate injury. Rather, a merciful mind-set allows you to become an intercessor rather than an accuser, and counts it a glory to pass by a transgression. Such a happy soul is God's channel of grace in a world full of hate.

GOD'S PRESCRIPTION FOR HEALING

> IT BECOMES CLEAR that the path to one's own inner healing is found in nurturing and assisting the healing of others.

The sixth beatitude is given as, "Blessed are the pure in heart, for they shall see God" (v. 8). This is a profound source of encouragement that will keep you moving toward alignment during those times when you find yourself tempted. Gazing at God's joyful countenance will focus you on keeping your heart pure. If you do not keep your eyes on God, you will be aimed toward those things that will ultimately defile you. The devil always shows you the *apple* but never the *worm* hidden inside that will destroy you. Many peaceful homes and marriages have been ruined by an eye that was diverted from God. Searching for—and seeing—the face of God, especially during times of temptation, brings spiritual pleasures that are infinitely more satisfying than trying to satiate an earthly appetite. An aligned mind will lead to the spiritual gifts, which ennoble and strengthen the soul.

The "peacemakers" have the happy benediction in the seventh beatitude: "Blessed are the peacemakers, for they shall be called sons of God" (v. 9). God's healing is found in the gospel of reconciliation. What a blessing it is to be what Paul calls "God's co-workers" as we seek to unite hard and bitter hearts (1 Cor. 3:9, TLB). Under God's blessing and power people become soft and tender toward one another. Such sweet fellowship is wonderful evidence that God can change the very bent of a soul. Peacemaking is a necessity to experience God's inner healing and peace, and to share them.

The final beatitude is pronounced on those who are persecuted for the sake of righteousness. "Blessed are the peacemakers, for they shall be called sons of God" (v. 9). One of the heaviest weights for the human spirit to bear is to be falsely accused. It is human nature to immediately defend our honor when challenged while conveniently forgetting the many times when we were wrong yet neither caught nor exposed. Such selective sight and memory cause us to defend ourselves with great energy to almost any limit.

> **GOD'S**
>
> THIS MENTAL alignment frees us from the destructive patterns of thought that ruin our lives and relationships, and distance us from the Creator.
>
> **PRESCRIPTION**

However, to humbly bear false accusation is to follow the Savior's example. We are often hated, persecuted, or hurt by others for doing what is right in God's eyes. Jesus tells us to rejoice and be exceedingly glad in these cases because He will reward us greatly in heaven. There is comfort in God's attitude toward us here.

This comfort is the foundation of all the beatitudes. We seek to please God and rest content that we know our God and love Him and aim to please Him. This is the mind-set toward a life aligned with God. This mental alignment frees you from the destructive patterns of thought that ruin your life and relationships, and distances you from the Creator. In this alignment you can experience a mind-set free to enjoy the liberty that God designed the soul to experience. The beatitudes outline an escape from the selfish patterns of thinking that imprison the mind and heart. Here is your key to freedom and inner healing.

> Come aside by yourselves to a deserted place and rest
> a while.
> —MARK 6:31

Jesus offered this invitation to His disciples to seek some rest and refreshment, a break from the noise and labor of life. Inevitably though, the spiritually hungry multitudes followed them on their escape. Jesus, moved by compassion, taught the eager crowd of more than five thousand, and fed them with two fish and five loaves of bread. Finally, after a long day, He drew apart once more for the much needed peace and solitude that He had not yet been able to find, going alone to the mountain to pray (Mark 6:46).

If Jesus, God's Son, required such quiet times, how much more do we? Nurturing the spirit of peaceful solitude is part of your healing. Only by recharging yourself are you ever going to be capable of helping and loving others when faced with their needs and demands. You need silence to hear God's voice.

In Jerusalem there was a very special pool where "lay a great multitude of sick people, blind, lame, paralyzed, waiting for the moving of the water" (John 5:3). The pool of Bethesda (*Beth* [house] *hesed* [of mercy]) drew those seeking healing. It provided cooling waters to those living in the middle of the city. This pool of Bethesda was a great mercy to the people of Jerusalem for its healing and restorative powers through God's grace.

The anguish and neuroses that we feel so deeply arise out of the time we spend overly focused upon ourselves. We tend to exaggerate our discomforts rather than enjoying peace and anointing. To dip in the pool is to dispense with all of your preoccupation with pain and simply rest in the Lord's arms. This is where you find physical, mental, and spiritual healing. You need to have a deserted place or a pool of healing in which to rest. God's Word is such a place of rest and restoration, for it is there that faith and grace abide. There, under God's sovereign hand, can be found every promise of God, sufficient for all your healings. Or your place of rest may be the place of prayer, meditation, and reflection upon God's gorgeous creation. Perhaps a simple walk on the beach or in the mountains is all that is necessary from time to time for you to slow down, relax, and reorient yourself to the Lord.

Wherever it may be, be sure you find a deserted place of calm and quiet—your pool of Bethesda. We live in a world of temptation, paranoia, confusion, chaos, and turmoil. With the Lord as the object of your focus, you will triumph. If you try to manage your difficulties separated from Him, out of alignment with His way, you will fail. The effects of such spiritual alignment are equivalent to a healing; losses incurred by neglecting this alignment are eternal.

GOD'S

YOU ARE REQUIRED
to do what God
has purposed
for you to do...
and to do it
with a
thankful heart.

PRESCRIPTION

How do you use your free time? What do most people do in their time outside their forty- to sixty-hour workweeks? Do they sit in front of the TV or hang out with the boys? What do you do? Many activities are meaningful, and many more merely seem meaningful. In the long run, what judges the activity is whether you grow through it—and whether you grow stronger or weaker. Well-used free time helps you get into condition physically, mentally, and spiritually. Time spent properly can refresh you and send you back into life rejuvenated.

During their free time, many people become bored, which leads frequently to a self-centered lifestyle rather than an abundant life. A self-centered lifestyle leads down the short, slippery slope to spiritual blindness. In that state you will worry about everything rather than offering the Creator thanksgiving for the blessings of this life. Make judicious use of your free time. Instead of thinking constantly about yourself, become one who looks to the anointed purpose and abundant life. "Therefore we do not lose heart. Even though our outward man is perishing, yet the inward man is being renewed day by day" (2 Cor. 4:16).

The abundant life can be experienced only after we have learned to rejoice and be thankful. "Rejoice in the Lord always. Again I will say, rejoice!" (Phil. 4:4). Don't waste your time in this life; it is your preparation for eternity. The Word tells you to, "Be anxious for nothing, but in everything by prayer and supplication, with thanksgiving, let your requests be made known to God" (Phil. 4:6). This is what is most important—praying, meditating, appreciating, and doing. "The things which you learned and received and heard and saw in me, these do, and the God of peace will be with you" (Phil 4:9). Such a mind-set is applicable to your activities twenty-four hours a day. Simply listening to what you ought to do, or even understanding what you ought to do, is insufficient. You are required to do what God has purposed for you to do…and to do it with a thankful heart.

The whole purpose of aligning your mind in such a way is to feel that the unction of God lives within you. You can only accomplish this in quiet, personal times spent in God's presence.

Chapter 10

SPIRITUAL ALIGNMENT WITH THE CREATOR'S DESIGN

I have been crucified with Christ; it is no longer I who live, but Christ lives in me; and the life which I now live in the flesh I live by faith in the Son of God, who loved me and gave Himself for me.

—GALATIANS 2:20

The Spirit of God has repeatedly sent messengers to us to teach us how to align ourselves spiritually with our God and Savior. Their voices cry in the wilderness just as did the voice of John the Baptist. "God is most glorified when we are most satisfied with Him," these faithful expositors of God's truth proclaim.[1] This is also understood to be the tenor of Jonathan Edwards' studies, which led him to conclude that we must "…align ourselves with Him in order to receive great joy."[2] Others, like C. S. Lewis, say that being with Him is like having an acceleration within one's heart. This meaningful acceleration is how Lewis defined joy. And it is the greatest of all joys. Without this joy as the foundation of our lives, all other instances and experiences of purported joy evaporate into nothingness.

Paul wrote a beautiful book to the ancient French tribe in Galatia. In Galatians 2:20 he wrote:

> I have been crucified with Christ [in Him I have shared His crucifixion]; it is no longer I who live, but Christ (the Messiah) lives in me; and the life I now live in the body I live by faith in (by adherence to and reliance on and complete trust in) the Son of God, Who loved me and gave Himself up for me.
>
> —AMP

The Galatians, like us, tended to become diverted by things other than Christ living in them. Paul was telling them that "now He is living in us by faith and by His grace. Let this be our focus before anything else." Later in Galatians 5:1, the apostle gives us the great imperative of the book where, in essence, the Savior says, "Stand fast in the liberty whereby I have set you free. And do not be entrapped anymore." Here we see the true nature of our liberty. It is the liberty to love by faith.

This liberty enables us to enjoy the fullness of God as it is described in Ephesians 3:16–19. There we hear the apostle's prayer for all of God's people. In effect, he says, "May you come to know God by faith, and may that faith be rooted and grounded in love. May you be granted, by God's glorious riches, to be strengthened by His Spirit in the inner person. May you live close to Jesus and experience His immeasurable and incomprehensible love. And may you be filled with all the fullness of God." His words are expressing the power of God living in you to make you stronger.

When you become stronger and filled with God's fullness, you are healed of the forces of fear, unbelief, and destructive desires. In joy, liberty, and faith your healing is meant to glorify God. He requires your cooperation to follow His direction for your mind, your thinking, behavior, lifestyle, and in your spirit—all in a controlled and inspired way. You must be brought into line, into understanding of and appreciation for the wisdom of His creation, evident in all life. Only once you have acknowledged the beauty and majesty in His design, which allowed sixty trillion cells and two hundred sophisticated tissue types to emerge from the genetic data of a single zygote to form your body, will you glorify the Creator. Only when you appreciate fully His intelligence, wisdom, and caring can you apprehend the purpose of life, which is anointed by God to give you strength and healing.

If you are focused on the Lord, you can avoid a huge impediment to fulfillment and satisfaction. One of the major roadblocks to this fulfillment is fear. It may be surprising to learn that fear is mostly self-generated. The fact that some are afraid of the dark and others love it means that

GOD'S

FOR HEALING

HERE WE SEE THE
true nature of
our liberty.
It is the
liberty to
love by faith.

PRESCRIPTION

our fears are unreasonable. Though we may not understand many of our fears, we can learn to defeat them with control and understanding of our anointed purpose in life. Your obsession with fear can be replaced with your focus upon God's anointed purpose for and in your life. Cling to the promise in John 10:27 to overcome your fears: "My sheep hear My voice, and I know them, and they follow Me." There are many solutions to your fears that can be found in God's Word—read it and heed it.

Obstacles to Alignment and God's Inner Healing

While alignment to the Lord and His principles through His mind-set is your key to inner healing, like others, you will experience many obstacles to this alignment. These obstacles are largely internal, self-induced, and persistent. These spiritual obstacles damage your being, injure others, and prevent the healing and the abundant life that Christ offers. They separate you from the Creator and blind you to His plan for your present and your future. I have taken an in-depth look at many of these obstacles in my book *Spiritual Blindness*.[3] The list of these self-deceptions is long, and mostly familiar: selfishness, self-pity, worry, fear, the need to control others, various compulsions and obsessions. We have already touched upon a couple of these, but there are a few more we need to look at since they are large, and very significant within the context of healing.

Pride

> Knowledge puffs up, but love edifies.
>
> —1 Corinthians 8:1

There is a mind-set that is aligned with the Creator's design for our healing. And, there is an enormous hindrance to attaining this mind-set. This obstacle is pride. What the Bible says about pride is extensive and profound, but it can be simply stated that pride prevents us from receiving the whole concept of God.

Pride, more than anything else, blinds us to the intricacies of creation and God's special purpose for it. Our scotomas, or blind spots, hide from us the irreducible complexity, power, and divine wisdom in the design of the human body, psyche, and spirit, which originated with a single, tiny zygote. It is pride that has allowed cold, indifferent theories of evolution to gain prominence and influence over generations of minds. It is pride, then, that prevents us from acknowledging the majesty of the Creator and from worshiping Him in awe and appreciation as He desires. So it is pride, more than anything else, that separates us from God's grace, His plan, and the meaning and purpose for our lives. It is pride, then, that separates us most ably from our healing.

The root of pride is selfishness and unwillingness, through fear and arrogance, to surrender to God's sovereignty. Pride is sin that originates within the heart. It may originate with undue trust in petty human knowledge and abilities (1 Cor. 8:1). Others develop their scotomas through a sense of self-righteousness, independence, or the artificial stature encouraged by power and wealth.

> GOD'S
>
> THE ROOT OF PRIDE is selfishness and unwillingness, through fear and arrogance, to surrender God's sovereignty.
>
> FOR HEALING
>
> PRESCRIPTION

These six things the LORD hates,
Yes, seven are an abomination to Him:
A proud look,
A lying tongue,
Hands that shed innocent blood,
A heart that devises wicked plans,
Feet that are swift in running to evil,
A false witness who speaks lies,
And one who sows discord among brethren.
                                        —PROVERBS 6:16–19

Jesus claimed:

Evil things come from within and defile a man.
                                        —MARK 7:23

What is the danger of human pride? It absolutely stands in the way of healing. There is no room for improvement under such a mind-set.

Do you see a man wise in his own eyes? There is more hope for a fool than for him.

—Proverbs 26:12

Pride will deceive you—blind you—while leading you into struggles with others, causing you to develop a spirit that criticizes and injures. Most significantly, though, pride causes you to reject the Creator and the reality of His Word. This mind-set amounts to a refusal to see His handiwork in the marvels of nature and the miraculous design for life and health. Without worshipful recognition of the source of healing, how can we experience such healing?

Unbridled pride will never result in growth, learning, or healing. Pride can only leave you with shame, debasement, and destruction (Prov. 11:2; 29:23; 16:18). Only your heart, designed and constructed by the Creator to be the seat of your inner man, holds the capacity for genuine understanding, wisdom to give entry to the Creator's plan for your life here and in eternity, and your capacity to love. You will be astonished at the healing you can experience through your love for your fellow man. How you respond to and love others is the measure of your alignment to God.

A critical spirit

At one point in his life, David Seamands's father left his successful career as an engineer to become a missionary in India, extracting his wife from her refined surroundings in the United States and settling them in a Third World country with a meager $100-a-month income. The two of them embarked on a mission that lacked not only a piano or a car, but even running water and indoor plumbing. Once in India, Mrs. Seamands complained loudly and incessantly. Surprisingly, even colleagues suggested to him that he would do well to divorce her.

Mr. Seamands's patient response to this was to say, "I can divorce her as you suggest, but that would not be what the Lord would want me to do. Alternatively, I can separate myself from her and her complaining and continue living the way that I want to live. Or, I can constantly pray for her and be an *intercessor* for her rather than her accuser." He decided to become this intercessor—to assist his wife rather than destroy her.

Through this difficult period in their life, Mr. Seamands Sr. surmounted the challenges and became stronger through them. As he constantly prayed for his wife, she also became stronger and more tolerant. The family ministry flourished through this couple, and then lived on in their son David. Mr. Seamands's love for his wife and his effort to align himself with God's more demanding and higher way had overcome her critical attitudes and constant bickering.

It is too easy to succumb to the temptation of a critical spirit. Therefore, it is important for you to grow above the complaints and criticisms of others. It is necessary to intercede rather than accuse. Accusations lead nowhere…except to acrimony and conflict. The only possible result of this bitter criticism is division and pain, and there is no healing to be found there.

Criticism of another may seem to have a momentary purpose if it makes you feel smarter or superior, but real purpose is found in alignment with God's desire that you love, forgive, and appreciate other people. By doing that you will find a truly anointed purpose to your life rather than a critical purpose. But learning to love, forgive, and appreciate others will require that you die to self and become one with the Lord. Only as you learn to move beyond the obstacle of a critical spirit will you find healing for yourself, your loved ones, and humanity.

> ## GOD'S
> ### FOR HEALING
> ENVY CONSUMES
> **the energies
> of body,
> mind,
> and heart.**
> ## PRESCRIPTION

A spirit of envy

One of our most intense inner battles is the one against a spirit of envy. Few inner states have the same potential to destroy and cause suffering to yourself and to those around you. It can rob you of health and well-being. The final, brutal influence of envy can be seen in the example of the world's first family. God had smiled on Abel and his offering of a lamb but was displeased with Cain and his offering of vegetables. Cain, consumed by his jealousy and overcome with anger, killed his own brother.

> A stone is heavy, and the sand weighty; but a fool's wrath
> is heavier than them both. Wrath is cruel, and anger is
> outrageous; but who is able to stand before envy?
>
> —PROVERBS 27:3–4, KJV

It is a simple task to prove the repercussions of wrath as a destroyer of hope and loving communication, but envy is an abyss, an overwhelming weight. Envy is a four-letter word that means selfishness. It represents a desire to possess that which does not belong to you. It is insatiable, never to be satisfied until something or someone has been wrecked in the vain pursuit to possess. Once that stage has been reached, of course, the object of desire is no longer worth possessing. As Cain discovered the hard way, nothing is solved by giving in to envy rather than seeking alignment with God and His ways. An envious heart is filled with anxiousness and tension begging to be released, and it results in physical illness, emotional extremes, impaired judgment, and the destruction of the peace and well-being of other people. Such an obstruction removes all possibility for the alignment necessary for healing. Envy consumes the energies of body, mind, and heart. The only possible outcome of unmitigated envy is illness, mental breakdown, and spiritual death. The only way out of envy's grip is in realignment with the Lord.

However, if you are already ailing, ill, or in pain, you may then be prone to envy as well. It is a small step toward envying others their vitality and physical or mental freedom. The phenomenon is not unusual; however, it demonstrates that part of the healing process includes the eradication of negative emotions and imaginings. Healing can occur only in the absence of envy. Healing is, therefore, in part the absence of envy.

The Great Physician

Our understanding of spiritual healing must include the diagnosis the Great Physician gives in Matthew 9. It is important to put it in the context of a description of the Pharisees of Jesus' day. Bound by an empty, outward conformity to religious rituals, these religious leaders were inflated with a sense of their own righteousness and moral standing in the community. However, their hearts were full of contradictions and evil. They suffered from excessive pride and a wrong attitude regarding a relationship with God. Jesus highlighted their hypocrisy when He claimed that they were intent on cleaning the outside of a cup while leaving the inside dirty.

In Matthew 9, Jesus said to these sanctimonious Pharisees, "Those who are well have no need of a physician, but those who are sick....I did not come to call the righteous, but sinners, to repentance" (Matt. 9:12–13). Jesus is telling them clearly that spiritual health includes repentance. The Pharisees did not believe that they needed the ministrations of the Great Physician. They were incapable of experiencing healing of the soul because they did not think they needed the heavenly cure.

Repentance

Why did they not see that they needed repentance? Do we? Each one of us has experienced guilt for wrongdoing. Do you, though, try to compensate with external actions that you believe to be right and good as the Pharisees did? Repentance involves turning from your sin to the Savior. You must turn to Him for forgiveness. You must turn to Him to satisfy you. You must turn to Him to renew you and to heal you. Every believer must do these things. The Son of God must cleanse the dirty, murky waters of our souls. He sends the Spirit to make rivers of living water, which flow out of your innermost being (John 7:37). Ask Him to give you a new nature—a new heart. This is the resurrected life. Your healing begins when you turn to God with your whole heart. It is then that you find the healing of the Great Physician. "You will seek Me and find Me, when you search for Me with all your heart" (Jer. 29:13).

> GOD'S
>
> FOR HEALING
>
> ASK HIM TO give you a new nature— a new heart. This is the resurrected life.
>
> PRESCRIPTION

Repentance always includes a new obedience to God. The apostle Paul calls us to present all of our members and faculties to be engaged in a life of holiness. (See Romans 6:19.) Peter reminds New Testament believers that what God said of old still applies to us:

"Be holy, for I am holy" (1 Pet. 1:16). It is interesting to note that the English words *wholeness* and *holy* derive from the same root: (1) In reference to God the word *holy* means worthy of whole devotion; in believers, it speaks of being wholly devoted to God. The original biblical words in both Hebrew and Greek mean "set apart." (2) They remind us that God is set apart above all His creation and set apart from sin. For believers it means to be set apart to God as your Lord and portion in life.

This is why the Bible teaches that true wholeness is found only in holiness. True happiness is found in holiness. Spiritual healing is found in holiness. God's ways appointed for us are designed to meet all of our needs. Behind each command are the Father's love and wisdom. Therefore, to seek our spiritual healing will always mean a realignment with the Word of God—with God Himself![4]

Repentance is never separated from faith. Faith is the act of casting ourselves upon Jesus. He says, "Come to Me...and I will give you rest" (Matt. 11:28). Faith is acting upon that invitation. John the Baptist described it as running to Him. Faith is receiving Him as the Bread of Life, our Savior, our Deliverer. All that we need is in Him.

God calls us to find our satisfaction in Him. Do you see your need of forgiveness? It is found through His suffering the penalty for your sin on the cross. "In Him we have redemption through His blood, the forgiveness of sins, according to the riches of His grace" (Eph. 1:7). Do you need a new heart? He is the one who pours down the Spirit from heaven to change you. Peter described this mighty work of the Son of God on the Day of Pentecost when he declared, "Therefore being exalted to the right hand of God, and having received from the Father the promise of the Holy Spirit, He poured out this which you now see and hear" (Acts 2:33). Do you need spiritual healing? He is the one who gives the Balm of Gilead (Jer. 8:22).

When God revealed His Son to us, He said, and still says, "This is My beloved Son, in whom I am well pleased" (Matt. 3:17). The question you must ask yourself is this: "Am I well pleased to make Jesus my all in all?" He promises to be all that we need to bring us to heaven's shore. By seeing your sin with an unobstructed eye and turning to the Great Physician, surrendering wholly to Him, you take your first steps to spiritual health and healing. You must be saved to be healed!

Salvation

Our English word *salvation* is derived from the Greek word *sozo,* defined variously as "cured," "made well," "get well," and "restored," as well as "saved" and "salvation." Salvation is our healing and health. Two aspects of salvation make it so.

The first crucial aspect of salvation is that *it was accomplished on the cross and is received by faith.* Salvation rests in the imputation of Christ's righteousness to our account. This justification means that God credits all who believe in the Savior as righteous. This is possible because of Jesus' work on the cross. He bore the penalty due your sins, and He offered up His perfect life as a sacrifice so that you could receive the righteousness of His obedience. All of salvation is based on Christ's death, because no one could be good enough to be saved by his or her own works. The Bible is quite emphatic on this foundational truth.

> GOD'S
>
> FOR HEALING
>
> RESTING IN redemption, discipleship, and caring for others form a threefold cord of Christian strength.
>
> PRESCRIPTION

Being justified freely by His grace through the redemption that is in Christ Jesus.

—ROMANS 3:24

Therefore, having been justified by faith, we have peace with God through our Lord Jesus Christ.

—ROMANS 5:1

For He made Him who knew no sin to be sin for us, that we might become the righteousness of God in Him.

—2 CORINTHIANS 5:21

The second aspect of salvation is its outworking. We must receive salvation by faith in a way that transforms us to the core. Many profess to believe yet are not saved. True faith and salvation change us from one who is self-centered to one who is God-centered and others-centered. In obedience to God there must be a focusing on our caring and compassion for others as well as our passion for God. The two greatest commandments God gave are: Love God with all of your heart; and love your neighbor as yourself (Matt. 22:37–39).

Real belief, salvation, results in a life that cares for others. Resting in redemption, discipleship, and caring for others form a threefold cord of Christian strength.

Forgiveness first

Ultimate healing—physically, mentally, emotionally, spiritually—will not take place until you have released any remnant of unforgiveness harbored in your heart. Until you truly accept God's forgiveness and then pass that on by your acceptance of others, you cannot live to the fullest degree possible. Unforgiveness is one of the primary obstacles to your health, healing, and meaningful life. Living a life of forgiveness becomes one of the first exercises to accomplish for healing, renewal, and communion with the Creator.

R. T. Kendall's book *Total Forgiveness* provides the definitive description of the importance of forgiveness for a full and anointed life.[5] The example provided by the Genesis story of Joseph's suffering betrayal, imprisonment, and defamation demonstrates the strength and character that can be forged in a forgiving heart. Total forgiveness is a biblical principle. To be capable of it may at times seem impossible. Yet, to forgive the assaults that we suffer at the hands of others is a necessity. God admonishes us, "If you forgive men their trespasses, your heavenly Father will also forgive you. But if you do not forgive men their trespasses, neither will your Father forgive your trespasses" (Matt. 6:14–15). To live in alignment—to meet the Creator face to face—we must have an aspect of total forgiveness toward all those who have harmed or hurt us. We must possess a disposition of joy and laughter that can see us through to a reconciled spirit, which is full of mercy toward others, just as God is merciful toward us.

GOD'S

FOR HEALING

THE IMPORTANCE OF being able to forgive and of being forgiven—by God and other people—cannot be underestimated in the process of our inner healing.

PRESCRIPTION

GOD'S PRESCRIPTION *for* HEALING

This is the only path to healing, because bitterness corrupts and refuses the existence of a thankful heart. Outstanding grudges and grievances can only cause or facilitate anger, illness, and despondency. Depression and a festering vengefulness will drag one into darkest despair. A spirit that is bound in such a manner cannot allow the Father to teach or the Holy Spirit to anoint. There is no healing, then, in a heart filled with the malice and ill will that arise out of unforgiveness.

There is, of course, an additional dimension to forgiveness in our healing. Receiving forgiveness for our mistakes, for the wrongs that we have committed before God's eyes and at the expense of others, is as vital to spiritual healing as being able to forgive. My friend Dr. James Avery, a hospice physician, points to the observation that those who are dying often have huge regrets that revolve around a lack of receiving or giving forgiveness. Unforgiveness is an immense spiritual weight, and there can be no healing until that weight is laid aside. Dr. Avery has a prescription for people who are struggling with unforgiveness during the process of dying, which he borrowed from another hospice physician, Ira Byock. The prescription is simply a list of five things to say to loved ones:

- Please forgive me.
- I forgive you.
- Thank you.
- I love you.
- Good-bye.

Human nature is sinful. We must actively seek forgiveness from those we have hurt and, more, from God. Forgiveness is a necessary precondition to healing. The noetic of sin—which is the mental and, perhaps, physical manifestations of sin—leads to depression and illness. These shadows not only prevent a process of healing, they are the antithesis—the opposite—of any healing. The noetic of sin and its inner illnesses can only be eliminated by an appeal to God's grace.

The importance of being able to forgive and of being forgiven—by God and other people—cannot be underestimated in the process of our inner healing. A lack of forgiveness is a great obstacle that makes healing impossible. It is pride, again, that does not allow us to ask for or offer forgiveness, receive our healing, and assist in the healing of others.

After the honeymoon

Healing is a process rather than an event, so it is continuous. Changes begin after the new birth and must be ceaselessly nurtured. As a new believer—after the honeymoon—you will learn that there is much to do to grow into Christlikeness. There are many areas of the old life that you must relinquish to put on the new life. Just as health will deteriorate in middle age through neglect and harmful habits, spiritual healing and continued health require vigilance, diligence, and constant attention. Every day of your life you will have a daily and desperate need of the heavenly Physician. You also have a present and pressing need of the Spirit's anointing to renew and increase your spiritual health.

We often have difficulty with the discipline this demands. If you struggle with being able to *receive* or *embrace* Him with your whole heart, it is simply because it is human nature for you to rest in your own resources rather than turn to God. By that human nature, you suffer from blind spots, obstructions, unbelief, hardness of heart, pride, and the distraction of seeking your satisfaction in earthly pleasures. However, God has a way of humbling us to bring us to the place where we have nothing else to hold on to but Him. It is necessary to realize that illness and trials sometimes accomplish this in your life, and to recognize that healing occurs when you turn wholeheartedly to God.

It is in your trials and, yes, through illness that you may draw closer to Jesus. Joni Eareckson Tada's life is a glowing testimony to this. She has lived life confined to a wheelchair as a quadriplegic since a terrible diving accident in 1967. Though the radical changes in her life were painful to accept, in that initial bleakness Joni asked God, "Show me how to live."[6] In the years since her accident Joni has accomplished much. She is a painter, public speaker, author, disability advocate, columnist, and wife. It was through her immense challenges that Joni has sought to live closer to her Savior within His plan for her. She knows that by putting one's trust in Christ, concerns of the body take "a backseat."[7] As she writes, "Life is intricately and intimately linked with Jesus. In fact, Jesus is life—He says so Himself. So when we look for a life worth living, we must look for it not in happy or heartbreaking circumstances, health, or even relationships. Life is in Christ."[8]

In ease and abundance we tend to feel independent. When life becomes difficult, it presses us up against Jesus, though. In hard times, crisis, brokenness, and suffering we learn to depend upon God and His plan. This is healing.

"'Is not My word like a fire?' says the LORD, 'and like a hammer that breaks the rock in pieces?'" (Jer. 23:29). God sends His Spirit and His Word to be a hammer and a fire to break down our obstructions to faith. The soul's malady is purged by these heavenly weapons. Yet, God also draws us to Him by the sweetness of His promises, wrapped in the Lord Jesus: "All the promises of God in Him are Yes, and in Him Amen, to the glory of God through us" (2 Cor. 1:20).

Once you have come to know the Savior, your challenge will be to continue to grow and maintain your spiritual health. *You will experience many assaults to your well-being, and each is a test.* Only by abiding in Jesus will you continue to bear spiritual fruit—and to live a healthy, fruitful life.

Resting in the Bosom of the Trinity

To experience inner healing you need to have the healing touch of each person of the Trinity upon your soul. The Triune God—the Father, Son, and Holy Spirit—is *Jehovah Rapha*, "the Lord our healer." We must learn to rest in the healing bosom of the Trinity. That is the essence of our healing.

We often begin our relationship with the Great Physician by coming to the Son of God as the only One who can forgive us. We realize that only His death on the cross can remove the penalty of our sins and grace us with the righteousness of God. To know this forgiveness is to extinguish the guilt that plagues us, as well as removing shame and a sense of rejection. We know that by being forgiven we are cleansed and welcomed at the throne of God.

However, many people arrive at an understanding of God as *Father* only after finding forgiveness. There may be things about your earthly parental upbringing that still cause you pain or skepticism. But God's Word has

GOD'S

> WE MUST LEARN
> to rest in
> the healing bosom
> of the Trinity.
> That is the
> essence of
> our healing.

FOR HEALING

PRESCRIPTION

made it very clear that each one of us still needs parenting from the hand of God throughout our lives. You were created in such a way that you have an inner longing for God the Father's acceptance and outpoured love. Even in the midst of illness and suffering, when you sense your limitations and disabilities, yet you can rejoice that the Father-heart of God has purposed the trial that you need in order to grow. He has promised to work everything for good (Rom. 8:28). He is God the Father Almighty, and His sovereignty teaches you to trust Him and to "fear not." You can cast all your cares on Him because you know that He cares for you (1 Pet. 5:7). No beloved child will feel more secure or encouraged than the believing, forgiven child of God who knows how to rest in the Father-heart of God.

The longer you live the Christian life in this world as it is, the more you will learn how much you need the Holy Spirit, and how much your inner peace and healing depend upon Him. The Christian is called to serve others. The Lord Jesus did not come to be served, but to serve. It is laid out so plainly for us in Galatians 6:2: "Bear one another's burdens, and so fulfill the law of Christ." The same is found in Galatians 5:13, "Through love serve one another." However, as you serve others you will find that they do not always appreciate your efforts. There will be times when you need healing for the wounds that result from your efforts, so that you do not become weary in well doing (Gal. 6:9, KJV).

As you offer up your service to God as a sacrifice to please Him, you will be consoled by the Holy Spirit. Live your life to please God. He is your "audience of one." By living your life to please Him, you will subsequently be pleasing His people also. He will show you how to serve others also.

In your service to others, there will be times when you feel the pain of watching others persist in self-destructive behaviors that destroy themselves or their families. You cannot change another person's heart if that person does not desire to change. The Holy Spirit is the power of God who, in answer to prayer, can change the heart of stone into one of flesh. He can turn the hardened heart and bring reconciliation when all of your efforts have failed. As you learn to rest in dependence upon the Holy Spirit's intervention, you will be able to persevere despite any discouragement you may feel. The Holy Spirit brings healing to the dejected servant of God who feels like he has expended himself in vain.

The Spirit also brings healing to your soul when you fall into spiritual decline and seem to dry up. At times you may fear that you have left your first love and cannot seem to revive the freshness of your "spring-time" communion with the Savior. The prophet Isaiah said that when the Spirit is poured out from on high, He turns the wilderness into a fruitful field (Isa. 32:15). He pours out upon the dry ground of the thirsty (Isa. 44:3). He revives us again so that we may rejoice in Him (Ps. 85:6). This spiritual healing is available to every true child of God who is grieved by his or her own backsliding heart and who is unsatisfied with superficial, shallow Christianity.

The healing work of the Holy Spirit in your inner man is the experiential side of salvation. He becomes in you "a fountain of water springing up into everlasting life" (John 4:14). He becomes a river of water flowing through your innermost being (John 7:37–39). The Spirit of God fills you, revives you, and renews you. He anoints you with His own gracious presence to give you a lively faith that sees this life in light of eternity. You will learn to live a life marked for eternity in the present moment. Abiding in Christ is the first and foremost imperative in your life.

> **GOD'S**
>
> FOR HEALING
>
> ABIDING IN CHRIST is the first and foremost imperative in your life.
>
> PRESCRIPTION

Your spiritual healing is also dependent upon you finding your anointed purpose in a "God-centered" and "others-centered" life. All human nature tends to be plagued with feelings of insignificance and uselessness. The antidote to these feelings is an awareness of God's anointed purpose for your life, which is conveyed to you by the blessed Spirit of God. To have an anointed purpose for life is one of the greatest rewards of life with God in the here and now.

Through your nature—the design of your heart, mind, and inner longing for communion with your Creator—you seek and are capable of receiving inner healing. *God's twofold gift of spiritual healing— forgiveness and a new life—are found in union with Christ through the cross.* A new heart, an anointed purpose, wholeness, and eternal life result.

Chapter 11

UNVEILING THE NEW HEART

Therefore, if anyone is in Christ, he is a new creation; old things have passed away; behold, all things have become new.

—2 Corinthians 5:17

In the late 1600s, Scotsman Henry Scougal wrote a letter to a friend (published as *The Life of God in the Soul of Man*) that stands today as a great summary of what it means to have a new heart and a new life from God.[1] It explains the true nature of a vital relationship with God, as well as eternal life. George Whitefield once commented that he never understood the real nature of life with God until he read this little treatise.

The letter begins with a description of the many common misunderstandings about the meaning of oneness with God. Some believe that true religion lies in orthodoxy, as the Pharisees did. Others believe that the essence of true religion is fleshed out in our acts and duties. Still others think that it lies in generating fervent, religious feelings within ourselves. All of these are mistaken.

The nature of wholeness, Scougal writes, lies in union of the soul with God. We must be branches joined to the Vine, which is Christ, and draw our life and strength from Him (John 15:5). We must be living members of the body drawing nourishment from Christ the Head (Col. 2:19). Christ must be in us as the "hope of glory" (Col. 1:27). We must be made new creatures, then "old things are passed away; behold, all things are become new" (2 Cor. 5:17, KJV).

When you have the life of God within you, which is achieved in union with the Son of God, you will be able to say, like Paul, "I live; yet not I, but Christ liveth in me" (Gal. 2:20, KJV). You become a partaker of the divine nature (2 Pet. 1:4). That is the life of God in the soul of man—in your soul! It is called the seed of God within us (1 John 3:9).

This principle of new life is permanent and stable; it does not waver or wither. This principle of the life of God in the soul of man is wrought in you by the Holy Spirit at the new birth (John 3:3). The spiritual signs of the regenerate soul contrast markedly with a natural life principle that is probably more familiar to us.

Spiritual vs. Natural

Natural life exists in the realm of the senses. The inclinations and tendencies that arise from the senses exist in a wide variety among humans. Some people may take interest in religious things as a result of their education or because they have fond memories of their upbringing. Others may be drawn to religion by curiosity or intellectual engagement. Some seek the approval and social commendation that may accompany a "religious" life. Others are motivated by respect for Christian character qualities such as virtue and moral justice. However, Scougal claims that a person might be motivated by any or all of these and still not be an authentic Christian at all.[2] The natural tendencies are not bad in themselves; rather, they simply cannot be confused with a living relationship with God.

In comparison, the divine life within us consists in faith, which produces four branches: *love for God, charity to men, purity, and humility.* It is Christ who provides the pattern for this life of God in the soul of man. In Him we see all these qualities exemplified—expressed in their clearest, crystalline form.

GOD'S

FOR HEALING

JESUS SHOWS US **what true love to people is in His unbounded charity, patience with His enemies, and His ultimate self-sacrifice.**

PRESCRIPTION

The Lord Jesus demonstrates love to God in constant devotion, prayer, and communion with Him. The fire of delight was never extinguished in Jesus, and He remained diligent in doing His Father's will, even to death. Jesus shows us what true love to people is in His unbounded charity, patience with His enemies, and His ultimate self-sacrifice. Christ remained pure, never to fall out of alignment by seeking sinful pleasures. And finally, the Son of God said to us, "Learn of me;

for I am meek and lowly in heart" (Matt. 11:29, KJV). He demonstrated the reality of this attitude when He knelt to wash His disciples' feet after the Last Supper. (See John 13:4–5.)

When we discover the character of God, we discover that He is exactly who He claims to be. Our deep assurance of that is our faith, which gives rest to the soul bringing everything into alignment with Him, enabling the growth of the four divine branches in the soul. This faith originates in looking at Jesus' death on the cross, His pardon for our sins, and His example.

The character of God will be seen in your life if you truly love God and express your love in prayer and worship. Adherence to His will follows as the true delight of your soul. Worship and service to God become delights to your new heart. Humbleness before God and others is expressed in the new free-flowing, self-moving principle of life. Then love—love for God and love for one's fellow humans—is the summary and apex of the new life.

Love

Scougal ended his treatise with an expansion on the great summary-grace of love. He stated that the capacity of love is so immense that it can only be satisfied with an infinite, perfect object. Love wants a suitable return and only finds satisfaction in God, who is ever present to the believing soul. There is an exchange of hearts in love. In that exchange you are refreshed and enlivened by the joy God possesses and the delight He shows in you. God's love to you far exceeds the love you can offer Him, yet even the tears of repentance and its sorrows have a sacred sweetness when you pour them out before the divine Beloved. Once your soul finds its satisfaction in God, then you can live from the strength of that felicity. You are renewed and healed.

Your love to others becomes an overflow of this love and delight in God. If you start at the wrong place and do not seek love and satisfaction in God first, you will experience perpetual frustration, because no human being can bring this satisfaction. When God Himself is your first love and chief portion, then you find overflowing joy and love within to channel to others, independent of their appreciation. This is the new life! This relationship with God is the fountain of refreshment for your spiritual life and the well from which you must draw your motives for living. When you know the nature and reality of your new life and how to nourish and revive it in love, you then will know how to perpetually find restoration and wholeness. This is the health of the soul!

Loving God = Inner Healing

The essence of being healed spiritually and living life anew is in a retreat from loving self toward loving God. What does it really mean to love God? In a taped lecture, John Piper asks the questions: "Is it actions? Is it things or gifts from God? Is it doing for God? Is it God doing for us? If these are not the essence of love for God, what is? What is left?"[3]

Piper goes on to say that love is the heart's esteem in God before it produces anything else. Love is your delight in God Himself, beyond His gifts. Every one of us desires forgiveness and an escape from hell to heaven, but heaven without Jesus is no salvation. Love is not a deed. Love is a reflex of the newly born heart responding to the beauty of God in Christ. A deed of love can be imitated, but a reflex of the heart cannot be. Love arises from the cell of the heart to the beauty of God in Christ. To truly love God we must delight in a relationship with God that satisfies.

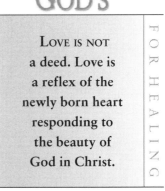

GOD'S

LOVE IS NOT a deed. Love is a reflex of the newly born heart responding to the beauty of God in Christ.

FOR HEALING

PRESCRIPTION

Loving God is delighting in, cherishing, savoring, treasuring, revering, and admiring God beyond any gift—life and health notwithstanding.[4] When we truly love God with all of our heart, independent of our requests and expectations, above our own needs, then we will find satisfaction, meaning, and purpose. We find, there, both eternal life and the inner healing for which we pine.

The medieval writer Dante knew the human race to have been created by a loving God. He therefore considered the seven deadly sins to be choices that are ultimately offenses against love. He grouped them accordingly. Pride, envy, and wrath are perverted love. Sloth is insufficient love. Greed, gluttony, and lust represent an excessive love of earthly goods.[5]

Loving God is our state of awe, contentment, and the tranquility personified in an existence next to Him. This is resting in the bosom of the Trinity. It is to have Him and not need anything else.

The Purpose of Our Lives and Eternity

The inner healing found through the new life—the life of God in one's soul—is ultimately expressed in an anointed purpose. There is the deepest richness associated with an anointed purpose in your life, because it has an impact now and for eternity.

The meaning of the anointed life can be seen in the comparison of the second king of Israel, David, with the first king, Saul, in the Old Testament. Saul was impressive outwardly. He stood head and shoulders above his countrymen and walked with aplomb. He had been appointed to his lofty position by the people. Saul, however, inevitably failed miserably. David, on the other hand, had a special anointing from God. He had made nearness to God his primary goal in life and consequently became the greatest king of Israel. The difference between *appointed* and *anointed* meant everything.

> THE ANOINTED life is, in essence, being a real Christian rather than superficially practicing a religion.

The anointed life means asking God to anoint everything you do rather than attempting to live by your own strength. This leads to an epiphany of your purpose. The anointed life is, in essence, being a real Christian rather than superficially practicing a religion. This added significance of life, meaning in life, and love in life is only found when you ask for the anointing and receive the anointing in Christ. Then life has real purpose.

The anointing of a purpose makes your life in the present more meaningful, more productive, and more passionate. You develop as a person and accomplish to a far greater degree than that which could be possible from your own strength alone.

There is a beautiful eternal significance to this anointed purpose of life. This is the reward of a godly life. In the third part of my book

Imaginations: More Than You Think, I discuss how the ways we allow ourselves to think and meditate now will have a commensurate reward in heaven.[6] Scripture confirms it:

> But without faith it is impossible to please Him, for he who comes to God must believe that He is, and that He is a rewarder of those who diligently seek Him.
>
> —HEBREWS 11:6

> And behold, I am coming quickly, and My reward is with Me, to give to every one according to his work.
>
> —REVELATION 22:12

Your responsibility is huge: your mind-set now will be your mind-set in eternity. Where are you focused? Do you sense your life has a purpose? Is your life meaningful? Will it be? It all begins with Jesus' call to you in Matthew 11:28, "Come to Me, all you who labor and are heavy laden, and I will give you rest."

A book written by Bruce Wilkinson, *A Life God Rewards: Why Everything You Do Today Matters Forever*, discusses God's rewards for our godly behavior in this life. Equally as important, *The Purpose-Driven Life* by Rick Warren points out the importance of purpose in a life for Christ:

> The purpose of your life is far greater than your own personal fulfillment, your peace of mind, or even your happiness. It's far greater than your family, your career, or even your wildest dreams and ambitions. If you want to know why you were placed on this planet, you must begin with God. You were born by His purpose and for His purpose.[7]

The anointed purpose of life in Christ gives meaning now and for eternity.

Everything you do in life will be judged by the Lord when you stand before Him in Glory. He not only enables you to live faithfully for Him here on earth, but He will reward you in heaven for doing so. His Word clearly describes the path of life that brings blessing and reward: "You will show me the path of life; in Your presence is fullness of joy; at Your right hand are pleasures forevermore" (Ps. 16:11). Spiritual blindness keeps us from perceiving His best for us. The Holy Spirit is yours, and He reveals the seemingly hidden diamonds of truth if you prayerfully search the Scriptures for understanding. All the criteria for blessing and reward are present in God.

Those who reject the Lord in this life will be judged and receive eternal judgment according to that life here on earth. Those who have received Jesus as their Lord and Savior will also be judged for every thought, word, deed, and action done here on earth. In the New Testament, Paul understood this judgment and pleaded with the church to see life from an eternal perspective. The believers who had spiritual blind spots often missed Paul's challenge, as had the disciples when Jesus preached the Sermon on the Mount recorded in Matthew.

> GOD'S
>
> FOR HEALING
>
> THE ANOINTED
> purpose
> of life in Christ
> gives meaning
> now and
> for eternity.
>
> PRESCRIPTION

Paul, well aware of God's grace, knew what it meant to be brought before a court of law and judged for one's actions. In the Greek city of Corinth, his enemies dragged him into court for preaching the gospel. Scholars believe that a raised marble platform still visible today in the ruins of Corinth was the place where Paul's case was tried. The platform was referred to as the *bema*, which is the Greek word for judgment seat. The *bema* represented authority, justice, and reward. Later Paul sent a letter to the church in Corinth and spoke of another *bema* in heaven—the judgment seat for Christians and the great white throne for nonbelievers.

You will be judged by how you behave during your time here on earth (your imaginations) and rewarded accordingly. Spiritual sight for the believer, your inner health, is achieved by an eternal desire to live today with eternity's values in view. And God's eternal reward system is extravagant! (See Matthew 11:21–22; 16:27; 23:14; Luke 6:23; John 5:22; 2 Corinthians 5:10; Revelation 20:11,15.)

Where you spend eternity is determined by belief—Acts 16:31: "Believe on the Lord Jesus Christ, and you will be saved."

How you spend eternity is determined by your faithfulness—Matthew 25:23: "Well done, good and faithful servant! You have been faithful with a few things; I will put you in charge of many things. Come and share your master's happiness!" (NIV).

To be anointed is to have meaning, direction, and purpose that God appoints, prepares, superintends, and revives along the way. It is the interpenetration of God's Spirit and yours. You are thus equipped so that you are not left to yourself. You are *in-presenced* with the Most High with whom nothing is impossible. Anointing is God saying, "I have chosen you, and I am going to be with you!" Our inner peace, spiritual healing, and health derive from the harmony, joy, completeness, and anointed purpose in our alignment with God.

> GOD'S PRESCRIPTION FOR HEALING
>
> ANOINTING IS God saying, "I have chosen you, and I am going to be with you!"

Two Penetrating Insights

The Savior has many penetrating insights into the real center of life recorded in the four Gospels. They refer to true satisfaction and the nature of the divine healing of which we all stand in need. Two of these insights provide a focus on inner healing for us here.

The first insight concerns what Jesus called "the one thing that is necessary"—namely to sit at His feet and to feed on His Word and His Person. (See Luke 10:38–42.) While Martha bustled with the details of her hospitality for Jesus when He came to visit her home, her sister, Mary, sat at Jesus' feet and listened to His Word.

Martha was distracted with much serving, and she approached Him and said, "Lord, do You not care that my sister has left me to serve alone? Therefore tell her to help me" (v. 40). Jesus answered her with gentle admonishment, "Martha, Martha, you are worried and troubled about many things. But one thing is needed, and Mary has chosen that good part, which will not be taken away from her" (vv. 41–42).

For you to receive all the good that the Great Physician has in store for you, you must choose "that good part." You must sit at Jesus' feet daily and learn from Him the joy of His fellowship, the wisdom of His design for your life, and His anointed purpose for your life. What do you feed your soul—God's Word or your own worries? The Son of God speaks very personally to each of us: "It is written, 'Man shall not live by bread alone, but by every word that proceeds from the mouth of God'" (Matt. 4:4). The question you must ask yourself each day is this: "Am I going to be a Mary today and sit at Jesus' feet, taking Him in, or a distracted and burdened Martha instead?"

Martha's actions in the account were founded on self-reliance and, therefore, were full of frustration. Mary's alternative of communion with her Lord and delighting in His presence represents a life full of satisfaction and contentment. In contrast to the busyness that Martha hoped would be generous to her guests, Mary's way generates a spirit permeated with the Lord, which provides us the best preparation for serving others.

> As LONG AS WE have Him, we will be rich and full and satisfied. This must be healing, or nothing is.

The second insight derived from a crucial passage from the Gospels is found in Matthew in the parable of the treasure hidden in the field. (See Matthew 13:44.) Through that parable Jesus taught that our tendencies to pursue one thing after the other—in a ceaseless search for the satisfaction of desire—inevitably end in frustration and disappointment. In Jesus' allegory, a certain man stumbled upon a treasure hidden in a field. Overcome with joy he sold all that he possessed so that he could buy that field. Jesus is the treasure hidden in the field—we must choose Him with passion as the only thing worth having. We will count it a joy to abandon all else as the source of our meaning when we find our all in all in Him. As long as we have Him, we will be rich and full and satisfied. This must be healing, or nothing is!

Jesus is the Shepherd who will guide you to green pastures and beside still waters. He is the King who, by His power, transforms your disappointments in life into something good (Rom. 8:28). He is the heavenly Bridegroom who fills you with the love of heaven. He is the Captain of your salvation who will lead you to be more than a conqueror. When He is yours, you can say, even in your weakest moments, that He is your strength. Jesus says to us, as He did to Paul: "My grace is sufficient for you, for My strength is made perfect in weakness" (2 Cor. 12:9). May you respond as the apostle did: "Therefore most gladly I will rather boast in my infirmities, that the power of Christ may rest upon me....For when I am weak, then I am strong" (2 Cor. 12:9–10). This is why Paul could say, "By the grace of God I am what I am, and His grace toward me was not in vain; but I labored more abundantly than they all, yet not I, but the grace of God which was with me" (1 Cor. 15:10).

The grace of God enables you to fulfill the anointed purpose for your life, through your experiences of illness and breakdown, into healing and health. Paul interpreted the disposition of spiritual vitality as "rejoice always, pray without ceasing, in everything give thanks" (1 Thess. 5:16–18). By such a life you may receive the grace of God daily, which empowers you to enjoy the restoration of your soul's health. This restoration is peace, and peace is "perfect well-being, all necessary good, all spiritual prosperity, and freedom from fears and agitating passions and moral conflicts" (2 Pet. 1:2, AMP). Anyone that can claim that peace is healed.

Chapter 12

THE HEALING OF THE WORD

*Your words were found…and Your word was to me the
joy and rejoicing of my heart; for I am called by Your
name, O Lord God of hosts.*

—Jeremiah 15:16

It is encouraging to find that many of the passages of Scripture that
deal with healing point us to the healing power of God's Word. The
reason it is so encouraging is that we have the Word of God in our hands
and so can plead with God to fulfill these promises in our lives by faith
and the work of His Spirit. Solomon counsels us to cling to God's Word
in our hearts (Prov. 3:1).

The mercy and truth that God speaks forth to you from the Word
are designed to work in you a life that will "trust in the Lord with all your
heart, and lean not on your own understanding; in all your ways acknowledge Him, and He shall direct your paths" (Prov. 3:5–6). The Truth
embraced and lived is health. "It shall be health to thy navel, and marrow
to thy bones" (Prov. 3:8, kjv). *The Message* paraphrases it like this: "Your
body will glow with health, your very bones will vibrate with life!" The
ways of God marked out for you in His Word are said to be "ways of pleas-
antness, and…peace. She is a tree of life to those who take hold of her, and
happy are all who retain her" (Prov. 3:17–18). Matthew Henry (who lived
in the late 1600s and early 1700s) shows us that God's promises will not
only strengthen our souls but our bodies as well, for they are intertwined
together in marvelous ways beyond our comprehension.

> For our encouragement thus to live in the fear of God
> it is here promised [Prov. 3:8] that it shall be as service-
> able even to the outward man as our necessary food. It
> will be nourishing: It shall be health to thy navel. It will
> be strengthening: It shall be marrow to thy bones. The

prudence, temperance, and sobriety, the calmness and composure of mind, and the good government of the appetites and passions, which religion teaches, tend very much not only to the health of the soul, but to a good habit of body, which is very desirable, and without which our other enjoyments in this world are insipid. Envy is the rottenness of the bones; the sorrow of the world dries them; but hope and joy in God are marrow to them.

—MATTHEW HENRY, COMMENTARY

Embracing God's truth activates all that is good, all that is honoring to God, and all that is concerned with true joy. Here is how you find the satisfaction, contentment, and appreciation of God and His created gifts and joys. By doing so you implement what God calls you to and you know the fulfillment of God's promises. You will know the joys of serving your wife or husband, family, and community (Ps. 112). By embracing God's truth you will know the love of God poured out into your heart (Rom. 5:5). You will know how to deal with fear: "He will not be afraid of evil tidings; his heart is steadfast, trusting in the LORD" (Ps. 112:7; see also Ps. 91:3–7). You will know how to trust in God at all times and pour your heart out to God (rather than "worry yourself sick," as we say) (Ps. 62:8). You know your need of renewal daily and how to be renewed—"Will You not revive us again, that Your people may rejoice in You?" (Ps. 85:6). You know the fountain of life that is found in "the law of the wise" (the Bible itself!) and in the fear of the Lord (Prov. 13:14; 14:27). These two passages in Proverbs teach us that God will attend a serious pursuit of His Word with what can only be called a fountain of life. It is life renewed to enjoy daily the majesty of God in appreciation of all His gifts to us and callings that rest upon us in a life with anointed purpose.

GOD'S

PRESCRIPTION

FOR HEALING

HAPPINESS, BIBLICALLY speaking, is being restored through the healing of the Word—embraced, applied, engaged in, and lived out!

Just as your body is perfectly integrated by the Creator's design, your life is designed to be integrated into the lives of others. It is not healthy to live a solitary isolated life. Proverbs 18:1 says, "A man who isolates himself seeks his own desire; he rages against all wise judgment." The believer who knows the healing power of God's Word applied by His Spirit to our lives is a person who has the qualities that make a good friend, and so enjoys the healing blessings of friendships. "Ointment and perfume delight the heart, and the sweetness of a man's friend gives delight by hearty counsel" (Prov. 27:9). Happiness, biblically speaking, is being restored through the healing of the Word—embraced, applied, engaged in, and lived out!

The healing that comes from the Word of God is described in Nehemiah. The captives who returned from Babylon gathered to hear the Word of God read and explained. The effect of that day was to teach them that "the joy of the Lord is your strength" (Neh. 8:10).

The message of the healing power of God's Word is found throughout the Bible. We have noted before that "a merry heart does good, like *medicine*" (Prov. 17:22, emphasis added). Jeremiah found the source of a merry heart by embracing God's Word. "Your words were found, and I ate them, and Your word was to me the joy and rejoicing of my heart; for I am called by Your name, O Lord God of hosts" (Jer. 15:16). This was the "medicine" he needed as he faced the difficult trials of the coming Babylonian invasion and destruction of Jerusalem. He knew the reality of God's intervention in his time of extremity, which is described in Psalm 107:20: "He [God] sent His word and *healed* them" (emphasis added). God sends His Word to us! We are often jarred off-center when illness comes our way; we easily get discouraged and flounder in a disoriented perspective of our lives.

The downcast disciples on the road home to Emmaus from Jerusalem after the crucifixion of Jesus found renewed healing by the Word of God. The risen Jesus Himself came near to them and did not allow them to recognize Him. He asked them why they were sad and "expounded to them in all the Scriptures the things concerning Himself" (Luke 24:27). They later recognized that it was Jesus Himself who had come alongside them to reorient them to God's Word. As they reflected on this experience, they summarized it in this way: "Did not

GOD'S PRESCRIPTION *for* HEALING

our heart burn within us while He talked with us on the road, and while He opened the Scriptures to us?" (v. 32). God used His Word to stir the fire of faith in them again. In other words, "He sent His Word and healed them!"

As with these disheartened disciples who were soul-sick, in your times of illness you need to sense God's consoling presence anew. You need to be made functional again and hopeful and useful to the Master. It is the power of God at work in your soul that brings healing to the "illness-side" of your disease. Your mind, emotions, and heart need the counteractions of faith and hope to renew afresh in you the "health to our navel and marrow to our bones" that He has promised you. Your hands, which hang down, are lifted anew in praise, and your feet, which are prone to stumble on rocky roads and be injured, are now put on the solid road to God's design for healing. "Therefore strengthen the hands which hang down, and the feeble knees, and make straight paths for your feet, so that what is lame may not be dislocated, but rather be *healed*" (Heb. 12:12–13, emphasis added).

> ## GOD'S
> ### PRESCRIPTION
> ### FOR HEALING
>
> NEGATIVE DISPOSITIONS are the things that destroy you; joy, prayer, and gratitude are the graces that enliven you and keep you living in the presence of God.

How we need to be healed from our backslidings of doubting God's goodness and despairing of His wisdom and sovereignty! Hosea calls us to this reengagement toward the living God: "In You the fatherless finds mercy. I will *heal* their backsliding, I will love them freely" (Hos. 14:3–4, emphasis added). When your expectations of health and usefulness are set aside by illness, you may say with Solomon, "Hope deferred makes the heart sick." But he goes on to say, "But when the desire comes, it is a tree of life" (Prov. 13:12). We have all known the heart sickness of disappointed goals from illness, but now with the powerful truths we have learned in God's design for healing let us look to God to send the healing of His Word to our lives when we face each illness. He will be glorified, and we will be blessed. Then we will find our newly sanctified desires fulfilled, for He has promised:

Delight yourself also in the LORD, and He shall give you
the desires of your heart.

—PSALM 37:4

Prayer is the opposite of self-reliance. Joy is the opposite of self-pity. A thankful spirit is the opposite of cynicism. These negative dispositions are the things that destroy you; joy, prayer, and gratitude are the graces that enliven you and keep you living in the presence of God who is your only source of lasting and satisfying peace. When this new principle dwells in you, you see the folly and vanity of life and understand that everything is contingent upon divine goodness and grace. When your heart is infused with God's life, you observe a wholeness and balance and understand that the love and joy you experience today, and the appreciation you can offer in worship now, are elements in your eternal life with Him.

Our benediction toward those who are seeking God's healing touch should be:

> *Let the anointing of Christ be in you, and peace be in*
> *you, and the love of the anointed Christ who lives in*
> *you give you peace*

This is the opposite of the sensation of anxiety, fear, and frenzy. This is healing.

PART IV

IMPROBABLE HEALING

Chapter 13

IMPROBABLE HEALING
IN THE SCRIPTURES

If you diligently heed the voice of the LORD your God and do what is right in His sight, give ear to His commandments and keep all His statutes, I will put none of the diseases on you which I have brought on the Egyptians. For I am the LORD who heals you.
—EXODUS 15:26

In this section, we are referring to healings that modern medicine and science—human understanding—neither brought about directly nor could have predicted. Examples of improbable healing show us men and women who would not give up. Or, if they did at some point, they were renewed and revived in the hope and passion of their meaning and purpose in the Lord.

Perhaps you are more familiar with a biblical context for this. In God's Word we read about our Great Physician, Jesus. Our Healer's ministry to His flock meant, among much else, fearlessly and lovingly touching the "untouchables." His love had no barriers, colors, definitions, or exceptions. Jesus inevitably gave comfort to the ruined, wasted, and suffering. Leprosy was a huge scourge in Jesus' time. We can reasonably expect that infection was also a major cause of illness and death. It was unlikely, especially in that era, that those who needed help would find it during their lifetime. Yet, there were many healings of an "improbable" nature, and those suffering found help in the most marvelous ways.

You will note that, although leprosy is still a plight in our present-day Third World—humans continue to be wasted by it—its prevention and healing are no longer improbable for us in the West. You may ask, are we not beyond, or can we not explain, improbable healings of the Bible? What connection do "improbable" healings two thousand years ago have to us in our modern world of hospitals and antibiotics? The truth is that, for one thing, nature is not standing still. While we are free from or relatively unbothered by some ailments today, others have replaced them, and we are still in the battle for survival. Today in the Western world it is the explosion of cancer rates and the recent emergences of deadly viruses such as SARS and AIDS with which our Western cultures are occupied. In our lives, there is as great a need for healing as in Jesus' day, and some of that is just as improbable and beyond our powers of explanation as events in the past.

In fact, all around us are examples of improbable healings. It is even likely that you may have experienced such a thing without knowing it or, rather, admitting it to yourself. How could that happen? Simply, most of us are not aware of the Creator's careful design—and deep, deep love for us—and, therefore, we do not appreciate the events that occur within ourselves, and around us, moment by moment, day by day.

> IN OUR LIVES, there is as great a need for healing as in Jesus' day.

It is easier for most of us, sadly, to beseech and bow only when we are already broken. Why do we not worship with authentic appreciation and love for the Creator and the intelligence of His design? I think that you can agree that the silent, incessant fight of your immune system, which developed from the microscopic instructions encoded in a zygote, is proof enough of ongoing "miracles." We do not appreciate—and so we do not understand. We do not appreciate, and so we are neither in the position to experience healing nor to recognize it when it does occur.

In both biblical accounts and modern medical testimony, there are healings and elements of healing that are beyond our immediate understanding and outside a certain statistical probability. But this does not mean that all mysteries will forever remain so. However, when we ask the Lord for healing, and receive it, the actual results may exceed what we could normally expect or doctors predict. In these cases—as in the "common" healing of a cut finger—we see a display of the Creator's mighty power, His amazing love, His tender compassion, and His saving grace. *God's love, grace, and mercy toward us in the episodes of healing that our science does not predict is His fourth gift of healing.*

Improbable Healing in the Bible

Healing and appreciation

There is a world of insight that emerges from the account of the cleansing of the ten lepers. In Luke 17:11–19, Jesus healed ten lepers and told them to show themselves to the priests so that they could offer the ritual cleansing they needed to be restored to society. It was only as the lepers were on their way to see the priests that they became aware of their healing. They all were elated as they saw their restoration to wholeness. We may well imagine how eager they were to break their mandatory quarantine and rejoin their families. But they lacked the important thing. Only one of the ten healed by Jesus returned to Him, fell at His feet, and worshiped Him. Only one said *thanks*; only one was grateful; only one was gripped with appreciation!

The Savior asked the sole returning leper a penetrating question, one which all of us should take to heart: "Were there not ten cleansed? But where are the nine?" (v. 17). Here we see an essential point. External, physical cleansing was not the only healing that was needed. The illness in the ungrateful nine was more than skin deep. They did not appreciate. They did not have a spirit of gratitude. Sadly, they reflect all of us in too many situations in our lives. We lack appreciation toward God and proudly go on our way, for example, when skillful surgeons and effective pharmaceuticals are successful in removing diseases of the body. To go on proudly, with an unthankful spirit to God, is to show ourselves in need of the inner healing that the tenth leper experienced. He obtained a grateful heart, which brought him to a truly satisfied condition of soul. The others still continued in their restless, unsatisfied, empty existence as men cleansed but not made "whole." Without appreciation of God's grace, we are not healed.

Forgiveness, purpose, and "direction"

There is another account of unexpected and improbable healing in the ministry of Jesus that highlights the power of forgiveness and the encouragements that are given to caregivers in the healing of others. Due to a heavy crowd, a man who was paralyzed and bedridden could not enter a home where Jesus was speaking. Insightfully, his friends lowered him from the roof so that he might approach the Great Physician Jesus (Mark 2:1–12). Jesus showed that He also noticed the "caregivers" and fellow supporters of this invalid. The Scriptures take note that "when Jesus saw *their* faith" (including the faith of the man lowered from the uncovered roof), He said, "Son, your sins are forgiven you" (v. 5). It was a surprise to all who heard it that a man could know that all his sins could be forgiven in the "here and now," but equally surprising were the words, "I say to you, arise, take up your bed, and go your way to your house" (v. 11).

To really appreciate the significance of this narrative you need to see that the effect of having his sins forgiven made as much of an impact on the man as the restoration of the use of his body. This beautiful gift of forgiveness enables us to have a peace that passes all understanding and a joy that flows from true satisfaction of heart. This inner healing of the soul irradiates in a hundred ways throughout one's life. It gives a sense of God's presence attending you wherever you are. Your words of encouragement and comfort to others are enhanced with a sense of the reality of a life with purpose. After receiving this forgiveness and the renewed use of his limbs, this former paralytic knew what his purpose was in life. He knew how useful he could be through helping others, since he had been helped by these "believing friends." He now knew how he could continue to live out a life of resting in the redemption of Jesus.

> GOD'S
>
> FOR HEALING
>
> To KNOW AND embrace God's purpose for your life is to have an inner fountain of motives springing up to spur you on to a meaningful life.
>
> PRESCRIPTION

You can ask yourself what good would have been accomplished by the restoration of this man's motor functions without the reception of forgiveness and reconciliation with God. Without the spiritual healing, this man would have movement without "direction." To know and embrace God's purpose for your life is to have an inner fountain of motives springing up to spur you on to a meaningful life. You are called to be a steward of the grace of God given to you. You are called to be a channel of blessing that shares the purpose you have found with others. You may have been carried to God for help, but you can walk away with an anointed purpose of being useful to others by letting your own acceptance with God shine forth. You are called to be useful as a caregiver who will "go and do likewise" as was done for us.

Cleansing and compassion

Mark 1:40–45 is another example of Jesus cleansing a leper and demonstrating that He had a heavenly sympathy and compassion that few people possessed in His day. Obviously He possessed the power that no one else did since He was the Son of God. The leper said, "If You are willing, You can make me clean" (v. 40). In effect he was saying, "No one cares for lepers; do You? I know You have the power, but do You care? Are You willing?" Jesus' answer to this man who was unloved and unwanted in his society was first of all a compassionate touch. This was an unheard of means of personal identification with an outcast. Then Jesus said, "I am willing; be cleansed" (v. 41). The man was cleansed of his leprosy immediately. Consequently we see that the man was not only healed externally, but he was given the comfort and consolation that he was cared for as a person. He departed rejoicing in the love of God that was poured out in his heart.

Favoring the neglected

In every society and in every age, there are many who are passed over and left to themselves. They are the neglected and forgotten. Wherever Jesus went, this was no longer the pattern. It seems that the more neglected the person was, the more Jesus took interest in that person. Restoring the sight of a blind beggar named Bartimaeus is an example of the Savior's principle of taking time to take notice and stopping the parade of life to include the person viewed by society as marginal. In Mark 10:46–52, Jesus showed that He takes note of the one that others are not interested in. The blind beggar named Bartimaeus heard Jesus was coming, and he cried out, "Son of David, have mercy on me!" (v. 48). The people in effect told him, "Shut up, old man." But he cried out all the more. Jesus stopped and said, "Bring him here."

Bartimaeus went to Jesus with such expectation that he cast away his beggar's cloak. We may assume he had heard of Christ's compassion and believed he would no longer need that cloak, which was the signature of his craft and trade. He anticipated that he would not be going back to that lifestyle again. Bartimaeus was not disappointed.

When Jesus restored his sight, Bartimaeus did not go on his way. Instead he followed Jesus with his newfound sight on the road to Jerusalem. The Savior could easily have just kept walking. This would have been viewed as an interruption by most, but not the Son of God. He puts the world on hold to give attention to the person neglected by others who is now calling on Him. He is never too busy for the person in the corner, the person on the outskirts of the crowd, or the person who has nothing to commend himself. To many, this person is a drain of their energy and a distraction from their busy schedules. That is not so to Jesus. He repeatedly befriended individuals with whom many would not want to "get involved." He took time to listen. He is an example to us of One who is willing to turn and take a look at what He can do to help others who are "left behind." Here is a glimpse of the true Healer of souls—one who affirms and favors the neglected.

Restoration and hope

In the story of the healing of the woman with an issue of blood for twelve years, Jesus showed that He cared for the one who others had given up on (Mark 5:25–34). No one could help her. But she had hope that with Jesus nothing shall be impossible. She came behind in the crowd and touched the hem of His garment, and virtue flowed forth from Him and healed her instantly. He called her before others and said, "Daughter, your faith has made you well" (v. 34). This not only gave her assurance of His love, but it also publicly restored her to all the functions of society. With an issue of blood in Jewish culture, she would be excluded from some of the most important functions in her society (such as attendance upon temple worship). Jesus brought a healing to her that made her whole in the fullest sense of the word.

Some students of Scripture believe that she probably was not married, or was unlikely to have stayed married because she was considered unclean. All of this had changed now that she found the healing virtue of Christ. She was even eligible for marriage; she was restored to all that made her human and in the image of God. This is the transforming power of Jesus' healing.

Jesus tends to all needs. He fed the five thousand with five loaves and two fishes. This unexplainable multiplication of loaves was designed to be a dramatic picture of the greatness, fullness, and sufficiency of Jesus to meet the deepest needs of our souls so that we will never hunger again. Later when the crowds who had seen Him feed the throngs sought Him, He told them, "I am the bread of life. He who comes to Me shall never hunger, and he who believes in Me shall never thirst" (John 6:35).

Jesus said that He was the resurrection and the life and then raised Lazarus from the dead (John 11). This unpredictable surprise of restoring Lazarus to his sisters was a demonstration that He alone can raise us from the dead spiritually and give us the resurrected life in the "here and now." This is what Paul sought to live by in Philippians 3—the power of His resurrection. Jesus said He was the light of the world, then He healed the man born blind (John 9). Here He demonstrated that we will remain in darkness until He gives us spiritual sight and sends light from heaven into our souls. These signs marked out Jesus as the Messiah. He did what no one else could do and showed He is the only Savior.

> GOD'S
>
> FOR HEALING
>
> THIS UNEXPLAINABLE **multiplication of loaves was designed to be a dramatic picture of the greatness, fullness, and sufficiency of Jesus to meet the deepest needs of our souls so that we will never hunger again.**
>
> PRESCRIPTION

> And truly Jesus did many other signs in the presence of His disciples, which are not written in this book; but these are written that you may believe that Jesus is the Christ, the Son of God, and that believing you may have life in His name.
>
> —JOHN 20:30–31

Improbable healing and our understanding

Healing may sometimes be a mysterious process that eludes our attempts to explain. This is what I mean by "improbable healing." Perhaps you are familiar with the story of Hannah, Samuel's mother. She could not conceive a child, and she suffered emotionally and socially from that. Still, Hannah continued to love the Lord.

> But to Hannah he would give a double portion, for he loved Hannah, although the Lord had closed her womb. And her rival also provoked her severely, to make her miserable, because the Lord had closed her womb.
>
> —1 Samuel 1:5–6

> Then they rose early in the morning, and worshiped before the Lord, and returned and came to their house at Ramah. And Elkanah knew Hannah his wife, and the Lord remembered her. So it came to pass in the process of time that Hannah conceived and bore a son, and called his name Samuel, saying, "Because I have asked for him from the Lord."
>
> —1 Samuel 1:19–20

Why Hannah could not have a child for years is unknown to us, but it is clear that God loved her. What we *do* know, now, is that apparent infertility can be due to evanescent conditions that are not systemic or permanent. As Dr. Rowsey explains, there are factors that seem to impede fertility. Stress, anxiety, and internal states such as anger work negatively in a woman's body. Infection of the uterus can be a problem. In addition to those, poor nutrition and alcohol abuse may also contribute to *anovulation*, which is a condition of unreleased eggs. God has shown us that the seemingly impossible or improbable need not be so. Hannah's healing and her pregnancy were improbable and certainly unexpected. However, if you are also desiring a child and are not achieving a successful pregnancy, there is always hope. Rest, relaxation, changes in lifestyle, and of course prayer may all have positive, happy effects in the end.

To experience healing we need faith; we need to understand that the Creator cares for us and has also designed provisions for healing in our body. We also need to understand that design of our bodies and tend to them with care. We must *appreciate*.[1]

Today, God still does wondrous things. His design within us is capable of much. He is still the God who answers prayer. He still shows Himself strong on behalf of those whose hearts are "at peace" with Him (2 Chron. 16:9).

The unexpected healings of the Old Testament, as well as those that accompanied the teachings of Jesus, show us that nothing is impossible to the Creator. They are signs of His compassion. And they are previews of what is yet to come, for ultimate healing is promised to all who enter His glorious heaven.

Chapter 14

MODERN EXAMPLES OF IMPROBABLE HEALING

Bless the LORD, *O my soul;*
And all that is within me, bless His holy name!
Bless the LORD, *O my soul...*
Who heals all your diseases.

—PSALM 103:1–3

Lance Armstrong is a modern example of improbable healing. Raised by his single mother, Lance demonstrated an aptitude for cycling, as well as a strong will at an early age. Now a national and world champion cyclist, two-time Olympian, renowned humanitarian, and role model, this man probably represents the greatest form of redemption seen in a physical body. Lance survived lethal cancers in his brain and in his testes to become a husband and father, and to continue to win races.

In 1996 Lance Armstrong was ranked as the number one cyclist in the world. He recaptured his success at the Tour Du Pont (the first person to do so), was the first American to win the traditional Belgian spring classic Fleche Wallone, and competed as a member of the U.S. cycling team in the Atlanta summer Olympic games. In 1996, the year of his twenty-fifth birthday—an age when few men achieve such status and recognition, and even fewer are faced with their own mortality—Lance encountered the battle of his life and for his life.

The man who had been described as the "Du Pont Dominator" and "The Golden Boy of American Cycling," was literally forced off his bike in excruciating pain in October of 1996. Tests revealed advanced testicular cancer that had spread to his lungs and his brain. He was operated on twice in the coming weeks—once to remove the malignant testicle, and then dramatic brain surgery to remove the cancer that had spread upward. Chances for his recovery were far less than 50/50 as a frightened but determined Lance began an aggressive form of chemotherapy. While it weakened him well beyond anything he had ever experienced, he had a deep well of reserves and the unconditional support of family and friends. Remarkably, the chemotherapy began to work, and Lance gradually allowed his thoughts to return to racing. He began riding and training only five months after his diagnosis, still uncertain of his future in the sport, but a profoundly grateful and resolute man.

Cancer left him scarred physically and emotionally, but he now maintains it was an unexpected gift; a viewpoint that is shared by many cancer survivors. Getting cancer was "…the best thing that ever happened to me," Lance said, in relation to the maturity and life focus the disease forced him to face. Throughout this life threatening ordeal, Lance knew his priorities were changing. His physical well-being, something that had never been challenged, was suddenly fragile. He was given the chance to fully appreciate the blessings of good health, a loving family, and close friends. Lance described his bout with cancer as "a special wake-up call." He heeded the call to activism by becoming a spokesperson for testicular and other forms of cancer.[1]

Lance celebrated his victory over cancer in 1998 by winning the Sprint 56K Criterium in Austin and later the Tour de France in 1999. In 2003 he won the Tour de France a fifth time. These were stunning achievements for a man who thought he was "through." His beautiful attitude toward life and his passion are a model for all of us. Lance's purpose and determination demonstrate to us that our bodies are designed to be renewed and restored through a beautiful spirit.

As Christians we talk about the *anointed* purpose in having Christ live in us. But Lance shows us that our bodies are designed to be renewed and restored through a beautiful spirit joined with a lifestyle that reflects a faithful stewardship of the body as the temple in which God dwells for believers. If you live continually in God's presence, you have the resources of hope and courage, which are perpetually renewed by prayer. You have the resources for the heart, soul, and disposition that it takes to experience this kind of improbable healing. Trust God to work out His sovereign will in you as you demonstrate to others that "with God nothing shall be impossible."

GOD'S

FOR HEALING

TRUST GOD TO work out His sovereign will in you as you demonstrate to others that "with God nothing shall be impossible."

PRESCRIPTION

The life of Reese Patterson provides another example of modern, unexpected, and improbable healing. Reese was a state champion tennis player, a great ophthalmologist, and a beautiful man of 6 feet, 3 inches, and 220 pounds when, in 1987, he developed a gastric carcinoma—stomach cancer. Surgeons removed 90 percent of his stomach, including the sphincter, which keeps food from moving back into the esophagus. His body eventually weakened and withered to a mere 90 pounds.

Reese gives us the details in his own words:

> As a busy physician (ophthalmologist) I never expected to have my career abruptly halted; however, in July 1987 at age 61, I was diagnosed with adenocarcinoma of the proximal stomach. A total gastrectomy was performed that included removal of the esophageal sphincter. The adjacent lymph nodes were found to be positive for local metastasis, which made the prognosis guarded.
>
> The surgery itself was far more devastating than anything I could ever have imagined. The weeks and months that followed made me realize how complex and baffling the postgastrectomy syndrome can be for both

the patient and the doctor. The physical and emotional aspects of the problem were at times overwhelming, and the implications of the lymph node involvement were a constant cloud over my head. But these thoughts were soon drowned out by the immediate and direct problems of food and liquid intake. This resulted in nausea and vomiting, cramping and diarrhea, and incessant fluctuations in blood glucose levels, along with self-induced hypoglycemic insulin shock. All of this was followed by massive weight loss.

My own medical education and knowledge took away what little hope I had. During the first six months I had to be dilated four times under anesthesia because of an inadequate opening in the esophagojejunostomy anastomosis, a complication that can often occur with this type of surgery. I wish I had been informed about this potential problem prior to the operation. Ultimately, I retreated to the bedroom to die. I desperately needed advice but did not know to whom I could turn. It was all too painful and bewildering. The immediate need for counseling when a diagnosis of cancer is made has become quite obvious to me in hindsight.

My long-time friend and tennis doubles partner pulled me out of the bedroom and back onto the tennis court six months after my surgery. This was the critical jump-start I needed to get back into the land of the living. I would never have made it without him. My life was reduced to the here and now. Massive eating and strenuous exercise became my vehicles for survival. I could not regain any lost weight until I began a moderate weight-lifting program. I was unable to put fat storage on my body. Contrary to my doctor's statement about the difficulty of regaining lost weight after a total gastrectomy, I was able to regain 100 percent of my lost weight with the extreme eating and weight-lifting program. This information I have shared with dozens of other gastrectomy patients, that is, unless the patients were obviously terminal.

Next, I had to learn how to fine-tune my nutrition with a totally different approach to fat, carbohydrate, and protein intake with the emphasis on a higher percentage of protein relative to carbohydrate. Fat consumption had to be reduced because of bloating, cramping, and diarrhea, secondary to dumping and fat malabsorption in the postgastrectomy syndrome.

As my exercise and tennis routine increased, I was compelled to formulate a liquid recipe consisting of predigested proteins and carbohydrates that could be consumed throughout an exercise activity lasting over a period of several hours. This technique not only consistently maintained my blood glucose levels, but, in addition, it translated into enhanced stamina when compared to the use of only water or Gatorade. This approach enabled me to play the seniors' tennis tournament circuit again, winning several national championships in doubles and ranking high in the singles division.

In 1991 my partner and I were ranked number 1 in the nation in our age group in doubles, and I was ranked number 13 in singles. The nationwide publicity that ensued allowed hundreds of fellow cancer patients and dozens of stomach cancer patients to make contact with me. So, this is my life now in forced retirement, working with other cancer patients, mutually learning from them and sharing with them how to deal with this disease.[2]

As a physician, Reese knew that textbooks would not predict such a successful recovery with physical strength and weight gain. And yet, they occurred. Reese's indomitable spirit would not allow him to succumb, and he turned to tennis as his vehicle of therapeutic healing.

When Reese first returned to the tennis court, he was physically capable of only one stroke. With time that became two strokes. Then it became more and more as he slowly built himself up. Later he went on to win the Tennessee doubles. Later still, Reese and his playing partner, also a cancer survivor, went on to win a national event on hard court. Eventually they won the nationals on grass as well. In that event, the two men won though they were both stiff from the disease and surgeries.

They had been virtually unknown prior to the finals in that tournament. But now, disbelieving New Yorkers approached the two for their story. Reese and his partner told them how they had almost died yet were restored. They described their interest in nutrition, exercise, and positive thinking. They explained that, at the end of their recovery time, they were better than ever, and due to their positive attitudes and excellence in nutrition, they felt better now than they had before the cancer.

The day after the interview in New York, these two men, who had never played on grass before, won the grass match and tournament. After they had won this match, the papers recorded this: "2 men who should be dead of cancer win Triple Crown in tennis." Since then, this pair has won many doubles events in tennis all over the world, and they have been able to witness to many people of their recovery. The importance of nutrition, exercise, and a positive mental attitude have been pointed out in many press releases and other events as a result of their stories.

GOD'S

DUE TO THEIR positive attitudes and excellence in nutrition, they felt better now than they had before the cancer.

FOR HEALING

PRESCRIPTION

Reese's commitment to these principles and his purpose in life show us how the Creator intended us to face seemingly impossible physical challenges. This hope-filled attitude and lifestyle led him back to being a very healthy man who is almost eighty, playing tournament tennis all over the world—and winning! Reese's is a special story from which we can all learn.

We have that message to share here as well. This perspective on life is exactly what God calls us to when He says, "Rejoice in the Lord always. Again I will say, rejoice!" (Phil. 4:4). "In everything give thanks; for this is the will of God" (1 Thess. 5:18). "I can do all things through Christ who strengthens me" (Phil. 4:13).

In cases of improbable healing, determination, positive thinking, and reshaped lifestyles are not the only elements for success. Appreciation and thankfulness for the body and its marvelous abilities for self-healing, for physicians and their skill and science in assisted healing, and sometimes for the least obvious details of our lives, which are invariably far richer than we tend to acknowledge, are also vital keys in the healing process—especially when hope may be most elusive.

In her book *When God and Cancer Meet*, Lynn Eib relates her story of her triumph over that disease that strikes fear in the hearts of people perhaps more than any other.[3] Informed that she had stage-three colon cancer, Lynn became aware that thanksgiving is normally not one of the many emotions that accompany the initial diagnosis or the months of treatment, uncertainty, and weakness. She did believe, however, that a thankful heart was essential to her ability to cope with her trial and also to her potential recovery.

Lynn found it difficult to find something to be grateful for inside of her grim circumstances. She was ill at a young age after having diligently taken care of herself; her daughters might grow up motherless; she had painful treatment with toxic chemicals to look forward to—not much to be thankful about, it seemed. Persevering, though, she realized that Dr. Hirsch, a Messianic Jewish oncologist, lived only seven miles from her home—a blessing. Lynn had found her reason to be thankful to God: Dr. Hirsch would be giving her the best treatment available. Lynn eventually beat the odds and survived her cancer, all the while realizing the vital role that an upbeat and appreciative heart had played in the process.

The stories of Lance Armstrong, Reese Patterson, and Lynn Eib should inspire all of those who are in need of improbable healing. For the believer there is a call to prayer when we need the help of the Great Physician, *Jehovah Rapha*: "Call upon Me in the day of trouble; I will deliver you, and you shall glorify Me" (Ps. 50:15). This has been called Robinson Crusoe's text, because Robert Louis Stevenson used it to portray Crusoe's cry for help from above while on his deserted island. We may feel as alone as Crusoe, but this text tells us to not trust our feelings.

GOD'S PRESCRIPTION *for* HEALING

Instead we are summoned to trust in the living God. There have been numerous studies done at universities and in other medical settings to show that patients who prayed received more help in their recovery than those who did not. This should not surprise us because God delights to answer believing prayer.

Improbable Deliverance From Addiction

Many lives are in constant bondage to addiction and compulsion. Finding freedom from such shackles seems as distant and improbable as anything for those suffering and those close to the suffering. The only way to "come back to life" is to be healed and set free.

For over forty years, my good friend Mickey Evans has been teaching men who are bound in addictions to alcohol, drugs, or sex how to give up running their own lives and establish a glorious oneness with God. He and his staff seek to introduce them to Jesus—the Way, the Truth, and the Life, and then to show them how they can hear from God personally. At Dunklin Memorial Camp in Okeechobee, Florida, lives are daily being transformed. Hopes are restored. Dreams are redeemed. God is transforming broken men from the inside out.

Soon after a man arrives at this "city of refuge," he discovers there is hope. The men are taught how to give their hearts to Jesus, to prayerfully read God's Word, and to listen to His Holy Spirit. It isn't many days before they discover that God is personally interested in healing their brokenness, forgiving them for their failures, and helping them to forgive those who have let them down. The Holy Spirit of God is the enabling power to help them to live a successful, satisfying, enjoyable life on their way to spend eternity.

The twelve-step program has been helpful to many people to overcome addictions. To the individual and his or her family, a real change has seemed *improbable*. In God's mercy they have found that what seemed impossible became a reality and a testimony to God's goodness and power. The common twelve-step program has come under criticism because it is used by some groups without any reference to the God of the Bible or to the Savior Jesus Christ. In these cases some people are encouraged to "turn yourself over to God as you understand Him," which may give the impression to certain people that what is really being said is "whoever you think He is." However, it *does* matter who God is, and some believers have refined the twelve steps to clearly state that we look to the true and living God of the Bible. Mickey Evans gives God all the glory, though, and summarizes the twelve steps in biblical terms as a testimony to God's mercy and intervention. Here is the way he states it:

1. We admitted we were powerless over our separation from God, that our lives had become unmanageable. "I know nothing good lives in me, that is, in my sinful nature. For I have the desire to do what is good, but I cannot carry it out" (Rom. 7:18, NIV).

2. We came to believe that a power greater than ourselves could restore us to sanity. "For it is God who works in you to will and to act according to his good purpose" (Phil 2:13, NIV).

3. We made a decision to turn our will and our lives over to the care of God, as He is revealed in the Bible. "Therefore, I urge you, brothers, in view of God's mercy, to offer your bodies as living sacrifices, holy and pleasing to God—this is your spiritual act of worship" (Rom. 12:1, NIV).

4. We made a searching and fearless moral inventory of ourselves. "Let us examine our ways and test them, and let us return to the LORD" (Lam. 3:40, NIV).

5. We admitted to God, to ourselves, and to another human being the exact nature of our wrongs. "Therefore confess your sins to each other and pray for each other so that you may be healed" (James 5:16, NIV).

6. We are entirely ready to have God remove all these defects of character. "Humble yourselves before the Lord, and he will lift you up" (James 4:10, NIV).

7. We humbly ask Him to remove our shortcomings.

"If we confess our sins, He is faithful and just and will forgive us our sins and purify us from all unrighteousness" (1 John 1:9, NIV).

8. We made a list of all persons we had harmed and became willing to make amends to them all. "Do to others as you would have them do to you" (Luke 6:31, NIV).

9. We made direct amends to such people wherever possible, except when to do so would injure them or others. "First go and be reconciled to your brother; then come and offer your gift" (Matt. 5:24, NIV).

10. We continued to take a personal inventory and when we were wrong, we promptly admitted it. "So, if you think you are standing firm, be careful that you don't fall" (1 Cor. 10:12, NIV).

11. We sought through prayer and meditation to improve our conscious contact with God, as He is revealed in the Bible, praying only for knowledge of His will for us and the power to carry that out. "Let the word of Christ dwell in you richly" (Col. 3:16, NIV).

12. Having had a spiritual awakening as the result of these steps, we tried to carry this message to others and to practice these principles in all our affairs. "Brothers, if someone is caught in a sin, you who are spiritual should restore him gently. But watch yourself, or you also may be tempted" (Gal. 6:1, NIV).[4]

It is a joy to hear of individuals set free and families reunited in the grace of God. Anyone who has struggled with addiction and its shattering effects on a life knows that deliverance really does come by God's grace alone.

An interesting and inspiring story of God's grace in the improbable healing of addiction comes to us from nineteenth-century China.

Pastor Hsi was a philosopher and a well-respected member of his community in Western Chang province—and he was an opium addict. Over time he watched his own life begin to disintegrate through his body's slavery to cravings. Eventually however, he was exposed to the influence of Christian missionaries, and he began to read the Scriptures. Pastor Hsi came to realize that Christ alone could deliver him from opium. He prayed; he wrestled with the physical need; he finally pleaded with the Savior for greater power than he possessed within himself.

In a moment of crisis, of great pain, he cried out, "Devil, what can you do against me? My life is in the hand of God. And truly I am willing to break off opium and die, but not willing to continue in sin and live!"[5] In the agony of his soul, he found a strength from heaven and rose above the life of slavery and self-destruction. He fully understood the transformation to be impossible "without real faith in Jesus."[6]

With his body healed and a new peace and joy, Pastor Hsi sought to minister to other opium addicts. He helped the people who came to him to rid their homes of idols, and he taught them of the mercy and power that the Savior offers to those who come to him in repentance and faith. Through Pastor Hsi's ministry many lives were changed, and many families were spared the devastation that opium had forced upon them. Pastor Hsi knew the importance of support groups, vocational training, and "staying clean by helping others." The practical help we all need was considered and implemented, but the decisive help was the power of God intervening to transform the inner man from a self-centered life to a God-centered life.

None of us can point in judgment to a substance addiction, for we all labor under the weight of preoccupations that divert us from God and His healing grace. Therefore, these principles are for all of us. We all need this healing that God sends to us through His Word. We are purposed by God to receive eternal life with Him. And, while we have controls and passions in life, the controls are automatically in place as we love Him. (See Ephesians 5:1–2.) Thus we have no place for a limited life. It is important to have a life of total abandonment to Christ. In abandonment we have our obedience, physically, mentally, and spiritually. With Him, the improbable occurs and rewards are eternal.

Chapter 15

HOW DO WE SEEK AN IMPROBABLE HEALING?

*Call to Me, and I will answer you, and show you great
and mighty things, which you do not know.*

—JEREMIAH 33:3

When we appreciate the Lord and His mercy toward us, our hearts, minds, and bodies are open to the possibilities of improbable healing. When we truly learn wonder, we are able to see healing in unexpected places. What are we to do to seek healing that initially appears unlikely, improbable, or impossible?

1. We are to pray: "Call upon Me in the day of trouble; I will deliver you, and you shall glorify Me" (Ps. 50:15).

2. We are to align ourselves with God's design for healing in diet, exercise, emotional, and spiritual alignment. This means we are to live without bitterness or envy or worry. We are to seek forgiveness from God so that we may live near to Him and find our satisfaction in Him. We are to live in gratitude and appreciation toward God and to live a life of serving others. We are to align our inner man with the Word of God.

3. We honor God by seeking counsel. "In the multitude of counselors there is safety" (Prov. 11:14). If the wisest counsel is to seek physician-assisted healing, we honor God by pursuing this wise path. Physicians can assist. Only God can heal. The wise physician seeks to align the body as God intended, as with a broken arm. They seek

to assist the body's immune system in dealing with overreaction to injury. They seek to remove that which would hinder the normal processes that God has made, such as the cleaning of vessels that nourish the heart muscles. The removal of a cancerous tumor with "clean margins" as you pray for God to bless your surgeon's skill is as much of a "divine" intervention as a "successful remission" in answer to prayer.

4. We must not forget to rejoice daily in the constant battle for our healing. It is being waged and won by all of the agents of our natural capacities, all impeccably designed by the Creator and placed in us with purpose and love. *We were designed for healing.*

PART V

ULTIMATE HEALING

Chapter 16

DESIGNED FOR ETERNITY

Unless you are converted and become as little children,
you will by no means enter the kingdom of heaven.
Therefore whoever humbles himself as this little child
is the greatest in the kingdom of heaven.

—MATTHEW 18:3–4

This world makes no sense without eternity. Intrinsic in every human soul is the desire to live forever. This too is part of your design—the Creator put this desire in you. Only He can fulfill it. It doesn't take long in life before we are distracted from this deepest of all longings. However, we will not have ultimate healing until we do return to it.

We are reminded of our mortality in many ways by the variety of diseases we experience. Few realize that each recovery is due ultimately to God's design for healing already prewritten in our sixty trillion cells. Physician-assisted healing is our way of using our greatest wisdom—to learn to cooperate with the way the Great Designer has made and integrated the cells and systems of the body. Your soul and body are interwoven together in a marvelous way, as the psalmist reminds us (Ps. 139). In spite of the wonderful design for healing that is inherent in our cells and systems, too often we do not cooperate with that design. We actually work against our own health by irresponsible lifestyles and habits.

Some of the greatest hindrances to your health are your inner stresses, worries, fears, bitterness, and lack of forgiveness toward others. All of these things point you to the need for returning to your Creator as

GOD'S PRESCRIPTION FOR HEALING

CHRIST CALLS you to total healing, beginning with total forgiveness.

173

your Savior. To return to an alignment with God's design for you, you must first of all seek the removal of your alienation from God. This reconciliation, union, and forgiveness come from surrender to the Great Physician, the Lord Jesus Christ. He calls you to total healing, beginning with total forgiveness. The healing begins now and will be completed when you enter heaven.

It is so important to realize that to attain to total healing you must first receive this total forgiveness. This is the basis of God's design for healing. Where there is total forgiveness—thus total healing, you are set totally free to be at one with your Lord. You will begin to taste the beauty of this relationship in this life—and it is the best part of life. Ultimately, however, that oneness will not be enjoyed in its fullness until you no longer look through a glass darkly.

> Now we see through a glass, darkly; but then face to face: now I know in part; but then shall I know even as also I am known.
>
> —1 Corinthians 13:12, kjv

In this life we really do only see through a glass darkly. Today, we too often superficially "practice" faith in a rote fashion rather than living it in vital communion with the Savior. We run around learning things about God and rolling up our sleeves and doing God's work, when He really wants us to be intimate with Him, just as He wanted intimacy from Mary rather than Martha's busyness. (See Luke 10:42.)

Three Feasts and Three Courts

In Charles Newbold's book *The Crucified Ones*, the author reminds us that communion with God in heaven is our ultimate goal and that we must begin "tabernacling" with Him now.[1] To set our minds in this direction, let's follow the author's thoughts as he walks us through a parallel study of the three feasts of Israel in the Old Testament, the three courts of the tabernacle, and the three great doctrines of knowing God. Each progression is designed to bring us to eternity with a heart prepared "to enjoy God forever." To fulfill the divine design for each of our lives now and forever we must live in appreciation for all that God is to us in Jesus.

We need to live in appreciation because we are part of the fold. This is the Passover. By the blood of the Lamb, He will pass over us and not bring us into judgment. This is to be forgiven of all our sins! To experience the Passover is to know and experience Christ's glorious work on the cross on our behalf. This is represented by the court of the altar of bronze at the tabernacle. Here the sacrifices were offered that portrayed the death of Jesus on the cross to pay for our sins. This is justification.

We need to live in appreciation because we love Him and have His power in us. This is the result of the Spirit's work of anointing us—this is Pentecost. This is living in the next court as we progress into God's presence—the Holy Place where the showbread is; the golden lampstand, and the altar of incense. This is sanctification.

We need to live in appreciation because we live in Him and He in us both now and for eternity. This corresponds to the Feast of Tabernacles. This corresponds to living in the most inner court of all—living in the holy of holies. This is living in satisfaction. And this is glorification. This is the bride enjoying communion and intimacy with the Bridegroom. We enjoy this through a glass darkly today. But we will enjoy it face to face in eternity.

The purpose for Passover and Pentecost is to enter into the satisfaction of

GOD'S

F O R   H E A L I N G

To TABERNACLE through life and eternity with our King we must have no competing interests that exclude God or crowd Him out to be a marginal influence in our lives.

PRESCRIPTION

Tabernacles. The purpose of justification and sanctification is to enter into the satisfaction of glorification. The purpose of the outer court and the inner court is to draw us on into the holy of holies—the full satisfaction and appreciation of the Lord Jesus. This is the glory of eternity begun now and that will grow for endless ages in heaven in its incomprehensible fullness.

Let us not forget that to enter this satisfaction in Jesus we must die to self. The Savior said, "Whoever of you does not forsake all that he has cannot be My disciple" (Luke 14:33). We must be determined that God will have no rivals in our life. To tabernacle through life and eternity with our King we must have no competing interests that exclude God or crowd Him out to be a marginal influence in our lives. The apostle Paul said that he counted all things as loss or "damaged goods" compared to Christ—He even said that he "[counted] them as rubbish, that I may gain Christ" (Phil. 3:8). This must be our focus—to "know Him and the power of His resurrection" (v. 10)!

Graduation Day!

The most beautiful part of life will be experienced as it ends. This is ultimate healing. It is like a person's graduation day from college. In Psalm 116:15, we read, "Precious in the sight of the LORD is the death of His saints." When we look at the death of a believer from God's standpoint, we realize that it is a special day to God—it is the day He brings His beloved child home. It must be precious in our sight too.

My friend Winnie Gillet understands this. Winnie is a lovely, sweet woman who works in our clinic assisting our patients; she is one of our most special caregivers. Winnie's life was changed and deepened with the loss of her thirty-two-year-old daughter, June, more than eighteen years ago. Doctors discovered a malignancy in June's brain, behind the optic nerve of one of her eyes. She eventually had surgery three times and was able to rebound to live and work again. Ultimately, though, the disease ran its course, and June began to die. One Sunday afternoon, as she lay in her hospital bed, I visited June with eleven other people. We stood around her bed and prayed. At one point, June sat up and said to us: "I am going to miss you all very much, *but I am healed*—I am going to be with Jesus." Shortly thereafter, June left her mother and all of us to be with the Lord. She was finally, and completely, healed.

Joni Eareckson Tada anticipates that day, too. She notes that while our bodies scream for our attention now, it counts for little. She encourages, "Be patient. Don't give up. This life's not over yet. It will get better. One day you will enjoy the most perfect exit."[2] Joni looks forward to "a new body. A new mind. A new heart. A new language. A new home. Even new ways to serve."[3] For her, paralysis merely brings her closer to heaven and to Jesus.

The believer's death is his graduation from the college of the world—the life experiences of our earthly life. A long, difficult time of training climaxes in a day of honor and joy. This will be our day of celebration in eternity.

A Beautiful Design

The Creator heals us through His beautiful design in so many different ways, which cannot be fully imagined. There is such beautiful complexity there that you can only stand in awe and admiration. Worship the Designer who gave you this beautiful life, and, because you trust Him, He will also give you eternity with Himself. You will find your place in eternity engulfed with Him and intermeshed with Him; you will come to know Him as you are known.

Your ultimate healing in eternity will restore your body to the Designer's perfect template—the arthritis, weak kidneys, tuberculosis, scarred skin, and ulcers will not exist. All of these things are completely healed as you take on a new body, a body like His. Your mind, will, and emotions will be given that perfect gift of *shalom*, or peace. In 2 Peter 1:2, the Amplified Bible describes this perfect peace as "perfect well-being, all necessary good, all spiritual prosperity, and freedom from fears and agitating passions and moral conflicts." On that day in eternity you will enter a spiritual oneness and intimacy with God that cannot be fully described or appreciated.

> GOD'S
> FOR HEALING
>
> YOU SHOULD PUT more emphasis on your spiritual training than you do on your physical training.
>
> PRESCRIPTION

The apostle Paul said this: "Eye has not seen, nor ear heard, nor have entered into the heart of man the things which God has prepared for those who love Him" (1 Cor. 2:9). You should begin to prepare for this life in heaven with God now by having spiritual mentors. A spiritual mentor would allow you to think with him of how it will be to be with Christ forever. We have coaches and physical trainers, but we don't have enough spiritual trainers to allow us to become close to the Lord. The spiritual aspects of life and preparation for eternity may be more important than anything else you do. You should put more emphasis on your spiritual training than you do on your physical training.

Paul said that the physical body only lasts for a short time, but the spiritual is for eternity (1 Tim. 4:8). This is so true—we may spend much time on training our physical bodies, yet we fail to engulf ourselves fully in a spiritual realm on earth like the one we will experience in heaven. In heaven we will be truly engrossed with God to such an extent that we no longer think of earth; it will be a total communion with Him in heaven. That beautiful state of mind is where we all need to be instead of trying to serve God with a hectic spirit and a fragmented and frustrated heart.

Don't become so busy *doing* so many things *for* God that you forget to *be* in communion *with* Him in your spiritual life. I believe that our greatest healing occurs when we can, on this earth, become engulfed in the spiritual nature, letting everything else become secondary. Those rare people who do this usually have no agendas. They think along spiritual lines and spend most of their time with Christ, realizing that the rest of life isn't very important. In fact, much of it is just useless momentum and activities. It is only with this focus on your relationship with God that you can produce anything satisfying. It is this state of mind that sets the tone for your ultimate healing, yet to come in eternity.

How Will He Reward You?

Understand this important principle: How you prepare yourself here on earth will determine how you relate to God in eternity. There will be rewards given for a godly life. In the last chapter of the Bible, God says, "And behold, I am coming quickly, and My reward is with Me, to give to every one according to his work" (Rev. 22:12). In the Gospel of John, Jesus said, "This is the work of God, that you believe in Him whom He sent" (John 6:29). James shows us that the fruit that flows from faith is a life full of works of love and mercy: "Thus also faith by itself, if it does not have works, is dead" (James 2:17).

Rewards are not the basis for entering heaven. We enter heaven only by faith in the work of Christ on the cross. The rewards for believers are rewards for Christian service and stewardship. What is required in a steward is that he is found faithful (1 Cor. 4:2). Jesus promised to come and reward His faithful servants in the parable of the talents found in Matthew 25. There is a continuity of this life with the next. What we sow in this life we will reap in eternity (Gal. 6:7–9). People often ask:

GOD'S PRESCRIPTION *for* HEALING

"How can there be any differences in heaven? If you are in glory, it is glorious." This is true. However, there can be a difference in the capacity to appreciate what is there. A trained musician who understands classical music can go to a concert and appreciate all the movements and immense variety of contribution made by the different instruments. An untrained person who also loves music can go to a concert, appreciate the beauty, and enjoy the experience, but his or her capacity to take it all in is less than that of the musician.

As a believer you will be filled to your capacity in heaven. However, we are developing different capacities here on earth by our stewardship. This deepened capacity will continue in glory. A faithful steward of the study of God's Word has a greater capacity to know God now, and this will continue in heaven, but it will be proportionately enriched with the intensity and immensity of eternity and glorification. Take to heart the great opportunity you have each day to prepare for a richer, more glorious eternity.

The Facts About Rewards

In his book *The Life God Rewards*, Bruce Wilkinson shows that there are very clear promises of God-given rewards in eternity to a life devoted to Him. There are various acts of service mentioned in the Bible that are each taken note of by God. Here are some of the kinds of good works that He rewards:

1. Seeking Him through spiritual acts such as fasting and praying (Matt. 6:6; Heb. 11:6)
2. Submitting to your employer as a faithful steward (Matt. 24:45–47; Eph. 6:8; Col. 3:22–24)
3. Self-denial in His service (Matt. 16:24–27)
4. Serving those in need in His name (Mark 9:41)
5. Suffering for His name and reputation (Luke 6:22–23)
6. Sacrifices you make for Him (Luke 6:35); a hundredfold reward (Matt. 19:29).
7. Sharing of your time, talent, and treasure to further His kingdom (Matt. 6:3–4; 1 Tim. 6:18–19)[4]

You can see why the Bible emphatically declares that "He is a rewarder of those who diligently seek Him" (Heb. 11:6). Perhaps one of the most familiar passages about eternal rewards highlights the fact that even the least act upon this earth that is done in Jesus' name will not be overlooked and forgotten—even offering a cup of cold water: "For whoever gives you a cup of water to drink in My name, because you belong to Christ, assuredly, I say to you, he will by no means lose his reward" (Mark 9:41). Wilkinson summarizes the pivotal principles very succinctly when he says, "Belief determines WHERE you will spend eternity. Behavior determines HOW you will spend eternity."[5]

> ## GOD'S
>
> A LIFE OF FERVENT cleaving to God in this life will be rewarded in glory with its counterpart of what only God can bestow in a way that only God knows how to bestow.
>
> ## PRESCRIPTION

The capacity of this eternal heavenly state of knowing and enjoying God is surely the gift of God's grace. But the deepened capacity is the reward of God upon our faithfulness as stewards "of the manifold grace of God" (1 Pet. 4:10). What a challenging summons to stir us up to shake off our lethargy! A life of fervent cleaving to God in this life will be rewarded in glory with its counterpart of what only God can bestow in a way that only God knows how to bestow. God will show that it was indeed worthwhile to heed His Word to walk worthy of the calling with which we are called (Eph. 4:1).

The rewards you receive in heaven are like the ones you receive while yet here below—especially the reward of giving you greater nearness to Him and a greater sense of His presence. One of the most important parts of your life here is that God rewards you not materially, but spiritually. So many people talk about materialistic things of Christ, which I think are absolutely ridiculous—God is not a materialistic God; He is a spiritual God. His rewards are spiritual, and they are eternal. Those who have suggested that God is a materialistic God have done Him a disservice. Although about one-third of His Word relates to materialistic things, He is truly spiritual, and His rewards are spiritual. How you set your mind now will help to determine what your spiritual rewards will be, which will be eternal.

A Date to Keep!

Your date for eternity with God is the most important date you will ever have. Your anticipation of that date with Him is the most important mind-set and feeling that you can ever become associated with. That important date far exceeds any engagement you may have here on this earth. You have a date to become the bride of Christ. If you come to Christ in total surrender, saying, "I am Yours," you have accepted your date to spend eternal life with Him in heaven.

The greatest commendation that you as a believer will ever receive will be given to you by God Himself at the entrance into heaven. He will welcome you in with these words: "Well done, good and faithful servant....Enter into the joy of your lord" (Matt. 25:21). This passage is so important because it comes in context with the verses that say, "Inasmuch as you did it to one of the least of these My brethren, you did it to Me" (v. 40, cf. v. 45).

The reward of entering into the joy of our Lord in eternity is set before us at the end of the parable of the talents. This parable tells us that this joy is the result of how we have lived our lives. A significant portion of this life of stewardship has to do with how we have cared for other people. We cannot overestimate the importance of the rewards we receive for being close to Him, and it's obvious from His words that we have to be doers of God's work. But we also have to be engulfed with Him. Spiritual engulfment! Spiritual training is one of the most neglected things in our society today. We train people in Bible studies; we train people in outreach; we train people in raising money; we train people in building big churches. But how well are we trained to be spiritually intimate with God?

Chapter 17

ETERNITY'S ANOINTED PURPOSE FOR LIFE

We do not look at the things which are seen, but at the things which are not seen. For the things which are seen are temporary, but the things which are not seen are eternal.

—2 CORINTHIANS 4:18

When you bring eternity into your life today, you begin to live today with the same purpose you will have for all eternity. You need God to anoint you and to equip you to live out this purpose with your eyes on Him. Even more, you must live it "with Him." The anointed purpose of life is to live a fulfilled life, feeling like you have a purpose. That purpose should not climax here on earth, but it should reach its peak when you look into the eyes of Jesus. C. S. Lewis said, "Heaven is the only thing I have ever longed for." He was longing for the glorious realities and relationships he would experience in heaven, those that he never found in his relationships here below.

In other words, to paraphrase what Lewis was saying:

> All that I longed for in life and never found will be found in heaven. So in reality, what I was longing for was heaven. Finally there I will have a Father like God, which I did not have here below. I will have a heavenly Bridegroom, which I did not have here below. I will have a heavenly Friend like I did not have here below. I will commune with another Person, the glorious Person of God. I will be welcomed and accepted! I will be delighted in. This is what I have longed for, and it cannot be had to this degree except in heaven. So I was really longing for heaven, and did not always know

it. I will be enabled finally to find my complete satis-faction in the Lord Jesus and will be half-hearted no longer; I will not be so easily distracted and diverted any longer. I will not dishonor him ever again with my sin. I will never again foolishly believe the lies that are so suited to sinful desires remaining in me. I long to enter the final and most full stage of salvation! I long for heaven.

So, as I've sought, I know I've failed to find anything that com-pares to what the Father in heaven will be like. The intimacy we will feel in heaven is something we seek here on earth. So many people seek it in different ways. Some patients, for example, come to doctors who will spend time with them just because they want companionship and love and caring. That is a wonderful characteristic, a beautiful charac-teristic of a person. Most people, however, are really more interested in getting on with the program, being tended to, and going on their way. Catering to both types, doctors may be living out the anointed purpose of their lives. But the question remains: "Is my purpose in life a purpose that is focused on eternity?"

The Temporal, the Eternal

Paul shows us how he answered this question in 2 Corinthians 4:16–18:

> Therefore we do not lose heart. Even though our out-ward man is perishing, yet the inward man is being renewed day by day. For our light affliction, which is but for a moment, is working for us a far more exceeding and eternal weight of glory, while we do not look at the things which are seen, but at the things which are not seen. For the things which are seen are temporary, but the things which are not seen are eternal.

Paul realized that the sorrows, trials, and afflictions that attended "his outward man perishing" as life moved on were really being used by God to prepare him for a more wonderful eternity. He is saying that these afflictions are helpful to us. They make us more humble and bring us to renewed submission to God's will. We learn to say again and again, "Nevertheless, not my will but Thine be done." These trials compel us to seek God as our comfort and portion. We draw nearer to God through them. Thus we are living more and more from the standpoint of eternity. Ask yourself, "How will this trial help me to live for eternity?" God sees and delights to reward the faithfulness of His children during their trials. This will make heaven more glorious.

Paul learned to have a distinct spiritual gaze and focus toward life. He aligned his soul in the direction of eternity. He admonishes us not to focus on the things seen, but to give our positive consideration to the things that are unseen. Keep looking at the unseen, or you will become discouraged. Don't be easily distracted and thereby lose your focus. When you worry, covet, or fear, you are fixated on the earthly side of things and will lose sight of God's sovereignty. Lose your focus, and you will lose sight of God's goodness and intervening power. Doing so will take you away from serving and worshiping. When you look on the eternal things, you will keep focused on God and His rule over all. Keep your eyes on Jesus, and fellowship with Him in the midst of your disappointments and sorrows. A focus like this will strengthen you and enable you to go forward with God.

To keep from being easily distracted, you must remember as Paul did that what you see is temporal; what you don't see is eternal. Eternity takes faith to contemplate. Eternity will never end. Ask yourself: Which is most important, the passing pleasures of sin, or the glory of God as His servant and worshiper and friend?

Motivated by Hope or Despair?

When Paul says that we do not lose heart, he shows that the believer's motivation is one filled with hope because our focus is different. The passage speaks of two motivations. First, it speaks of the despair that comes when we focus on our bodies—"the outward man" (v. 16). That would include the times we focus on our pains—"afflictions" (v. 17)—or the times we focus on what we can see with our eyes, basing our thinking on that alone (v. 18). It also includes the despair that comes when we focus on our clocks—"the temporal."

However, there is a second motivation that fills our hearts with hope—a focus on pleasing God and hearing Him express His pleasure in us forever. This is a focus toward our souls rather than solely toward our bodies (v. 16). The reward we receive for a focus on pleasing God is one of the weightiest rewards in glory (v. 17). With it, we do not lose heart, and we are filled with hope by focusing on the invisible, the hidden springs of God's Spirit, present and working (v. 18). We look to the Savior who is interceding at the right hand of God. This is focusing on the long run or what really will matter as time goes on and eternity arrives.

Focusing on immediate gain is a natural impulse, but it is not the best in the long run, as can be illustrated in everyday life. Think of two high-school classmates. One wishes to leave school, get a job, and start earning money. The other one goes to college and is not receiving a weekly paycheck. But the committed student is not really falling behind because in the long run he gets ahead through discipline and thorough preparation for his life career. There are exceptions to this rule in regard to vocational pursuits, but in the spiritual realm it is always true. The unbeliever wants to live by his own impulses, which are often self-destructive. But the believer is preparing for the long

> **GOD'S PRESCRIPTION FOR HEALING**
>
> In the final analysis, the one who goes after the things that last for eternity gets more now and then.

run. He is living in light of eternity. His discipleship has an eternal focus. This analogy holds in the study of music also, for the one who learns to read music goes further in the long run than the one who learns to "play by ear."

In the final analysis, the one who goes after the things that last for eternity gets more now and then. There is no doubt that we will live longer in eternity than we will in the United States, England, Hungary, or in our mortal bodies.

Let me sum up the important message of 2 Corinthians 4:16–18: Heaven is a message of ultimate healing for all of our illnesses, both physical and spiritual. Therefore it is a message of hope. Hope looks forward with expectation to the good that God has promised us. Hope is joined to joy in Scripture (cf. "rejoicing in hope" in Romans 12:12). Hope possesses in advance that which is yet to come. The patient who has hope has the foundational disposition for the healing of his inner man and is predisposed to activate all of the resources that enhance healing. Paul describes this hope as an active grace that is spurring him more and more toward an eternal perspective for all of life.

Our Perspective: Living in Light of Eternity

In a very practical way, Paul was saying this: It is natural to look at pain, rejection, discouragement, and setbacks. But in the face of those, Paul said that he focused on these things: God's hand at work; God's promised goodness in His Word; the work of the Spirit within us to sanctify us by our trials; and the goodness of God to give us the privilege to serve Him and be His ambassadors. He also kept in mind that every ounce of spiritual strength he received was obtained for him by the Savior's work on the cross. It was sent down from heaven as the fruit of the Savior's intercession in heaven on our behalf. He saw himself enveloped by the constant activity of the Triune God for him, in him, and on his behalf. His benediction for each day of his life was this: "The grace of the Lord Jesus Christ, and the love of God, and the communion of the Holy Spirit be with you all. Amen" (2 Cor. 13:14).

If you live by the principles given to you in 2 Corinthians 4:16–18, the following powerful truths will be written on your heart:

1. Your life is one of hope; you do not lose heart. Your life is marked by what is strengthened, glorious (you are working at something that will be glorious), and forever.

2. Your life is one of mystery, in that your help is invisible, unseen, and nourished by hidden springs in the soul. Therein lie your strength and confidence.

3. Your life is one of contradiction and paradox. The paradox is that the greatest part of your life is the unseen part of life. A progressive strengthening and aim for glory are going on in the midst

of your life on earth, which seems full of contradictions and trials because your outward man is perishing.

4. Your life as a believer is one that is eternal. It will not end. Your trials will be long forgotten one day. As Matthew Henry reminds us, "The things that are seen are men, money, and things of earth. The things that are not seen are God, grace, and heaven." Where is your focus? Where is the alignment of your heart?

Chapter 18

A WALK THROUGH GLORY

And he showed me a pure river of water of life, clear as crystal, proceeding from the throne of God and of the Lamb. In the middle of its street, and on either side of the river, was the tree of life.

—REVELATION 22:1–2

It is one of our great joys on this side of eternity to pause and meditate on the blessedness that awaits us. One of the best ways to engage in this refreshing anticipation is to take a walk through Revelation 21 and 22—the last two chapters of the Bible. Let's look at John's description of what lies ahead.

When the Great Physician puts on His surgery clothes for His last operation, He will come out of the operating room with "new heavens and a new earth in which righteousness dwells" (2 Pet. 3:13). No pediatrician has ever held forth such a perfect newborn to the wondering eyes of all around as God will on that day. The new creation of God's glorious kingdom will be the ultimate and final healing work of *Jehovah Rapha*.

The new creation in eternity is described for us in Revelation 21:1–4.

> Now I saw a new heaven and a new earth, for the first heaven and the first earth had passed away. Also there was no more sea. Then I, John, saw the holy city, New Jerusalem, coming down out of heaven from God, prepared as a bride adorned for her husband. And I heard a loud voice from heaven saying, "Behold, the tabernacle of God is with men, and He will dwell with them, and they shall be His people. God Himself will be with them and be their God. And God will wipe away every tear from their eyes; there shall be no more death, nor

sorrow, nor crying. There shall be no more pain, for
the former things have passed away.

The context of this passage follows the opening of the Lamb's
Book of Life. After the Lamb's Book of Life is opened, the names
written in it are the ones that will obtain ultimate healing (Rev. 21:27).
The last verses of chapter 20 and chapter 21 signal the Lamb's Book
of Life as the deciding factor of who enters glory. Why is this so?
Because Jesus is the Lamb of God, and only His death on the cross as
the Passover Lamb can remove our sins. To
those who have received Him, God will say
to them, as He said to the Israelites many
years before, "When I see the blood, I will
pass over you" (Exod. 12:13).

The healing of the inner man as well
as the healing of the outer man will be
complete on that day. Believers, formerly
assaulted by fears, will be healed from
their fears when they see the lost cast away
but hear the Lamb say to them: "Come, you
blessed of My Father, inherit the kingdom
prepared for you from the foundation of
the world" (Matt. 25:34). Then fear will be no longer possible. We will
be made perfect in love. We will have a faith that now sees God face to
face. Those experiences will convince us of His determination to dwell
with us forever.

As a believer, you will receive your ultimate healing in the context of
being prepared as a bride adorned for her husband (Rev. 21:2). You will
be fully satisfied with the greatest intimacy with your blessed Savior that
is possible—but it will still be incomprehensible. Your joy will be complete. You will no longer be homesick for Him. You will no longer pine
away in your sense of distance from Him. You will be with Him forever.

> ## GOD'S PRESCRIPTION FOR HEALING
>
> THE NEW CREATION of God's glorious kingdom will be the ultimate and final healing work of Jehovah Rapha.

Good-bye, Trouble and Sorrow!

In one verse of Scripture, this ultimate healing in glory is described in
six ways (Rev. 21:4):

1. God will wipe away every tear from our eyes.
2. There shall be no more death,
3. ...no sorrow,
4. ...no crying.
5. There shall be no more pain.
6. The former things have passed away.

But there is more! The intimacy of your eternal relationship is the climax of it all. After describing the removal of all that would harm us, John proceeds to unfold the blessedness of our sonship and what it means to be the bride of the King of kings (Rev. 21:7, 9).

Throughout the Bible God says that He takes note of our sorrows. Now on this day there will be the final healing of sorrow. God will wipe away every tear from our eyes. Healing will be given from all the effects of death entering the world—and death itself will be removed. Deprivation, grief, and loss, with all of the wounds that attend them, will end. There will be no more sorrow from broken relationships and bereavement. There will be an end to the sorrow in our lives that arises from the sad consequences of our own foolish choices, missed opportunities, and mistreatment of others. All of this will all be removed because the blood of Christ that forgave it will now obliterate the very core of sin. The sorrows of rejection, ridicule, betrayal, and unforgiveness will be removed.

Great joy will break forth as the reign of eternal comfort begins. God says, "There will be no more sorrow"—none at all!

This beautiful chapter in the Book of Revelation on the subject of ultimate healing declares that there will be no more pain. For some this means final, total relief from the many avenues that bring pain to our bodies. The oppressed will no longer be beaten. Relief will come from the aches and pains of exhaustion. The Book of Revelation often refers to those who are put to death for their loyalty to the Savior. The martyrs who have been bruised and pressed beyond all limits here below will enter a new existence where all of these sufferings for the Savior's sake will be wiped away.

Others who have suffered from the effects of living in a fallen world will experience the end of pain. There will be no more injuries due to falls, concussions, migraine headaches, or end-stage cancer. Gone will be the pain of hunger and thirst.

There will be no more tears from the sorrow of chronic pain, fever, and the exhausting effects of chemotherapies and needles. All will be healed and made whole with the touch of the King. There will be no more tears of loneliness, homesickness, desertion, or war. These tears, indeed, *all* tears will suddenly be removed, and you will be infused with a joy filled with praise. The former things that assaulted you, hindered you, or were obstacles to you will be removed forever. The glorious truth on that day will be: "The former things have passed away."

Inconceivable Blessing

The glories of heaven are so great that we cannot fully conceive of them. The picture John gives in Revelation 21:4 is like a negative exposure of film. Each item in verse 4 is a negative experience (sorrow, pain, death) that is negated or said to be done away with. Therefore, we are called to look forward to the positive counterpart when the film is developed. He will not just wipe away our tears; God will make His face to shine on us and revive our joy to last forever. As Isaiah says, "The ransomed of the LORD shall return, and come to Zion with singing, with everlasting joy on their heads. They shall obtain joy and gladness, and sorrow and sighing shall flee away" (Isa. 35:10).

GOD'S FOR HEALING

He WILL NOT JUST wipe away our tears; God will make His face to shine on us and revive our joy to last forever.

PRESCRIPTION

Not only will there be no more death, but there will be the glorious resurrection when "this mortal must put on immortality" (1 Cor. 15:53). Not only will there be no more crying, but also there will be the singing of praise, the shouting of glory, and the offering up of endless *Hallelujahs* to the Redeemer. Sorrow will be gone, and in its place will be the outpouring of God's joyful presence. As David says, "In Your presence is fullness of joy; at Your right hand are pleasures forevermore" (Ps. 16:11).

Not only does the Book of Revelation tell us that the former things will be passed away, but we also read: "Then He who sat on the throne said, 'Behold, I make all things new'" (Rev. 21:5). In other verses in His Word, God tells us that His glory will cover the earth as the waters cover the sea (Hab. 2:14; Num. 14:21). It is when our lives and our souls are filled to overflowing with God's glory that we will be filled with satisfaction. God summons us to come to Him with our thirsty souls and drink deeply from His supply: "I will give of the fountain of the water of life freely to him who thirsts" (Rev. 21:6). This satisfaction is found in our intimate relationship with our Maker and our King.

Can Anything Be Added to This?

God makes an even more profound statement in Revelation 21:7. He says that we will experience and enjoy all that it means to be His sons: "I will be his God and he shall be My son." All that a Father can be to a son, God will be to us. We begin the Christian life by crying out, "Abba, Father." We will continue it in heaven by knowing the Father-heart of God revealed to us with increasing intimacy for all eternity.

There is more. Next, an angel says to John: "Come, I will show you the bride, the Lamb's wife" (v. 9). Who can describe what it will be like to be the bride of the King of kings? God's people will live forever with their heavenly bridegroom, the Son of God.

Now, to our surprise, John has one more chapter to write about heaven. He describes heaven in the last chapter of the Bible as a return to Paradise. It is like a return to the Garden of Eden, but in eternal glory.

> And he showed me a pure river of water of life, clear as crystal, proceeding from the throne of God and of the Lamb. In the middle of its street, and on either side of the river, was the tree of life, which bore twelve fruits, each tree yielding its fruit every month. The leaves of the tree were for the healing of the nations. And there shall be no more curse, but the throne of God and of the Lamb shall be in it, and His servants shall serve Him. They shall see His face, and His name shall be on their foreheads. There shall be no night there: They need no lamp nor light of the sun, for the Lord God gives them light. And they shall reign forever and ever.
> —REVELATION 22:1–5

In these verses we see five more glories with which God will crown our eternity. God promises us:

1.   Refreshment from the heavenly fountain, which flows from the throne of God
2.   Total healing from the Great Physician
3.   The continued privilege of serving Him in glory
4.   The intimate fellowship of seeing Him face to face
5.   The security and felicity of sharing His victory in the blessed reign of God forever

These five things represent total healing and complete wholeness. This is *shalom*, or perfect peace that will have no end. This is the longing of our hearts now. We must have a taste of this daily to maintain our calm steady pursuit of our anointed purpose in life as we live in light of eternity. Let this be our mind-set now—and our mind-set for eternity.

Charles Spurgeon shows us how to begin to enjoy God's healing now and taste the glory of heaven before we ever arrive there. He says it must be through maintaining a prayerful spirit.

> The very act of prayer is a blessing....To pray is to mount on eagle's wings above the clouds and get into the clear heaven where God dwells. To pray is to enter the treasure-house of God and to enrich one's self out of an inexhaustible storehouse. To pray is to grasp heaven in one's arms, to embrace the Deity within one's soul, and to feel one's body made a temple of the Holy Spirit. To pray is to cast off your burdens, it is to tear away your rags, it is to shake off your diseases, it is to be filled with spiritual vigor, it is to reach the highest point of Christian health. God give us to be much in the holy art of prayer.[1]

John Piper ends his book *Future Grace* by ruminating on how the promises of God will all find their abundant fulfillment in our lives in eternity. He titles the chapter, "Why I Think About What Comes After

Death." Catch the spirit of what he says, and reflect on your own inter-twining with God's purposes both now and eternally.

> My faith grows in the soil of God's promises and gives hope and confidence. Fear goes, hope in God over-flows, we live differently. Our treasure in God is more precious than the fleeting things of the world and sin. Our dreams are not wrapped up with accomplishments and relationships that perish. Don't fret over what this life fails to give us. Marriage, wealth, health, fame. Instead we savor the wonder that the owner and ruler of the universe loves me and has destined me for the enjoy-ment of his glory—and is working infallibly to bring us to his eternal kingdom. We live to meet the needs of others because God is living to meet our needs. (See Isaiah 31:10; 64:4; 2 Chronicles 16:9; Psalm 23:6.)
>
> We are satisfied with all that God will be for me in the ages to come. This truth makes you free. Free from the short shallow suicidal pleasures of sin, and free for the sacrifices of mission and ministry, these cause people to give glory to God. That freedom, that love, and that glory must be the aim of our lives.
>
> Why did God make us? He had a delight in making something outside himself that would communicate a fullness of his divinity, flow out, emanate, and display his glory. He wanted to fill it with his own skill and beauty and then let it shine forth. That's what God did with our creation. He has never changed his mind. He will fulfill that delight by our resurrection and removal of sin (Isa. 43:7). There is a definite continuity.[2]

Dr. Piper ends his description of heaven with an imaginative encounter with the glories that lie ahead in the Celestial City.

> And as I knelt beside the brook
> To drink eternal life I took
> A glance across the golden grass

  GOD'S PRESCRIPTION *for* HEALING

And saw my dog old Blackie fast
As she could come she leaped the stream
Almost—and what a happy gleam
Was in her eye. I knelt to drink
and knew that I was on the brink
of endless joy and everywhere
I turned I saw a wonder there
A big man running on the lawn
That's old John Younge with both legs on
The blind can see a bird on wing
The dumb can lift their voice and sing.
The diabetic eats at will
The coronary runs uphill.
The lame can walk, the deaf can hear
The cancer-ridden bone is clear
Arthritic joints are lithe and free
And every pain has ceased to be
And every sorrow deep within
And every trace of lingering sin
Is gone and all that's left is joy
And endless ages to employ
The mind and heart and understand
And love the sovereign Lord who planned
That it should take eternity
To lavish all his grace on me.

O God of wonder, God of might
Grant us some elevated sight
Of endless days and let us see
The joy of what is yet to be
And may your future make us free
And guard us by the hope that we
Through grace on lands that you restore
And justified for evermore.[3]

In the Book of 2 Timothy, Paul was soon to face his execution by Nero. When we have grasped the message of eternity for our lives, we can see why Paul had such eager anticipation and confidence that the Savior would give him the blessed realities of heaven, just as He promised. In confidence Paul asserted: "I know whom I have believed and am persuaded that He is able to keep what I have committed to Him until that Day" (2 Tim. 1:12). Paul believed what he knew to be true!

GOD'S PRESCRIPTION *for* HEALING

Conclusion

FINAL WORDS

I shall never believe that God plays dice with the world.
—ALBERT EINSTEIN, 1947[1]

It might seem somewhat odd to end a book that touches on God's eternal purpose for you with the reflections of Einstein alongside Jesus' admonition that we become childlike. However, in a way, nothing could be more pertinent or to the point for us. Einstein's investigations into the clockwork of the universe seem complex to the point of being incomprehensible for most people. The astonishing fact is that though it is difficult to view it as such, he merely asked hugely simple, "transparent, innocent questions."[2] These were questions that most of us choose to forget as we leave our childhood for our allegedly "sophisticated" lives as adults.

Hearing God Think

What are we saying? Certainly, Einstein's theories are not simple to understand, and the complexity of the human design, likewise, is not easy to fully explain. Yet, what we must come to see is that underneath it all is a very simple principle: God created us and the entire universe that surrounds us. To see that is to live in wonder. Einstein spoke often of God, and he surveyed God's handiwork in the cosmos with such wonder. How is it that we do not? It was in his deepest appreciation for the apparent symmetry, beauty, and perfect design of space, time, matter, and energy that Einstein looked for answers and preserved in his own heart the deepest respect for the Creator's wisdom. "And what his life showed, and his work, is that when the answers are simple too, *then you hear God thinking*" (emphasis added).[3]

The evidence of the Creator's mastery is, in many ways, immediately before the eyes of those who can look at it with childlike wonder through

197

the simplicity and clarity that genuine gratitude provides. This is the ability to approach "the stuff of life" with excitement and humility before its underlying truth. We definitely need our intellect and tools to look at God's creation, but real understanding means coming to God Himself—and His handiwork—as children, relinquishing selfishness and pride. This Jesus told us. This means appreciating the Creator's vision of life in a way that is so integral to the soul that it is expressed reflexively in eyes that widen, hands that seek to touch, a probing mind full of excited interest and awe, and a heart full of worshipful adoration. Only with such a heart could we ever hope to truly see the Father's impression on our joys, our paths through hurt, our salvation, our eternal future—and our healing.

The Lord Has a Plan for Your Cut Finger, and for Your Life!

In the beginning God created the heavens and the earth.

—GENESIS 1:1

Bless the LORD, O my soul;
And all that is within me, bless His holy name!
Bless the LORD, O my soul,
And forget not all His benefits:
Who forgives all your iniquities,
Who heals all your diseases,
Who redeems your life from destruction,
Who crowns you with lovingkindness and tender
    mercies,
Who satisfies your mouth with good things,
So that your youth is renewed like the eagle's.

—PSALM 103:1–5, EMPHASIS ADDED

God is the Creator, and God is the Healer of His creation. In David's song of praise and adoration for the many graces that the Lord bestows upon us, we are reminded that God forgives our sins, protects us, sustains and comforts us, and renews our hearts, minds, and bodies. God certainly heals us. He has a plan for each one of us, in this moment and for eternity. Yet, to see God, we must learn that our suffering is as meaningful as any triumph over infirmity or adversity. To understand this too is healing.

In John 9 is the story of a man, blind from birth, who saw Jesus as He truly is and believed in Him. Others around this man suffered from a much more debilitating blindness—spiritual blindness—and could neither see nor glorify the Lord. We too are so often spiritually blind and cannot see our own need to be healed and to embrace God's purpose in our lives.

It is in seeing your need for healing and supplicating God, worshiping Him, that you find your purpose and the purpose of the universe—of all creation. Christianity can be summarized in one word: *faith*. Faith that we live in Him and He in us. From this flows our love for Him as Creator and Savior, and we look forward to being with Him for eternity. In faith, we can come to know His purpose for our lives, for our suffering, and for our healing.

The human body is a marvel that exhibits astonishing and profound natural capacities for healing, as well as for the maintenance of a state of total health—a state of balance. They are all present from the beginning in the design of our DNA. The time will come when you must appeal to the knowledge and expertise of professionals trained to treat the ailments of

GOD'S

> WE DEFINITELY NEED our intellect and tools to look at God's creation but, real understanding means coming to God Himself—and His handiwork—as children, relinquishing selfishness and pride.

FOR HEALING

PRESCRIPTION

your body. God's plan for healing is seen working through the fingers of others. But is that enough? Healing is somewhat more difficult to achieve without some commitment and action by each potential patient. God made you a steward of your body, accountable for your health. He shows you how to maintain the gift that He has bestowed upon you. We settle for mere adequacy when God wants us to have abundance physically, mentally, and spiritually.

How aware are you that your mind can be an instrument to help or to hinder physical healing? In some cases, it is the mind itself that is ill; it too may need healing. Human pride and a lack of alignment with God will blind you spiritually and will be the source of a much deeper illness, a spiritual malaise, that can only be healed by God. God can heal your heart when you seek Him, and He can also heal your body directly as well when you have faith that can move mountains. You, along with every other person who ever lived, have experienced healing from the day of your birth. You have a present need of healing in one way or another, and you will continue to require healing until the day that you meet the Lord face to face in His perfection—the ultimate healing.

Healing and Wonder

This life's dim windows of the soul
Distort the heavens from pole to pole
And leads you to believe a lie
When you see with, not through, the eye.

—William Blake[4]

We exist, and we exist according to God's plan. God is omniscient, so good, His design so impenetrable and marvelous, and His purpose for us so glorious that we should be in ceaseless awe. God has created us as physical, mental, and spiritual beings with a beautiful, irreducibly complex design for reactions to injury. Yet we are often too blind to perceive it. We take nearly everything for granted and fail to acknowledge the wisdom of the One who is the Beginning and the End, the wisdom of God the Creator, of Jesus, God Incarnate, and the Holy Spirit, the Comforter.

The physical body you possess, and its integrated processes for healing, is your practical proof of His existence, His design of, and His love and continuing concern for His creation. God has endowed you, allowed you, the ability to see Him, to see His mind, and even to assist in healing. However, your understanding and effort must invariably remain tethered to God's holy purpose and guidance. "The fear of the LORD is the beginning of wisdom, and the knowledge of the Holy One is understanding. For by me your days will be multiplied, and years of life will be added to you" (Prov. 9:10–11).

Pride

Introducing his lecture on the "Strange Theory of Light and Matter," the renowned physicist Richard Feynman stated, "What I am going to tell you about is what we teach our physics students in the third or fourth year of graduate school....It is my task to convince you not to turn away because you don't understand it. You see, my physics students don't understand it....That is because I don't understand it. Nobody does."[5] Human pride will often crow that we know all, or can know all—but, really, only the Creator understands His creation, how it functions, how it heals, and how to heal it. If we could explain it, we would have no need for God; if we could explain it, there would be no beautiful mind of God to countenance. If we could explain it, there would be no beginning, no design, and no mystery or majesty. If we could explain it, there would be no anointing or eternal home. If we could explain it, we would be mere products of chance—accidental, mere cosmic mishaps—and we would have no purpose. If we could explain it, life would have no meaning.

Humanity, with an overabundance of faith in itself, its reasoning mind, and its science and manipulation of nature, has refused to acknowledge the God made evident in the healing of a cut finger. Instead, much of humanity has elected to refuse the Creator entrance into explanations of the integration and intrinsic complexity of life. Refusing to acknowledge God as He reveals Himself in our design may well be one of our greatest sins.

> ## GOD'S
> **YOU WILL CONTINUE to require healing until the day that you meet the Lord face to face in His perfection— the ultimate healing.**
>
> FOR HEALING
>
> ## PRESCRIPTION

Rather than simply being mere outcroppings of chance and bundles of chemical reactions, as the materialistic science of our day purports, we are created in His image with the capacity for love. It is in our understanding of advanced molecular systems that this becomes all the more evident, if we are willing to humble ourselves and peer at the design with spiritual clarity.

In fact, details of that design clearly refute any recourse to godless accident or chance in our emergence on the planet. The universe—from the outer galaxies, to the earth's fragile stratosphere, to the busy biological hothouse of the rainforest canopies, to the potatoes you eat and the digestive processes by which you transform them into nourishment—is, of a piece, the most eloquent testimony to a design far too complex to have arisen by any other means than God's own blueprint. Humanity cannot understand it fully and certainly cannot re-create it. However, in the anthropocentric world of our own imagining, humankind has averted its inherent accountability and seeks for answers to healing in its own corruptible wisdom. This has led to abomination, and it will lead to demise. Our blindness to God's thumbprint at all levels of our constitution is our folly.

Alignment to God

As John Piper has pointed out, God can lead us to pierce our spiritual cataracts and overcome the distortions of our souls through God's future grace. When you turn from satisfaction in yourself and things, and turn to satisfaction in Him, God speaks to you personally. It begins with a belief in His promises for you, and then the Holy Spirit comes to attend to that belief and to invigorate you within it. God's future grace is His assistance with your problems and the difficulties of life and its responsibilities.

There are so many sources of our spiritual cataracts, but they all are symptoms of sin and our divergence from God's will and plan. Human pride will not allow that we are lost and dissociated from God, or that there are problems that have no solution outside of His grace. Pride is the agent of our spiritual blindness. In addition to pride, an unforgiving attitude, defiance, escape into myriad addictions and compulsions, daily distractions, a need to transcend and control, envy, and a resort to the habitual, uninspired, legalistic practice of faith rather than engaged, vibrant, living faith all serve to cloud the eye to God's pure light. The most important aspect of your healing, in Christ, is humbling yourself and surrendering to His purpose and will. Blindness by pride is why most of us don't come to really know Jesus and why we are not able to claim our healing.

The ostensible aim of chiropractic is to put the skull and spine in proper alignment to affect proper body carriage and overall muscle and organ health. In much the same way, Jonathan Edwards says, we need to align ourselves to God to receive His blessing. Most of us are out of alignment with God—too concerned with ourselves, too prideful, and too consumed by fear and anxiety. The Lord delights to bless us and heal us, however. The key is humility and surrender to Him is this: "Humble yourselves in the sight of the Lord, and He will lift you up" (James 4:10). When you come to the Lord through His anointed Word and prayer, rest in His redemption, and abandon yourself to His power, His presence, and His love, then you experience *shalom*—true peace—and are aligned with God. Alignment with God is the only position that makes His healing power a reality in your life. God wants you to find your contentment in Him.

In God's healing, you relinquish yourself. You release and abandon yourself in faith, and, through the Holy Spirit, you move from a state lacking control into a state of control and peace in Him. You come to embrace God's mentality, His focus and vision, and His purpose. This is being united with Him by faith. *This is the healing vision of your life—who and what you are in Jesus Christ—and without it, without saving union with Him, you perish.* This is the vision that the Holy Spirit inspires through the Word of God, directing you to take on the mind of Christ (Phil. 2:5).

> # GOD'S
> ### ALIGNMENT WITH God is the only position that makes His healing power a reality in your life.
>
> FOR HEALING
>
> # PRESCRIPTION

God's Prescription

Through your episodes of illness and subsequent healing, the Lord wants you to learn to trust in Him rather than misplacing trust in yourself. This is the whole purpose of your mortal existence on earth. You can become stronger in pain and adversity, and the whole source of your strength is recognizing, receiving, and relying on the Holy Spirit. Fear and sin can allow the devil to exploit your physical weaknesses when you are not in close communication with God—when you are spiritually blind.

Illness is more than injury to, and weakness of, a biological mechanism; it is part of spiritual warfare. "For we do not wrestle against flesh and blood, but against principalities, against powers, against the rulers of the darkness of this age, against spiritual hosts of wickedness in the heavenly places" (Eph. 6:12).

We have God's promise that "I am the LORD who heals you" (Exod. 15:26). Belief in God's promises promotes future grace. It is faith that pleases God. "Without faith it is impossible to please Him, for he who comes to God must believe that He is, and that He is a rewarder of those who diligently seek Him" (Heb. 11:6). God rewards a godly life, a life of faith, both here and in eternity. Faith is of the greatest importance in God's plan for your deliverance and healing (Ps. 91). As a steward of the body He has designed, He will bless you with the capacity to serve Him faithfully during the run of your life.

Strong faith in God and His salvation, belief in the promises of His Word, and intimate communication in worship and prayer provide the basis for a healthy body and mind, and their healing when necessary. It is the purpose-driven life that prepares for eternity through the stewardship of body, mind, and spirit while we inhabit the earth.

God summons us to hear all that His Word says and to receive all that His Word promises. "My son, give attention to my words....For they are life to those who find them, and health to all their flesh" (Prov. 4:20, 22). God gives us a choice—the choice of life or death. "I have set before you life and death, blessing and cursing; therefore choose life, that both you and your descendants may live" (Deut. 30:19). First He provides the design nestled in your DNA; then He asks for your surrender and obedience. Jesus is your shining example of this: "And being found in appearance as a man, He humbled Himself and became obedient to the point of death, even the death of the cross" (Phil. 2:8). Jesus made the sacrifice that you might live now and forever: "Who Himself bore our sins in His own body on the tree, that we, having died to sins, might live for righteousness—by whose stripes you were healed" (1 Pet. 2:24).

Alignment brings blessing and healing, but *the key to healing is in acknowledging the wisdom of the Creator, having faith in Him, and appreciating and loving Him.* Without these, it is not possible to please God (Heb. 11:6), nor is it possible to be healed. The Pharisees of Jesus' day conformed rigidly to God's law, but they did not see Him and did not accept Him. With a faith so real and earnest that merely touching the hem of His garment was sufficient, a woman who had been suffering for years found healing (Mark 5:25–32). Her faith made her well. With faith the size of a tiny mustard seed, nothing is impossible (Matt. 17:20). As the substance of things hoped for and the evidence of things not seen, you can move mountains and be healed. Once you find a promise in God's Word, seek its fulfillment in your life by faith. "Ask, and it will be given to you" (Matt 7:7). You had faith in the Lord for your salvation; likewise seek Him for your healing. Be obedient to His Word, but exercise obedience out of love and surrender: "You are My friends if you do whatever I command you. No longer do I call you servants" (John 15:14–15).

Fear and worry can blind you to God's promises, plan, and purpose for your life. Your attitude, and how you approach Him, might well be the biggest factor in your healing. You come closer to God through your faith and an attitude of wonder, of thanksgiving, and of appreciation—*storge*. "Faith comes by hearing, and hearing by the word of God" (Rom. 10:17). Yet, as we read in Mark 4:19, the Word is lost on those who are consumed by the concerns of the world. It is with a spirit of *storge* that we may seek our healing.

S.T.O.R.G.E.

S   Spirit, the Holy Spirit made present in your life when you ask for unction

T   Thanksgiving and appreciation, worshiping God for the bad as well as the good

O   Demonstrating your love for God by Obedience

R   Righteousness

G   Goodness, godliness, and gentleness—products of the Holy Spirit within

E   Enthusiasm for God, the proof of your being in Christ

My Prayer for Heather

The main concern in my life concerns my wife, Heather. For seven years she has fought a tenacious microbacterium that has caused an occasionally debilitating chronic bronchiectesis. In the evenings before our dinner, we bow our heads, and I offer this prayer for Heather's healing—for her complete healing in the five ways that we have become familiar with in the preceding pages.

So we pray:

Dear Lord,

We thank You for who You are, the glorious Creator. Thank You, Lord, for Your beautiful mind in all Your majestic creation, including my wonderful wife. I thank You that I have her to share my life with and to love.

We are in awe of our wonderful bodies that You have created. Through Your intelligent design and the irreducible complexity of physical mechanisms, we are able to experience healing and live a full life. We worship You.

Lord, we want to thank You also for all the knowledge, techniques, and wisdom that You have offered humanity to be used in assisting in healing one other and easing the suffering of others. And we ask, Lord, that people in need everywhere, in addition to Heather, may benefit from these remarkable advances.

Lord, we ask that You show us the way to align ourselves to You through our lifestyle, eating, and exercise to best receive Your healing touch. Yet, Lord, may we seek to align ourselves with You spiritually more than physically. May we take on Your heart and invite You to live within us. We want You to become our Savior and, as our soul prospers, to be our guide to good health as well.

Help us, Lord, to release negative thoughts and to attain a spirit of caring and love for others. May we be rejuvenated as we care for others with humility.

Lord, we recognize that some instances of healing that occur are not very probable in most

eyes, yet we acknowledge with certainty that they are the product of the Creator's intelligent design in His creation.

Lord, heal Heather so she can continue as a mentor to the many people who depend upon her and as a grandmother to her growing grandchildren. With all that is within us, we cry out to You for this healing. You know that our prayers represent only the alignment of ourselves to You and our willingness to rest in Your redemption, by the power of the Holy Spirit. May we lie closer to Your feet and depend on You and Your salvation. May we want nothing other than to know You more, now and forever. What we really seek is a greater intimacy with You in this moment and lasting through eternity.

First Corinthians 13:12 tells us that now we see through a glass darkly; but then we shall see Him face to face and shall know as we are known. May we try to worship You now as we imagine we will be worshiping You then. Let us find ourselves worshiping You now as we come to You for Heather's healing. Let us find ourselves totally in Your hands for our healing, for our future—for our everything. Teach us to be people living in worship, praise, and thanksgiving to You.

This is my prayer for Heather, that she obtain this eternal life now and that she be physically healed, if that be Your will.

While we cry out to You, we seek not to change the mind of God, but to change our minds to align ourselves to You in a greater way. The hopes we hold for ourselves in healing are bound in the desire to draw closer to You, just as the apostle Paul did with the thorn in his flesh, which You did not allow to be healed. Though we ask for healing in a very selfish manner, may we rather cast ourselves on Your mercy. So, dear Lord, let me pray that Heather's lungs be healed, bringing us closer to You, for now and for eternity. We pray that we may be healed in this more important way—in the way that we'll have You now and share You for eternity.

Amen.

NOTES

Introduction

1. Ronald W. Clark, *Einstein: The Life and Times* (New York: Avon Books, 1984), 143–144.

2. "George W. Bush's Testimony," January 2003, www.psalms150-6.com/srories/test georgewbush.html (accessed March 3, 2003).

Chapter 1
An Intelligent Design—and Designer

1. Werner Gitt, "The Flight of Migratory Birds," September 1986, www.icr.org/pubs/imp/imp-159.htm (accessed July 12, 2003).

2. G. Ramel, "When and How Do Birds Migrate," June 2003, www.earthlife.net/birds/migration2.html (accessed July 12, 2003).

3. Ibid.

4. Ibid.

Chapter 2
Disease and Healing

1. Edmund D. Pellegrino and David C. Thomasa, *Helping and Healing: Religious Commitment in Health Care* (Washington, DC: Georgetown University Press, 1997), 20.

2. Daniel E. Fountain, *God, Medicine & Miracles: The Spiritual Factor in Healing* (Wheaton, IL: Harold Shaw Publishers, 1999), 39.

Chapter 3
Irreducible Complexity, Impeccable Design

1. William Blake, from *Auguries of Influence*, c. 1800.

2. James P. Gills and Tom Woodward, *Darwinism Under the Microscope* (Lake Mary, FL: Charisma House, 2002).

3. Michael Behe, *Darwin's Black Box: The Biochemical Challenge to Evolution* (New York: The Free Press, 1996), 239.

4. Richard A. Swenson, *More Than Meets the Eye: Fascinating*

Glimpses of God's Power and Design (Colorado Springs, CO: NavPress, 2000).

    5. John R. Cameron, James G. Skofronick, and Roderick M. Grant, *Physics of the Body* (Madison, WI: Medical Physics Publishing, 1999), 38. Quoted in Swenson, *More Than Meets the Eye*, 21.

    6. David Rosevear, "The Myth of Chemical Evolution," *Impact* (July 1999): iv. Quoted in Swenson, *More Than Meets the Eye*, 21.

    7. Matthew Kuure-Kinsey and Beth McCooey, "The Basics of Recombinant DNA," Fall 2000, www.rpi.edu/dept/chem-eng/Biotech-Environ/Projects00/rdna.html (accessed May 15, 2003).

    8. Quoted at "Christian Apologetics and Research Ministry," www.carm.org/evo_questions/darwineye.htm (accessed December 10, 2003).

Chapter 4
Examples of Design for Balance, Repair, and Cure

    1. Personal interview with Dr. Rowsey, May 30, 2003.

    2. William R. Clark, *At War Within: The Double Edged Sword of Immunity* (New York: Oxford University Press, 1995), 3.

    3. Jacqueline Sharon, *Basic Immunology* (Baltimore, MD: Williams & Wilkins, 1998), 3.

    4. Ibid., 4.

    5. Clark, *At War Within*, 36.

    6. Mark H. Beers, et al., eds., *Merck Manual of Diagnosis and Therapy* (Whitehouse Station, NY: Merck & Company, 1999), 1002.

    8. Stewart Sell and Edward E. Max, *Immunology, Immunopathology, and Immunity* (Washington, DC: ASM Press, 2001), 4.

    9. Ibid., 3.

    10. Ivan M. Roitt, Jonathan Brostoff, and David K. Male, *Immunology* (St. Louis, MO: Gower Medical Publications, 1985), 5–6.

    11. Sell and Max, *Immunology, Immunopathology, and Immunity*, 4.

    12. Clark, *At War Within*, 39.

    13. Ibid., 40.

    14. Ibid., 43.

15. Ibid., 46.

16. Ibid., 51.

17. Ibid., 53–54.

18. "Who Says SARS is Mutating?", *The Globe and Mail*, June 19, 2003, www.theglobeandmail.com?servlet/story/RTGAM.20030619.wsars0618/BNPrint/International.

19. Clark, *At War Within*, 40.

20. Cedric Mims, *The War Within Us* (San Diego, CA: Academic Press, 2000), 52.

21. Ibid., 83.

22. Ibid., 167–168.

23. *Merck Manual of Diagnosis and Therapy*, 1023–1024.

24. Douglas W. Brodie, "The Nature of Cancer," www.drbrodie.com/cancer-nature.htm (accessed March 3, 2003).

25. Mims, *The War Within Us*, 182.

26. Sell and Max, *Immunology, Immunopathology, and Immunity*, 676.

27. Mims, *The War Within Us*, 177.

Chapter 5
Designed for Health

1. Stephen Hawking, *A Brief History of Time: From the Big Bang to Black Holes* (New York: Bantam, 1988), 174.

2. Ravi Zacharias, *Recapture the Wonder* (Nashville, TN: Integrity Publishers, 2003), xv.

Chapter 6
Physician-Assisted Healing

1. John Bartlett, *Familiar Quotations*, edited by Emily Morison Beck (Boston: Little, Brown and Company, 1980), 591.

2. James P. Gills, Robert Fenzel, and Robert G. Martin, *Cataract Surgery: The State of the Art.* (Thorofare, NJ: SLACK Incorporated, 1998), 19.

3. Ibid., 2–3.

4. Richard Falk, "Genetics and Human Life—Part 2," 2000, www.biologie.uni-hamburg.de/b-online/library/falk/GenHumanLife/

genetics-2.htm (accessed July 14, 2003).

5. "Cloning of Genetically Engineered Molecules," April 1997, www.inventors.about.com/gi/dynamic/offsite.htm (accessed July 13, 2003).

6. "Recombinant DNA and Gene Cloning," March 7, 2003, www.users.rcn.com/jkimball.ma.ultranet/BiologyPages/R/RecombinantDNA.html (accessed June 1, 2003).

7. Falk, "Genetics and Human Life—Part 2."

8. "Cloning of Genetically Engineered Molecules."

9. "Frontiers in Immunology: Genetic Engineering," information from the NCI and NIAID, http://allergies.about.com/library/blncinihimmunegenetic.htm?iam=eboom_SKD&terms=Recombinant+dna (accessed May 15, 2003).

10. Ibid.

11. "Clinical Trial Results Suggest Recombinant DNA Gene Therapy is a Safe and Effective Treatment for Patients with 'Inoperable' Heart Disease," www.ctsnet.org/doc/3148 (accessed May 15, 2003).

12. Stephen Willingham, "Scientists Weave Spider Silk Into New Bulletproof Vests," September 2000, www.nationaldefensemagazine.org/article.cfm?Id=255 (accessed May 15, 2003).

13. Ibid.

14. S. Kay Toombs, *Handbook of Phenomenology and Medicine* (Dordrecht, The Netherlands: Kluwer Academic Publishers, 2001), 97.

15. Pellegrino and Thomasa, *Helping and Healing*, 20.

16. Ibid., 88.

17. Toombs, *Handbook of Phenomenology and Medicine*, 123.

18. Ibid., 117.

19. Pellegrino and Thomasa, *Helping and Healing*, 16.

20. Ibid.

21. Ibid.

22. Audrey W. Davis, *Dr. Kelly of Hopkins* (Baltimore, MD: The Johns Hopkins Press, 1959), 39–40.

23. Ibid, 29.

24. Ibid., 42.

25. Ibid., 53.

26. Ibid., 81–82.

27. Ibid.

28. Ibid., 3.

29. Pellegrino and Thomasa, *Helping and Healing*, 151.

30. Quoted in John Piper, *Brothers, We Are Not Professionals* (Nashville, TN: Broadman & Holman Publishers, 2002), 159.

31. Mark Griffiths, "The Emperor's Transgenic Clothes," January 1999, www.binternet.com/~nipwessex/Documents/gmlemmings.htm (accessed May 2, 2003).

32. Quoted at "Famous Quotes," www.1famousquote.com/f/maxfrisch-1.htm (accessed November 25, 2003).

33. Tim LaHaye, *The Battle for the Mind* (Old Tappan, NJ: Fleming H. Revell Co., 1980), 83.

34. Ibid.

Chapter 7
You Are Your Own Best Physician

1. James P. Gills and James Pitzer Gills III, *Temple Maintenance* (Tarpon Springs, FL: Love Press, 1989).

2. Charles Lasley, *120 Years of Longevity* (Self-published, 2000).

3. Richard Steiner, "An Ounce of Prevention," 2002, www.geocities.com/b_sherback/matol_update7.htm (accessed July 29, 2003).

4. Terry Dorian, *Total Health* (Lake Mary, FL: Siloam, 1996), 74.

5. Quoted at "The Quotable Franklin," www.ushistory.org/franklin/quotable/quote67.htm (accessed June 7, 2003).

6. Dorian, *Total Health*, 137.

7. Ted Broer, *Maximum Energy* (Lake Mary, FL: Siloam, 1999), 4.

8. Ibid., 14.

9. Paul Huddle and Roch Frey, *Starting Out Triathlon* (Miami, FL: Meyer and Meyer Sport, 2003), 94.

10. Ibid., 110.

11. Ibid., 123.

12. Ibid.

13. Ibid., vii.

14. Ibid., viii.

15. Ibid., xiii.

16. Ibid., xiv.

17. Ibid., xv.

18. Ibid., 13.

19. Ibid., 16.

20. Ibid., 27.

21. Reginald Cherry, *Healing Prayer* (Nashville, TN: Thomas Nelson Publishers, 1999), xii.

21. Broer, *Maximum Energy*, 10.

22. Ibid., 11.

23. Ibid., 18.

24. Ibid., 12.

25. Don Colbert, *The Bible Cure for Back Pain* (Lake Mary, FL: Siloam, 2002), 1.

26. Broer, *Maximum Energy*, 14.

Chapter 8
Mental Alignment With the Creator's Design

1. Ben Carson, *Gifted Hands* (Grand Rapids, MI: Zondervan, 1990), 53.

2. Ibid., 56.

3. Ibid., 60.

4. See, for example: Chris Woolston, "Illness: The Mind-Body Connection," *Lifestyle and Wellness*, March 2003, http://blueprint .bluecrossmn.com/topic/depills (accessed May 30, 2003); "Breast Cancer and Depression," *Artimis*—Feature Article, November 2000, www .hopkinsmedicine.org/breastcenter/artemis/200011/feature7.html (accessed May 30, 2003); and Chris Woolston, "Depression and Heart Disease," *Ills & Conditions*, March 2003, http://blueprint.bluecrossmn .com/topic/depheart (accessed May 30, 2003).

5. "Mind and Body Are Inseparable," Mental Health, A Report of the Surgeon General—Chapter 1, www.surgeon general.gov/Library/ MentalHealth/chapter1/sec1.html.

6. William Collinge, "The Dance of Soma and Psyche," Mind/ Body Medicine, Health World Online, www.healthy.net/asp/templates/

article (accessed June 9, 2003).

7. Andrew Newberg, Eugene D'Aquili, and Vince Rause, "Why God Won't Go Away: Brain Science and the Biology of Belief," complied by Thomas B. Roberts and Paula Jo Hruby at Council on Spiritual Practices, 2002, www.csp.org/chrestomathy/why_god.html (accessed March 25, 2002).

8. Daniel Fountain, *God, Medicine, and Miracles* (Wheaton, IL: Harold Shaw Publishers, 1999).

9. Rob Shaw, "Publix Store in Lutz Evacuated After Outbreak of Coughing," *Tampa Tribune*, Tuesday, June 3, 2003, 5.

10. W. Douglas Brodie, "The Cancer Personality: Its Importance in Healing," 2003, www.drbrodie.com/cancer-personality.htm (accessed March 20, 2003).

11. Larry Burkett, *Nothing to Fear: The Key to Cancer Survival* (Chicago, IL: Moody Publishers, 2003).

12. Reese Patterson, "Illness As a State of Woundedness," excerpts from a talk given to a medical group at a St. Louis hospital, October 26, 1995.

13. Collinge, "The Dance of Soma and Psyche."

14. James P. Gills, *Rx for Worry* (Tarpon Springs, FL: Love Press, 1998).

15. "Brother Lawrence: The Practice of the Presence of God," http://homechurch.com/spirituality/brother_lawrence.html (accessed December 3, 2003).

16. "Is Laughter the Best Medicine?" *Quest* Vol. 3, No. 4, Fall 1996, www.mdausa.org/publications?Quest/q34laughter.html (accessed September 22, 2003).

17. "But Seriously Folks...Humor Can Keep You Healthy," *Readers Digest*, September 2003, 62–71.

18. "Norman Cousins: The Power of Belief," www.potentialsmedia.com/NormanCousins.html (accessed September 22, 2003).

19. Peter McWilliams, *Chicken Soup for the Surviving Soul*, quoted at "Norman Cousins: Read On & Laugh," January 1999, www.myelitis.org/tmic/archive/22/0993.html (accessed September 22, 2003).

20. Annette Goodheart, *Laughter Therapy: How to Laugh*

About Everything in Your Life That Isn't Really Funny (Santa Barbara, CA: Less Stress Press, 1994).

21. Ibid.

22. Ibid.

23. Harold G. Koenig, Michael E. McCullough, and David B. Larson, *Handbook of Religion and Health* (New York: Oxford University Press, 2001), 205.

24. Ibid., 211.

25. Ibid., 205.

26. James A. Avery, "The 'H' in Hospice Stands for Hope," *Today's Christian Doctor,* Summer 2003, 24–27.

27. Dutch Shields, *Tell Your Heart to Beat Again* (Ventura, CA: Gospel Light, 2002), 20.

28. Robert J. Morgan, *Real Stories for the Soul* (Nashville, TN: Thomas Nelson Publishers, 2000), 53–55.

Chapter 9
The Prescription for Inner Healing

1. Usha Lee McFarling, "Doctors Find Power of Faith Hard to Ignore," December 23, 1998, www.tennessean.com/health/stories.98/trends1223.htm (accessed March 11, 2003).

2. Studies include the following titles: "Religion and Blood Pressure," "Religion and Survival," and "Religion and Immune Function." See H. G. Koenig, et al., "The Relationship Between Religious Activities and Blood Pressure in Older Adults," *International Journal of Psychiatry in Medicine* 28 (1998): 189–213, www.dukespiritualityandhealth.org/pastreports.html (accessed March 10, 2003).

3. H. G. Koenig, et al., "Does Religious Attendance Prolong Survival?" *Journal of Gerentology: Medical Sciences* 54A(7) (1999): M370-M376, www.dukespiritualityandhealth.org/pastreports.html (accessed March 10, 2003).

4. Randolph C. Byrd, "Positive Therapeutic Effects of Intercessory Prayer in a Coronary Care Unit Population," *Southern Medical Journal* 81 (1998): 826–828, www.godandscience.org/apologetics/smj.html (accessed March 10, 2003).

5. Ibid.

6. Ibid.

7. Dale A. Matthews, et al., "Effects of Intercessory Prayer on Patients With Rheumatoid Arthritis," *Southern Medical Journal* 93 (2003): 1177–1185.

8. Ibid.

9. William Standish Reed, *Surgery of the Soul: Healing the Whole Person* (Tampa, FL: Christian Medical Foundation Inc., 1987), 53.

10. H. Helm, et al., "Effects of Private Religious Activity on Mortality of Elderly Disabled and Nondisabled Adults," *Journal of Gerontology (Medical Sciences)* 55A (2000): M400-M405, www.dukespiritualityandhealth.org/pastreports.html (accessed March 10, 2003).

12. Ibid.

13. "The Forgotten Factor: Faith," St. Joseph's Mercy of Macomb, www.stjoe-macomb.com/services/faith.shtml (accessed August 15, 2002).

14. Larry Dossey, "Prayer As a Healing Force," July 1996, www.healthy.net/asp/templates/article.asp (accessed August 15, 2002).

15. Harold G. Koenig, Michael E. McCullough, and David B. Larson, *Handbook of Religion and Health* (New York: Oxford University Press, 2001), 254–255.

16. James P. Gills, *The Prayerful Spirit* (Tarpon Springs, FL: Love Press, 1995).

17. See for example: Linda K. George, "The Health-Promoting Effects of Social Bonds," www.cossa.org/linda%20george.pdf (accessed October 6, 2003); Sophia P. Glezos, "Social Relationships, Connectedness, and Health: The Bonds That Heal," Summary of a Presentation by Lisa F. Berkman, Harvard School of Public Health, 5/22/1997, http://obssr.od.nih.gov/Publications/SOCIAL.HTM (accessed May 30, 2003).

18. Ben Carson, *Think Big* (Grand Rapids, MI: Zondervan, 1993), 95–96.

19. Quoted in "The Best Medicine in the World—Love and Care," Pityriasis Rubra Pilaris: How a Support Group Can Help You, http://personal.nbnet.nb.ca/mdetjld/Webpage/S_group.htm (accessed May 30, 2003).

20. Reported at "Depression and Cancer," McMan's Depression

and Bipolar Web, http://www.mcmanweb.com/article-43.htm (accessed February 20, 2003).

21. Personal interview with Dr. James Rowsey, October 10, 2003.

Chapter 10
Spiritual Alignment With the Creator

1. John Piper, *God's Passion for His Glory* (Wheaton, IL: Crossway Books, 1998).

2 Ibid., 111.

3. James P. Gills, *Spiritual Blindness* (pending—yet unpublished, soon to be so).

4. *Merriam-Webster Online,* http://www.m-w.com/cgi-bin/dictionary (accessed December 2, 2003); Hebrew word *qodesh*, http://bible.crosswalk.com/Lexicons/Hebrew/heb.cgi?number=06944&version=kjv (accessed December 2, 2003); Greek word *hagiazo*, http://bible.crosswalk.com/Lexicons/Greek/grk.cgi?number=37&version=kjv (accessed December 2, 2003).

5. R. T. Kendall, *Total Forgiveness* (Lake Mary, FL: Charisma House, 2002).

6. Joni Eareckson Tada, *Choices, Changes* (Grand Rapids, MI: Zondervan Publishing, 1986), 176.

7. Ibid., 179.

8. Joni Eareckson Tada, *When Is It Right to Die?* (Grand Rapids, MI: Zondervan Publishing, 1992), 177.

Chapter 11
Unveiling the New Heart

1. Henry Scougal, *The Life of God in The Soul of Man* (Ross-shire, Scotland: Christian Focus Publications, 2002).

2. Ibid.

3. John Piper, *All Things for Good, Part One,* June 9, 2002, www.desiringgod.org/library/sermons/02/060902.html (accessed September 20, 2003).

4. Ibid.

5. "The Seven Deadly Sins," June 18, 1996, found at www.rushman.org/seven/ (accessed August 2, 2003).

6. James P. Gills, *Imaginations: More Than You Think* (Tarpon Springs, FL: Love Press, 2002).

7. Rick Warren, *The Purpose-Driven Life* (Grand Rapids, MI: Zondervan, 2002), 17.

Chapter 13
Improbable Healing in the Scriptures

1. Personal interview with Dr. James Rowsey, September 6, 2003.

Chapter 14
Modern Examples of Improbable Healing

1. "Lance Armstrong—A Biography," www.lancearmstrong .com/lance/online2nsf/html/bio (accessed July 7, 2003).

2. Reese Patterson, "Proposal for a Standardized Protocol in the Medical Intervention With Pre and Post Operative Esophageal and Stomach Cancer Patients," Prepared for National Cancer Institutes' Stomach/Esophageal Cancers Progress Review Group Roundtable Meeting, Washington D.C., May 5–7, 2002.

3. Lynn Eib, *When God and Cancer Meet* (Wheaton, IL: Tyndale House Publishers, 2002).

4. *The Twelve Steps—A Spiritual Journey* (San Diego CA: Recovery Publications, 1988), xiii–xiv.

5. Geraldine Taylor, *Pastor Hsi* (Singapore: Overseas Mission Fellowship, 1989), 52.

6. Ibid.

Chapter 16
Designed for Eternity

1. Charles Newbold, *The Crucified Ones* (Monterey, TN: Ingathering Press, 1990).

2. Tada, *When Is It Right to Die?*, 180.

3. Tada, *Choices, Changes*, 173.

4. Bruce Wilkinson, *A Life God Rewards* (Sisters, OR: Multnomah Publishers, 2002), 38–39.

5. Ibid., 15.

Chapter 18
A Walk Through Glory

1. Charles Spurgeon, "Order and Argument in Prayer," found at Grace Quotes, Holy Art of Prayer at www.biblebb.com/quotes/prayer.htm (accessed December 9, 2003).

2. John Piper, *Future Grace* (Sisters, OR: Multnomah Books, 1995), 374.

3. Ibid., 381–382.

Conclusion
Final Words

1. Quoted in Bartlett, *Familiar Quotations*, 763.

2. J. Bronowski, *The Ascent of Man* (London: Futura Publications, 1986), 155.

3. Ibid., 162.

4. Quoted in Bartlett, *Familiar Quotations*, 407.

5. Quoted at "Space Talk: Gravity Travels Faster Than Light," March 3, 2003, www.space-talk.com/ForumE/showthread.php3?postid =21326#post21326 (accessed May 11, 2003).

BIBLIOGRAPHY

Anderson, Dana K., ed. *Advances in Wound Healing and Tissue Repair*. New York: World Medical Press, 1993.

Bartlett, John. *Familiar Quotations*. Boston, MA: Little, Brown, and Company, 1980.

"Basics of Recombinant DNA." http://www.rpi.edu/dept/chem-eng/Biotech-Environ/Projects00/rdna/rdna.html

Behe, Michael J. *Darwin's Black Box: The Biochemical Challenge to Evolution*. New York: The Free Press, 1996. By far the strongest blow to Darwinism yet, this is the book that "uses a mousetrap to challenge evolutionary theory." Behe demonstrates in easy-to-read language that the biochemical world comprises an arsenal of chemical machines, made up of finely calibrated, interdependent parts—and that this "irreducible complexity" could not have been produced by gradualistic Darwinism.

Broer, Ted. *Maximum Energy*. Lake Mary, FL: Siloam, 1999.

Bronowski, Jacob. *The Ascent of Man*. London: Futura, 1986.

Buell, Jon, and Virginia Hearn, eds. *Darwinism: Science or Philosophy?* Richardson, TX: Foundation for Thought and Ethics, 1994. This is the high-powered collection of ten papers given at the SMU Darwinism Symposium that brought five Darwinists and five Intelligent Design scholars together to debate the central thesis of Johnson's *Darwin on Trial*. Johnson's and Behe's essays are the highlights of this rather technical volume.

Burkett, Larry. *Nothing to Fear: The Key to Cancer Survival*. Chicago, IL: Moody Publishers, 2003.

Burton, Dennis R., ed. *Antibodies in Viral Infection*. Berlin, Germany: Springer-Verlag, 2001.

Carson, Ben. *Gifted Hands*. Grand Rapids, MI: Zondervan, 1990.

———. *Think Big*. Grand Rapids, MI: Zondervan, 1992.

Cherry, Reginald. *Healing Prayer.* Nashville, TN: Thomas Nelson Publishers, 1999.

"Clinical Trial Results Suggest Recombinant DNA Gene Therapy is a Safe and Effective Treatment for Patients with 'Inoperable' Heart Disease." http://www.ctsnet.org/doc/3148.

"Cloning of Genetically Engineered Molecules." http://inventors .about.com/gi/dynamic/offsite.htm.

Colbert, Don. *The Bible Cure for Back Pain.* Lake Mary, FL: Siloam, 2002.

———. *The Bible Cure for Cancer.* Lake Mary, FL: Siloam, 1999.

———. *The Bible Cure For High Blood Pressure.* Lake Mary, FL: Siloam, 2001.

———. *Walking in Divine Health.* Lake Mary, FL: Siloam, 1999.

Cooper, Kenneth H. *Faith-based Fitness.* Nashville, TN: Thomas Nelson Publishers, 1995.

Davis, Audrey W. *Dr. Kelly of Hopkins.* Baltimore, MD: Johns Hopkins Press, 1959.

Davis, P. William, and Dean Kenyon. *Of Pandas and People,* 2nd ed. Dallas, TX: Haughton Publishers, 1994. This is the text developed for use in public schools as a supplement to biology texts on the topic of evolution. It presents the case for intelligent design in a very calm, careful, scientifically scrupulous way, so as to conform to Supreme Court guidelines. A must-read.

Dawkins, Richard. *The Blind Watchmaker.* New York: New York, 1987. The classic modern work on orthodox Darwinism. Highly recommended as an example of "evolution's best shot" today. A runaway bestseller, and easy, feisty read. Dawkins is a brilliant writer, which is helpful when evidence is thin.

Denton, Michael. *Evolution: A Theory in Crisis.* Bethesda, MD: Adler & Adler (through Woodbine House), 1986. Denton's work is the most powerfully sophisticated and complete critique of the scientific foundations of Darwinian evolution (with the possible exception of Phil Johnson's). Very readable and yet massive in its coverage of evidence.

Dorian, Terry. *Total Health and Restoration*. Lake Mary, FL: Siloam, 2002.

Falk, Richard H. "Genetics and Human Life—Part 2." http://www.biologie.uni-hamburg.de/b-online/library/falk/GenHumanLife/genetics-2.htm.

Fountain, Daniel E. *God, Medicine, and Miracles*. Wheaton, IL: Harold Shaw Publishers, 1999.

Gills, James P. *Cataract Surgery: The State of the Art*. Thorofare, NJ: Slack Inc., 1998.

Gitt, Werner. "The Flight of Migratory Birds." *Impact* 159. September 1986. Institute for Creation Research, http://www.icr.org/pubs/imp/imp-159.htm.

Gould, Stephen Jay. *Wonderful Life* (1990) and *The Panda's Thumb* (1983). Both published by Norton. Gould, Phil Johnson's attacker and the leading American (atheist) evolutionist/writer of our era, presents the gripping tale of the Burgess Shale Cambrian fossils in *Wonderful Life*, while *The Panda's Thumb* is a key collection of essays that include early expositions of his "Punctuated Equilibrium" mode of evolution.

Heeren, Fred. *Show Me God*. Wheeling, IL: Day Star Productions, 1995. There is really no book that is like Heeren's—no book entertains so powerfully while presenting the case for a designed, created universe (much as Hugh Ross does). It contains simply incredible interviews with major cosmologists and astronomers about the implications of recent discoveries for belief in God.

Henderson, Ronald E. *Attacking Myasthenia Gravis*. Montgomery, AL: Court Street Press, 2003.

Hepworth, Dana. *Healing in the Hogpen*. Royal Palm Beach, FL: D. Lyle and Associates, 2000.

"Introduction to DNA Structure." http://www.blc.arizona.edu/ Molecular_Graphics/DNA_Structure/DNA_Tutorial.

Janeway, Charles A., and Paul Travers. *Immunobiology: The Immune System in Health and Disease*, 2nd ed. New York: Current Biology Ltd., Garland Publishing, 1996.

Johnson, Phillip. *Evolution as Dogma*. Richardson, TX: Foundation for Thought and Ethics, 1991. This is a delightful booklet that contains a very abridged (17-page) summary of the essence of Johnson's argument in *Darwin on Trial* (minus the discussions of scientific evidence), followed by five responses from a variety of scholars.

Koenig, Harold G., Michael E. McCullough, and David B. Larson. *Handbook of Religion and Health*. New York: Oxford University Press, 2001.

Kreier, Julius P. *Infection, Resistance, and Immunity*, 2nd ed. New York: Taylor and Francis, 2002.

Larimore, Walt. *10 Essentials of Highly Healthy People*. Grand Rapids, MI: Zondervan, 2003.

Lewin, Roger. *Bones of Contention*. New York: Touchstone Books (Simon & Schuster), 1987. This is the classic modern treatment of hominid evolution from an evolutionist perspective, but one that admits the frauds, mistakes, and general problematic nature of this infant field.

Lubenow, Marvin. *Bones of Contention*. Grand Rapids, MI: Baker Book House, 1992. This minor masterpiece by a DTS graduate teaching at Christian Heritage College is an up-to-date, comprehensive, intellectually rigorous treatment of human evolution from a creationist perspective.

McMillen, S. I., and David E. Stern. *None of These Diseases*, Millennium Three Edition. Grand Rapids, MI: Fleming H. Revell, 2000.

Mims, Cedric. *The War Within Us: Everyman's Guide to Infection and Immunity*. San Diego, CA: Academic Press, 2000.

NCI and NIAID, "Frontiers in Immunology: Genetic Engineering." http://allergies.about.com/library/blnciniimmunegenetic .htm?iam=eboom_SKD&terms=Recombinant+dna.

Piper, John. *Future Grace*. Sisters, OR: Multnomah Books, 1995.

"Recombinant DNA and Gene Cloning." http://users.rcn.com/jkimball .ma.ultranet/BiologyPages/R/RecombinantDNA.html.

Ross, Hugh. *The Fingerprint of God* (1989); *The Creator and the Cosmos* (1992). Colorado Springs, CO: NavPress. Ross, an old-earth, old-universe creationist, has emerged as the most vocal and articulate writer/thinker on how the evidence of astronomy, physics, and cosmology all point to a created universe. He is controversial in strongly endorsing the Big Bang theory as evidence of God's handiwork.

Sell, Stewart. *Immunology, Immunopathology, and Immunity*. 6th ed. Washington, DC: ASM Press, 2001.

Shapiro, Robert. *Origins: A Skeptic's Guide to the Creation of Life on Earth*. New York: Bantam Books, 1986. This is the classic work by an honest evolutionist, about the scientific puzzles and problems of chemical evolution scenarios.

Stevens, David. *Jesus M.D.* Grand Rapids, MI: Zondervan, 2001.

Swenson, Richard A. *More Than Meets the Eye*. Colorado Springs, CO: NavPress, 2000.

Thaxton, Charles, Walter Bradley, and Roger Olsen. *The Mystery of Life's Origin*. Dallas, TX: Lewis and Stanley, reprinted 1992. This was the pioneering skeptical overview of chemical evolution that shook up the scientific community when it first appeared in the mid-1980s. It remains one of the most important books on chemical evolution ever published, even though it's ten years old.

Tournier, Paul. *The Meaning of Persons*. Cutchogue, NY: Buccaneer Books, 1957.

Warren, Rick. *The Purpose-Driven Life*. Grand Rapids, MI: Zondervan, 2002.

"When and How Do Birds Migrate?", http://www.earthlife.net/birds/migration2.html.

Whitcomb, John, and Henry Morris. *The Genesis Flood*. N.p.: Presbyterian and Reformed, 1961. This is the granddaddy of "recent creationist" critiques of Darwinism that employ a universal flood approach. Parts of the book are out-of-date now, but it is still a highly provocative and useful source for understanding the young earth position, especially in its historical section and discussion of the ark.

Willingham, Stephen. "Scientists Weave Spider Silk Into New Bulletproof Vests." http://www.nationaldefensemagazine.org/article.cfm?Id=255.